Academic Pathfinders

Academic Pathfinders

Knowledge Creation and Feminist Scholarship

Patricia J. Gumport

Greenwood Studies in Higher Education
Philip G. Altbach, Series Editor

Greenwood Press
Westport, Connecticut • London

Library of Congress Cataloging-in-Publication Data

Gumport, Patricia J.
    Academic pathfinders : knowledge creation and feminist scholarship / Patricia J.
Gumport.
        p.   cm.—(Greenwood studies in higher education, ISSN 1531–8087)
    Includes bibliographical references (p.) and index.
    ISBN 0–313–32096–9 (alk. paper)
    1. Women college teachers.   2. Women college students.   3. Women in education.   4.
Feminism and education.   5. Learning and scholarship.   I. Title.   II. Series.
    LB2332.3.G86   2002
    378'.0082—dc21   2001040583

British Library Cataloguing in Publication Data is available.

Library of Congress Catalog Card Number: 2001040583
ISBN: 0–313–32096–9
ISSN: 1531–8087

First published in 2002

Greenwood Press, 88 Post Road West, Westport, CT 06881
An imprint of Greenwood Publishing Group, Inc.
www.greenwood.com

Printed in the United States of America

The paper used in this book complies with the
Permanent Paper Standard issued by the National
Information Standards Organization (Z39.48–1984).

10 9 8 7 6 5 4 3 2 1

Published in cooperation with the Center for International Higher Education and the Program
in Higher Education, Boston College, Chestnut Hill, Massachusetts.

For Sandra,
and in loving memory of Cory

Contents

Series Foreword

Greenwood Studies in Higher Education publishes current research and analysis on higher and postsecondary education. Higher education in the twenty-first century is a multifaceted phenomenon, combining a variety of institutions and systems, increasing diversity of students, and a range of purposes and functions. The challenges of expansion, technology, accountability, and research, among others, require careful analysis. This series combines research-based monographs, analysis, and reference books related to all aspects of higher education. It is concerned with policy and practice in a global perspective. Greenwood Studies in Higher Education is dedicated to illuminating the reality of higher and postsecondary education in contemporary society.

Higher education is a central enterprise of the twenty-first century and a key part of the knowledge-based economy. Universities are the most important source of basic research, and are therefore key to the development of technology. They are also the repositories of the wisdom of society—their libraries and other facilities are in many ways the institutional memory of civilization. University faculty not only provide education and training, but also are involved in the creation and interpretation of knowledge. Universities are central to the civil society. Higher education is a key to the social mobility and progress of large numbers of people.

Universities and other postsecondary institutions are increasingly complex. They are large and multifaceted. Academe is also diverse, with a wide range of institutions, a less than homogenous student population, and a mixture of public and private support. This series is dedicated to illuminating these complexities. It is also committed to the improvement of one of the most important parts of society—postsecondary education.

Philip G. Altbach

Preface

The core of this manuscript is based on retrospective accounts from thirty-five women faculty who gave generously of their time for in-depth, semistructured interviews. Their willingness and candor enabled me to reconstruct their diverse career histories and intellectual biographies with sufficient detail to portray the historically specific mix of intellectual, organizational, and political conditions that shaped their work in their disciplines, and more broadly in the academy.

This study began as a doctoral dissertation and extended into further research as I launched my own academic career. Among the many debts I have acquired in the course of that research and the subsequent revision of the manuscript, one stands out as most deserving of public acknowledgment. Ann Swidler provided steadfast encouragement and guidance throughout the research and writing process. The following people also offered substantive editorial suggestions at critical junctures: Christine Beirne, Susan Christopher, Sandra Faulkner, Nel Noddings, Mary Kay Martin, Mary Ann Danowitz Sagaria, Sheila Slaughter, Myra Strober, and Barbara Townsend. Finally, I am indebted to Philip Altbach, who facilitated the book's publication.

Introduction

This book examines how academic knowledge is created from the perspective of the knowledge creators. Using feminist scholarship from the 1960s into the 1980s as a case study, the analysis depicts the ways in which this new academic specialty took form through the individual interests of those academic women who created feminist scholarship in their disciplines and, more broadly, in the academy. The core of the manuscript is based on the career histories and intellectual biographies of thirty-five academic women who entered universities during this period. Their diverse accounts portray how new knowledge is created on multiple levels: through personal reflection on life experiences, in disciplinary legacies and local organizational contexts, and within historically specific societal conditions.

The analysis suggests a forward-looking story of knowledge creation, beginning with those who contributed the initial breakthroughs of feminist scholarship. The core group, whom I call the Pathfinders, began graduate school in the mid-1960s, and came to generate a new knowledge specialty within and outside their disciplines. Some of these women explicitly defied admonishments that the subject matter was an oxymoron, energetically demanding inclusion and transformation within their disciplines. Other Pathfinders became proponents of a new separate field, with its intellectual and organizational home in women's studies programs.

In hindsight, the academic generation of these Pathfinders is often referred to as the "second-wave" of feminist scholarship. Despite intragenerational differences in experience and divisions based upon political perspective, "genera-tion" can serve as a compelling explanatory construct that signifies the gendered nature of coming of age professionally at different historical mo-ments. The white middle-class women who started their careers in this era of changing social and political conditions for women perceived solidarity in their gendered experience of the academy (Looser and Kaplan, 1997).

The perceptions and experiences of other women in the academy provide a contrast to the Pathfinders. As I interpret their accounts, two patterns are most apparent. The Forerunners were already established faculty in their disciplines when feminist scholarship took hold, and they varied in their reactions to it. The Pathtakers, who succeeded the Pathfinders, had several academic options, including pursuing feminist scholarship or not. Their intellectual biographies suggested that they found new ways to combine their individual interests, po-litical commitments, and career aspirations. On the other hand, some women disregarded developments in feminist scholarship, aware of, yet not contribut-ing to, either the intellectual or the broader political agenda. Still others carried out knowledge work that at times included gender as they moved from one project to the next, yet they did not self-identify either as a proponent of, nor as a contributor to, feminist scholarship.

My analysis of these diverse career histories and intellectual biographies makes evident a wide range of academic possibilities for women during these years as they faced historically specific opportunities and constraints. Al-though their years in graduate school were far from ideal, the Pathfinders did find conditions that enabled them to create a fusion between feminist politics and academic interests. These conditions included the following elements: a critical mass of women scholars, epistemological openings in selected disci-plines, an abundance of financial aid for doctoral candidates, and a supportive national political movement. Moreover, several factors within their campus settings supported women's studies as an area for interdisciplinary teaching. Organizational climates espoused academic pluralism, financial resources re-sponded to women's requests symbolically if not substantively, and campus leaders were tolerant of, if not willing to establish experimental programs, ad-junct teaching positions, courses cross-listed by departments, and academic appointments reflecting multidisciplinary expertise.

In spite of those facilitating conditions, the indictment of academic patriar-chy and the feminist advocacy agenda that accompanied some of the emerging feminist scholarship directly challenged many premises and practices of tradi-tional academic settings. Furthermore, the scholarly nature of the field and the academic suitability of its subject matter continue to be scrutinized by critics. Indeed, during the course of my research and writing, some of these critics have suggested that feminist scholarship is not a case of new knowledge, knowledge creation, or knowledge advancement. I disagree. And I hope this book will change their minds.

With the benefit of hindsight, we can see how the emergence of feminist scholarship during the 1960s and 1970s was quite remarkable. In the 1960s, no one at the time anticipated the difference women would make and the intellectual momentum that would be established by making gender visible within and across the disciplines. Much of the work by feminist scholars entailed an unprecedented mix of intellectual, organizational, and political interests. Although Black studies had paved the way for a women's studies agenda, the establishment of feminist scholarship as a knowledge specialty entailed intellectual disruption, interpersonal conflict, and curricular transformation on a scale that race and class have not yet achieved.

This book's account of the emergence of feminist scholarship focuses on the experiences and initial academic contributions of those women who began graduate school in the mid-1960s, most of whom were white middle-class women influenced by a leftist political agenda and antiwar sensibilities. Their accounts chronicle how feminist scholarship was created in academic settings that became populated by women students and academic communities whose members became receptive to a discourse of women's rights, including the right to be free of discrimination, to be included, to be heard, and to choose. This movement intersected with disciplinary openings concurrently forged by these women: establishing women as subjects of study, legitimating an authorial voice, and furthering methodologies with particularistic aims. During this period, as women students and faculty sought to establish a visible organizational presence, universities typically responded with additive solutions: new courses and later programs, new positions albeit often not tenure-track, and new organizational forms (such as women's centers and associations) that stabilized an expanding network.

Such expansion was effective at mediating gender-based conflict in many campus settings. However, by the mid- to late-1980s, there was increasingly widespread recognition that ongoing additive solutions would not be viable economically or politically as a long-term academic management strategy. Public scrutiny of higher education increased, with vocal criticism aimed at targets ranging from escalating costs to curricular reform, which had partially replaced classical works with politically correct subject matter. State revenues for public campuses fluctuated as the institutions were criticized for inefficiencies. Along with cost-cutting strategies and cost-effectiveness rationales, the new academic mandate became "change by substitution": the addition of something new meant that something else had to be eliminated.

By the 1990s, the dominant trends in academic management supported the restructuring of academic units to demonstrate an effort toward (if not the reality of) achieving cost savings and leaner organizational structures. Academic investment favored those fields that were revenue-generating and/or most likely to yield knowledge for industrial applications. More humanistic fields, especially those inclined toward particularistic knowledges and advocacy agendas, have gradually been scaled back. One option considered across campuses has been to consolidate into a generic organizational home and degree program, such as cultural studies, a structural move that some campus leaders saw as a potential common ground for the agenda of multiculturalism and identity politics. Ironically, of course, the emerging divisions among and within different academic feminisms—alongside a proliferation of postmodern perspectives—suggest that such academic units might achieve little to no intellectual coherence or shared sense of purpose, either in faculty teaching or research activities.

For the most part, faculty and administrators across colleges and universities continue to puzzle over the appropriate organizational arrangements for existing and emerging fields. Although decisions will continue to be incremental and local, they have cumulative consequences for what counts as knowledge, what categories of expertise are valued for academic degrees and future academic positions, and how upcoming generations of faculty are socialized.

By the close of the 20th century, an unprecedented blending of fiscal and academic interests have altered the criteria for reshaping the landscape for knowledge creation in universities. Nonetheless, it is still the case that yesterday's work at the margin may become tomorrow's core concern. Universities have a shared stake in determining the organizational conditions that facilitate the creation and transmission of new knowledge. As the contest over resources continues, what counts as knowledge is central to deliberations over which expertise is most suitable for degree programs, departments, and faculty billets, as well as which ideas are worthy of dissertations, tenure, and promotion.

This book thus speaks directly to many of the contemporary challenges inherent in pursuing an academic career in universities. A number of considerations have been foreshadowed in my analysis of feminist scholarship: how the attainment of legitimacy is as much an organizational and political achievement as an intellectual one; how the criteria for evaluating academic knowledge are ambiguous; how new ideas struggle to compete alongside established ones; and how transcending established boundaries can potentially produce intellectual vitality.

The different experiences of academic women in this study suggest that faculty of every academic generation bring to their work different preconceptions about the parameters of their disciplines and the appropriate foundations of scholarship. In the process of making their academic careers, the women in this book persevered to reconcile tensions within themselves, with others, and within their academic settings. In fact, it may be said that, in a fundamental sense, faculty who aspire to create knowledge must each in her or his own way become a pathfinder, engaged in an ongoing process of discovering a way through or into unexplored regions. As Gail Sheehy (1981) observed in her analysis of pathfinders, the process is one of seeking and risking as much as it is of locating ourselves in a world that is itself changing.

While such introspection has achieved currency in popular culture, as an analytical approach it also resonates with the broader sociological framework that anchors my study. Building upon C. Wright Mills' invitation to analyze the intersection of biography, history, and social structure, my analysis depicts how these women forged their academic careers within existing social conditions. Although their circumstances and knowledge-making paths differed, the critical insight is that biography and knowledge coevolve. That is, individuals' life paths in part shape their knowledge work; and their academic contributions in turn reshape the parameters of their careers. Such an approach not only brings to light the evolution of gendered struggles in the academy alongside changing academic landscapes, but it also suggests that other academic pursuits and knowledge breakthroughs may be similarly grounded in life experiences, and in unexpected ways.

ORGANIZATION OF THE BOOK

The book is organized as follows. In chapter 1, I establish the dynamic character of academic knowledge, the prevailing social science approaches to studying this phenomenon, and the theoretical framework that informs my analysis. Chapter 2 provides a larger context for the study, including antecedents to "second wave" feminist scholarship as well as its emerging consequences. Chapter 3 describes the research methods and sample of women for the study.

Chapter 4 moves directly into the core exploration of knowledge creation, by analyzing women scholars' intellectual biographies and career histories; first, the experiences and perceptions of the generation I call the Pathfinders. In describing their starting points and intellectual contributions, I explore how they came to generate feminist questions from their life experience as women, and then ultimately developed feminist scholarship. In chapter 5, I examine the disciplinary forces in the creation of new academic knowledge. History, sociology, and philosophy each presented different contexts for the Pathfinders. I consider the range of opportunities and constraints that they perceived as they sought to reconcile the tensions they experienced between their politics and the academic establishment.

Chapter 6 moves beyond the Pathfinders' initial integration of feminism and scholarship to examine how new knowledge was created in alternative academic pursuits. As feminist scholarship developed, it created new possibilities for other generations of academic women, both for the Pathtakers, who went to graduate school after the Pathfinders, and for the Forerunners, who were already well established in their disciplinary careers when academic feminist perspectives became an option.

In chapter 7, I revisit the question of how new academic knowledge is created and gains legitimacy within historically specific conditions. In this concluding chapter, I examine the political and organizational conditions that shape the formation of academic specialties. Returning to core concerns in the sociology of knowledge, I identify changes that occurred in the political and economic conditions of universities during the last quarter of the 20th century, and I argue that the parameters for knowledge creation have shifted. Subsequent generations of aspiring faculty are still expected to produce original work that pushes the edges of disciplinary knowledge, yet they must attempt to do so under conditions increasingly shaped by cost-conscious academic management practices and wider economic imperatives.

1

The Dynamic Nature of Academic Knowledge

Changes in what counts as knowledge have received increased attention over the past three decades, even capturing the attention of media. Within higher education, dramatic shifts—or at least perceptions of shifts—have been prominently featured depicting academic settings as a contested terrain between established fields, with departments and scholars facing a range of formidable challenges from academic reformers. While at any given time in any university, programmatic resources, general education requirements, or promotion decisions may be locally contested, such academic disagreements are symptomatic of the fact that the contours and content of academic landscapes are ever-changing. New fields emerge, such as women's studies, urban studies, biochemistry, computer science, and symbolic systems, whereas existing fields may recede or disappear entirely, as have geography and home economics. Moreover, even though some academic labels may remain the same, such as English, history, and chemistry, the content of courses and the degree requirements in those areas undergo constant revision.

The perennial challenge for universities and their participants is to determine and allocate the resources, academic positions, and organizational forms that are appropriate for existing knowledge as well as for emerging knowledge. Although decisions are made locally and incrementally, their effects are cumulative and ultimately redefine which ideas are considered most worthy and thus which are viable areas of expertise for degrees, academic departments, tenure-track positions, publications, and academic careers.

While it is clear that academic knowledge changes over time, *how* such knowledge change occurs requires a deeper examination of the development of ideas within particular social conditions. Such an inquiry must involve attention to the disciplinary legacies within which scholars work, particularly what occurs in the formative stages of graduate school, when scholars undertake their advanced studies and begin to shift from knowledge consumers to knowledge creators. Yet attention must also be focused upon the wider societal conditions surrounding universities, for these conditions define the pressures and expectations for universities as well as for their students and faculty. Finally, the analysis must be grounded in the experiences and perspectives of the knowledge creators themselves, as they encounter opportunities and constraints in their intellectual, organizational, and political circumstances.

Such a phenomenological approach is unusual in the scholarly investigation of knowledge. Although the body of work on the social construction of knowledge has grown in recent years, the bulk of it tends to be located within a functionalist or a critical theory paradigm rather than within an interpretive one. From Foucault (1973) to Fuller (1988), Giroux and McLaren (1994) to Gieryn (1983), concepts such as genealogy, social epistemology, identity politics, border crossing, and boundary work have gained currency to portray the establishment of knowledge as a social process that involves people, power, and institutions. As contemporary incarnations of core concerns within the sociology of knowledge, each of these disparate efforts is fueled by the fundamental scholarly recognition that what comes to count as knowledge is inescapably anchored in specific historical conditions. My analytic perspective builds on this work but emphasizes that the relationship between emerging knowledge and its respective historical conditions is mediated by individuals' life experiences and by the prevailing practices within established institutional settings (Swidler and Arditi, 1994). This emphasis is an important analytical departure because it proceeds along several levels of analysis simultaneously.

Specifically, academic disciplines and universities are conceptualized as primary arenas in which students, faculty, and campus leaders reproduce or transform what counts as knowledge. Such a conceptual convergence suitably frames an in-depth inquiry into the interplay between individuals' experiences and perceptions, disciplinary practices and intellectual legacies, and organizational conditions offering opportunities as well as constraints for new academic work, all of which churn within a wider set of societal forces that reshape what is expected of universities. By considering scholars themselves as mediators of these several levels of context, we can probe how new knowledge is created at the intersection of intellectual, organizational, and political forces.

Feminist scholarship serves as a powerful case for exploring these questions, to bring to light the dynamics that provide openings for scholars to develop new ideas within conditions that have institutionalized existing academic knowledge. It is especially striking to consider how in this case, academic women managed to gain scholarly visibility within their disciplines while they often explicitly challenged many long-held assumptions about theory and method. Bridging a wider social movement of women's liberation with the academic discourse of traditional disciplines, those who developed feminist scholarship found themselves charting new academic pathways that linked their life experiences as women to their knowledge work. Moreover, they did so despite the widespread unease over the interplay between biography and scholarship and the presumed bias it entailed. To varying degrees, they not only established places for themselves and career trajectories within the disciplines, but by doing so, they transformed the disciplines and the university settings within which they worked. Other women pursued alternative academic paths that are also worthy of careful examination. Some sought to establish an autonomous unit outside the disciplines, such as women's studies. Still others disregarded these developments entirely, aiming to maintain a separation between their gendered experience and their scholarship.

Before delving into my analysis of the diverse women scholars' accounts, I want to underscore the contribution of this study within the broader social science literature. In the context of prevailing conceptions of academic knowledge and social change, my approach puts more emphasis on the mix of historically specific conditions and on the potential for individual agency to remake the conditions of the academy. The general conceptual contribution that I seek to make is to sharpen our understanding of academic knowledge as a social construction that is simultaneously deeply personal in its sense-making value, potentially professional in its currency for academic careers, and ultimately political when it is used as a force for social reproduction or social change. Those readers with less interest in the intellectual ancestry of my approach and my intended contribution to academic literatures may want to move directly to chapter 2.

THE CENTRALITY OF KNOWLEDGE TO HIGHER EDUCATION

Within the study of higher education, an analytical focus on knowledge is rare. The conventional research tends to examine the major people-processing functions: how universities and colleges affect students through skill training, personal or career development, credentialing and human capital development, all having consequences for social mobility or the lack thereof. In contrast, my research addresses knowledge as the central concern. Among the diverse institutional settings in the United States, my interest for this book is in universities—both comprehensive universities and research universities—as these are settings for several types of knowledge creation activities: transmission (teaching of undergraduates and graduate students), production (research), and transfer (dissemination and application). Building on a conceptual advance articulated by Burton Clark (1983), I view knowledge and its constituent bundles of fields as defining the work of universities and the people in them. From this perspective, it is important to examine continuity and change: the types and categories of knowledge that universities support—and conversely, those that remain unsupported—as well as the organizational conditions that constrain or facilitate the creation of new knowledge.

This line of inquiry reflects an enduring interest among sociologists of knowledge to illuminate how the development of ideas is shaped by social and material conditions, including the social relations among knowledge producers. At the same time, within this foundational literature, a virtually unexplored area of study concerns what makes whole orderings of knowledge possible (Swidler and Arditi, 1994). The basic premise for this line of inquiry is to examine the interplay between social structures and individual agency in knowledge creation. From this perspective, knowledge creation is a bidirectional endeavor. Two dimensions of this phenomenon must be made explicit. On the one hand, social conditions in part frame what is possible for individual interests. As Gerson has argued of the gendered nature of social conditions, "in the context of structural constraint, women actively build their lives out of the materials provided by larger social forces" (1985, p. xiii). At the same time, such life paths reshape the parameters for their careers. Gerson continues: "In so doing, they in turn shape and under propitious circumstances reshape the world that shaped them" (p. xiii). In the context of knowledge work, we may understand this interplay as a coevolution of knowledge and biography within the broader context of changing social conditions and academic possibilities for women.

This approach has much to offer for the study of contemporary higher education in general and for the study of knowledge creation in particular. In the remainder of this chapter, I will identify the most relevant literature that helps refine this approach, and then I will lay out the framework that I used to anchor this study.

PRIOR LITERATURE ON ACADEMIC KNOWLEDGE

Historians of higher education, organizational theorists, and sociologists of science are among those who have contributed to our understanding of how academic knowledge has changed over time. While each type of literature demarcates important lines of analysis, each body of work also provides some partial insight into the historical development of specific academic specialties, the organizational features of universities that promote or constrain change, or the range of factors influencing knowledge production. Together, the literature points to a compelling intersection which I delineate in the last section of the chapter.

Historical Understandings of Curricular Change

One of the more stable features of postsecondary institutions is often thought to be the departmental structure, with departments as the basic units within which knowledge is organized. However, a closer historical inspection of the organization of departments, and the disciplines which have justified their institutionalization, reveals ongoing change. Over the past century, the dominant pattern has been expansion, the addition of fields of study and degree programs. Such a long historical perspective lends insight to my study in two ways. First, it emphasizes the ascendance of departmental and disciplinary autonomy as a dominant force in the organizational arrangement of modern universities. Second, it illuminates some factors integral to the emergence of and subsequent struggles for legitimacy in specific academic fields.

Rise of Departmental/Disciplinary Organization

The organization of knowledge into the departmental structure of the modern university did not become widespread until the 1880s. Prior to that time, distinctions were made among subjects of study, but not according to the disciplinary boundaries that underlie the current configuration of departments, and not according to divisions of responsibilities among faculty members, nor between faculty and the administration on a campus.

Prior to departmentalization, several distinct subjects of study can be discerned within the standard curriculum of the colonial colleges. The tightly ordered classical program of study included the following: ancient languages (Latin, Greek, and Hebrew), rhetoric, logic, mathematics, natural philosophy (Aristotelian physics), and theology. A student would usually study one subject each day, weekdays from eight to five, and half of Saturday. Controlled by a guild of professors, most of whom were ministers and "generalists" capable of teaching all of the subjects, the curriculum was designed and organized to convey the cultural heritage of Western civilization and to prepare the elite for professions such as the clergy or the law. New subjects were gradually added to this classical core curriculum, including modern languages (French, Spanish, Italian, German, and English), geography, and natural history (botany, geology, and chemistry) (Rudolph, 1981).

As early as the Yale Report of 1828, evidence existed of some dispute over the educational value of different subjects. For example, controversy flourished regarding the presumed greater value of ancient languages over the modern languages. In spite of this ongoing disagreement, consensus about underlying purposes prevailed: to develop mental faculties for communication and reason, and to impart a universal body of knowledge about "man and nature" (Carnegie Commission, 1977). Institutions across the country echoed the sanctity of the standard classical curriculum and extolled a hierarchical view of the subjects as progressive interdependent stages that would culminate in wisdom.

By 1825 the initial signs of departmentalization were evident at the University of Virginia, where instruction was organized into schools headed by professors; these included ancient languages, modern languages, mathematics, natural history, moral philosophy, medicine, anatomy, and law. Usually there was only one professor or chair to each "department" (Dressel, Johnson, and Marcus, 1970).

Dramatic academic changes occurred in the late 19th century, due to a shift toward utilitarianism and a new emphasis on original research—that is, research founded in "the ideal of pure science, or inductive, empirical research for its own sake" (Veysey, 1973). A knowledge explosion at this time brought about widespread departmentalization of colleges, increased specialization in course offerings, a hierarchical ranking of faculty members within departments, and faculty professionalization. Rudolph describes the need for departmentalization as a function of growth in size, specialization of knowledge, and faculty desires for autonomy:

A hierarchy of biologists, for instance, had to be held together by some formal authority; their interests had to find expression in some formally recognized locus of organization. But it was not enough to have a department of biology, for such a department could not adequately reflect the splintering of knowledge and the rivalry of attention for funds, for approval, that now ensued. . . . At the University of Chicago . . . the department of Biology split into five new departments—zoology, botany, anatomy, neurology, physiology. And that meant five new departmental chairmanships, five new little hierarchies, five new competing domains of knowledge and interest. Yet, in truth, scholarship could be served and the growth of knowledge assured in no other way. (Rudolph, 1962, p. 399)

While departmentalization was a method of organizing many academic specialists into the framework of university governance, the exact form and rate of organizational change varied across disciplines and across campuses. As Rudolph (1962) continued to explain:

[M]ultiplication of departments took place everywhere. The method chosen might be addition or division. Departments of Modern Languages became Departments of German and Departments of Romance Languages. Departments of History and Political Economy became Departments of History and Departments of Political Economy. Departments of History became Departments of European History and Departments of American History. Departments of Political Economy became Departments of Political Science, Departments of Economics, and Departments of Sociology. (Rudolph, 1962, p. 400)

No longer were professors generalists. As "a new breed of professors" began "to 'stake their claim' to new courses of study," the new emphasis on the production of knowledge brought about specialization and a "shift in faculty loyalty from their institution to their discipline" (Graham, 1978).

During the same period, new fields emerged in the social and behavioral sciences, such as sociology and psychology. There were also subdivisions and increased quantification within the natural sciences. At most large institutions, the number of major institutionally distinct subject areas was roughly 25 to 40, which would persist from about 1905 to 1950. After 1950 came another surge of increased specialization of knowledge, which resulted in a tremendous proliferation of new fields and subdisciplines. In the natural sciences alone the number of different institutionally recognized specializations grew from 50 in 1950 to nearly 1,000 in 1970 (Dressel, 1971; Veysey, 1973).

A commonly understood distinction emerged: the department is not the equivalent of the discipline; disciplines transcend universities, whereas departments exist within them (Light, 1974). Moreover, departments are not standard units across all universities: a department on one campus may be a school or even several departments on another. Departments also differ in terms of priorities, modes of operation, size, intellectual orientation within a discipline, and degree of status on campus (Dressel, Johnson, Marcus, 1970). And within disciplines, there is variation as well. Within one discipline there may be subdivisions as well as conflicting conceptions of disciplinary boundaries, priorities, various orientations toward what counts as knowledge, and preferred concepts, methods, and principles of inquiry. Lodahl and Gordon (1972) have suggested that there is an interaction between the character of disciplinary ideas and their organizational manifestation as distinct departmental activity on campus. Given this interdependence, they argue any proposed change must "take into account the intimate relations between the structure of knowledge in different fields and the vastly different styles with which university departments operate" (Lodahl and Gordon, 1972, p. 71).

Yet in spite of these variations in departmental styles and disciplinary orientations, for the most part, the compartmentalization of knowledge into a common array of departments has become widely accepted as a distinct structure that approximately parallels disciplinary lines (Trow, 1977). The persistence of some underlying disciplinary categories has won them the designation of "traditional" and on occasion the presumption that they are a reflection of the natural order of knowledge itself. Indeed, the preservation of boundaries for "traditional" disciplines has become a common referent in discussions of academic legitimacy, particularly in campus deliberations over the appropriate location for new subject matter.

More specifically, the departmental/disciplinary tradition carries its own organizational and intellectual momentum, making existing academic structures a conservative force against intellectual currents that seek to transcend those boundaries. For example, depending on the extent to which an emerging field is genuinely interdisciplinary, the departmental/disciplinary organization of universities may prove to be a source of theoretical and practical resistance to such a field's emergence and successful institutionalization. On the other hand, if an emerging area is cast as cross-disciplinary, its potential may be seen as an intellectual and organizational endeavor that can be readily accomplished by cross-listing courses from existing departments. So, while any emerging field is likely to receive scrutiny based on the fact that it is new, its trajectory may be determined based on whether it is positioned as a supplement to existing departments or as a threat. In this regard, it is also important to note that the initial establishment of a new area of study is simply one step in an ongoing process of programmatic review and performance evaluation; thus those who are located in existing departments can weigh in either favorably or unfavorably at many points throughout the process (Mandelbaum, 1979; Wood, 1979).

Factors Involved in the Emergence of New Fields

Although some academic subjects, such as Greek and moral philosophy, have existed for centuries, other subjects have been added as spin-offs, such as psychology and biophysics, whereas still others have been dropped, such as navigation and surveying. During the last 100 years, departmental designations have shifted to reflect corresponding knowledge growth and specialization. Overall departmental structures have become larger, more differentiated, and more complex. Controversy over what subjects to include in the formal organizational structure, and in what form they should be included, is reflected in the development of new academic fields. Although emerging fields have experienced different administrative arrangements across campuses, some generalizations can be made about their patterns of emergence, by tracing the factors influencing the origin and varying successes of a variety of fields.

Attempting to document broad changes that have occurred in the organization and production of knowledge, scholars have proposed that the emergence of new fields is linked to a wide range of societal and organizational factors, including changes in the functions of higher education in society (Dressel, 1971; Jencks and Reisman, 1977; Veysey, 1973); demands of the new professions (e.g., agriculture, business, forestry, architecture); changes in the availability of resources (Hefferlin, 1969); the presence of individual advocates who express support and interest in new knowledge (Hefferlin, 1969); strong leadership buttressed by outside (financial) support (Dressel, Johnson, Marcus, 1970); and new ways of connecting, classifying, or ordering experience (Foucault, 1973).

Other accounts have traced the development of a specific discipline by identifying one or more major factors in its evolution. Particular faculty interests, epistemological characteristics, and wider political concerns of scholars have each been cited as a major influential factor in the development of mainstream fields as well as more marginal fields and interdisciplinary fields.

Mainstream Fields

Some of the dynamics that function in the establishment of emerging fields can be seen at work in the inception of psychology, statistics, and sociology. While "institutional location" for these disciplines may vary across campuses—that is, some exist as departments, schools, or in another form—each of these academic areas has gained some recognition in the formal academic and social structure. A brief overview of the development of each discipline reveals influences that are intellectual (on the level of ideas) and social or organizational (informal or formal patterns of interrelationships among scholars).

The origin and development of psychology reflect a motivation for professional advancement. In fact, one study suggests that psychology is the product of a conscious strategy for scholars to achieve upward mobility and resolve role conflict (Ben-David and Collins, 1966). In the late 19th century, Wilhelm Wundt is credited as the central figure who established the field by applying empirical methods to questions of philosophy and thereby combining the intellectual traditions from speculative philosophy and physiology (Gardner, 1985, p. 102). Wundt's contributions opened up a new channel for expertise and therefore professional advancement. This motivation to create a new domain has been characterized as follows: "Mobility of scholars from one field to another will occur when the chances of success (i.e., gaining recognition, gaining a full chair at a relatively early age, making an outstanding contribution) in one discipline are poor, often as a result of overcrowding in a field in which the number of positions is stable. In such cases, many scholars will be likely to

move into any related fields in which the conditions of competition are better"
(Ben-David and Collins, 1966, p. 460).

Similar faculty aspirations for upward mobility have been cited in the
development of statistics (Ben-David, 1972). Prior to World War I, statisticians were located in several departments where historical data were used
for research—biology, education, agriculture, and social science. As the
number of statisticians grew, they developed a national reference group,
founding a professional association, scholarly journals, and, soon after, departments of statistics.

At least two types of faculty interests contributed to the development of sociology: not only the desire for upward mobility, but also the commitment to
practical reform efforts (Wood, 1979; Oberschall, 1972). Contributors to
early sociology, according to Oberschall (1972), included social reformers,
Protestant clergy, intellectuals who perceived their upward mobility to be
blocked, and muck-raking journalists. The scholars in the young field drew
professorships and chairs from a variety of existing departments: from schools
of political science (University of Michigan, 1881), political economy (University of Michigan, 1884), from the department of applied Christianity
(Iowa), history (Kansas, 1889), and political science (Columbia, 1894). By the
1920s sociologists had conceptualized a distinctive field, developed a sense of
research methods, and established a trust in findings based on those methods
(Faris, 1964). Concepts such as social process, interaction, and organization
were among the content that constituted the territory for sociology, and at that
time were the least apt to involve boundary disputes with neighboring academic fields. Respectability derived from establishing a stable base of recognition, and from there the specialists legitimated social reform activities. As
Gouldner (1970) assessed:

In two generations, American sociologists devised a number of research techniques
and invented another handful of complex theoretical perspectives; they completed and
published thousands of researches; they trained a cadre of full-time specialists at least
two or three times larger than that of all European countries combined; they established many new periodicals, research institutes, departments; they developed academic influence and won wide public attention, if not uniform respect; and they
committed every form of gaucherie and vulgarity that can be expected of an arriviste
discipline. Yet for all its vulnerabilities, it did establish itself firmly as a part of the
American culture, and each year sees it even more deeply institutionalized in the
United States. (p. 22)

The development of sociology and its struggle for legitimacy point to several processes that may effect the emergence and potential legitimacy of all new
fields. In the case of sociology, these can be summarized as fourfold. First,

scholars in the field were motivated by self-interest; they had an investment in the future of the field. Hagstrom (1965) observes that in every discipline scholars expend energy writing a "disciplinary ideology" that comes to serve as the tradition. Second, the development of intellectual content did not necessarily precede the recognition of sociology in an institutional form. Oberschall (1972) suggests that sociology was institutionalized before it had a distinctive intellectual content, a distinct method, or even a point of view. Third, the political climate outside the academy played a role in scholars' motivations to the extent that they viewed their academic work as a form of service to the community or had political interests outside the immediate campus or profession. And finally, problematically, the activist inclinations of some faculty potentially conflicted with established notions of academic work. Sociology's early ties to reform movements provoked accusations of its practitioners having an advocacy agenda and even subversive intentions. This is a recurring theme that has affected the life course of several emerging interdisciplinary fields as well, including history of science, ethnic studies, American studies, and women's studies.

Marginal Fields

In contrast to psychology, statistics, and sociology, several other fields (arts and criminology, for example) struggled not only for status and resources but also merely to be recognized as legitimate members of the academic order. Their development highlights both ongoing, pervasive scrutiny by those more established within institutions and the perennial challenge to determine the criteria for what fields should be supported and in what forms. The criteria for legitimacy are pertinent not only for emerging fields, but also for fields that have always struggled against marginality.

The performing and studio arts, for example, have a long history of marginal status and scrutiny for a presumed lack of intellectual rigor—not for their presumed vocational nature, but for an association with "anti-cognitive and anti-intellectual" currents (Morrison, 1973). As Ross (1997) skillfully observed in her historical analysis of dance, some fields have never been liberated from such academic scrutiny.

Other fields have been considered marginal due to a pragmatic or vocational orientation. At Berkeley, in the past several decades, for example, there have been steady efforts to "rid the letters and sciences catalog of inappropriately technical major subjects, so that criminology, journalism, home economics, education and the like were gradually dropped over the years; only a few such fields, including physical education and social welfare, managed to survive" (Veysey, 1973, p. 49).

The case of criminology is especially illustrative of an emerging field that has been unable to gain a foothold in the academy (Wood, 1979). Its initial development was linked to practical reform efforts as well as to the availability of federal funds—over $150 million from 1965 to 1975. One observer describes the field's applied fallibility within the confines of established university structures:

As a bureaucracy, the structure of the university is relatively frozen, as indicated by various departments that have existed longer than most can remember. Because criminal justice education . . . has come to be defined as outside the realm of any one of the traditional disciplines . . . [it] has, in some instances, been defined as unacceptable by those disciplines. The traditional disciplines have felt that their reputations might become tainted by contact with [criminology] because it requires applications of knowledge in field situations. (Culbertson, 1975, p. 172)

The lukewarm reception of criminology by higher-prestige institutions suggests a mix of factors that may influence the struggle of similar fields for academic legitimacy: a pragmatic or applied nature along with an apparent lack of disciplinary foundation within the existing departmental structure.

Even for fields with apparent disciplinary ties, the departmental structure itself may continue to function as a barrier, as illustrated by history of science or sociology of science. Even though these intellectual specialties could be considered spin-offs from either history, sociology, or the sciences, they have not been assured security within a home department. During the past several decades, programs for these studies have existed under shifting nomenclatures (such as science studies, science and technology studies, science technology and society), and undergraduate degrees in this area have not achieved a taken-for-granted status, nor have they been consistently recognized as a standard academic entity.

Interdisciplinary Fields

The factors influencing the emergence of interdisciplinary fields become evident in tracing the development of area studies, American studies, ethnic studies, and women's studies. Of all emerging academic fields, these interdisciplinary areas most clearly illustrate the interplay between intellectual interests and ideas, social interaction among scholars—both formal and informal—and wider political concerns capturing the attention of graduate students and faculty. Together these factors influence each other and provide energy for those seeking to establish a field's legitimacy. While other new knowledge areas may have proponents, these interdisciplinary fields are most commonly characterized as having key people on campus around whom the field's academic legitimacy is established.

Among the longer-standing interdisciplinary fields, area studies (e.g., Russian, Chinese) entered the academy due to external forces: a government mandate motivated by national defense concerns and "increased American concern over remote parts of the globe" (Veysey, 1973). Supported by government funds, programs were set up around the country, and when the funding was withdrawn, area studies programs experienced a dramatic decline. Although these programs were oriented more toward research than undergraduate teaching, the question was raised as to whether or not area studies as domains of knowledge possessed the concepts and intellectual substance necessary to sustain themselves over time (Rudolph, 1981). Other factors contributing to this tenuous status have been suggested: that the dual appointments held by area specialists created a tension in their work between the interdisciplinary program and the "academic department" (Bennett, 1951) and that the interdisciplinarity of both content and methods in area studies threatened the departmental organization of the university (Fenton, 1947).

While sharing a similar social/historical climate with area studies, American studies emerged as an interdisciplinary phenomenon primarily from departmental initiatives. Proponents for American studies can be traced to literature departments, where American literature was engaged in a long ascendance from being neglected, scorned, and ignored by curriculum-makers to gaining increasing recognition and status (Walker, 1958; Zabel, 1947). The intent of American studies proponents was to synthesize and integrate scholarly materials from existing departments—literature and history, at first. One professor, however, suggested the establishment of American departments: "When the name American department is once found on the American college campus, that is, when it can be read on an office door or in the catalogue . . . , everything that this name implies will eventually come with it. Courses in American literature, language, and culture will no longer be tied up with the European and world background" (Koester, 1940, in Zabel, 1947, p. 136).

During American studies' ongoing struggle for legitimacy, several obstacles were noted by Zabel (1947): perceptions of traditions; need for institutional resources; biases in assessments of the intrinsic worth of scholarship; and lack of "adequately trained" specialists. Since the 1930s, American studies has provided an "integrative interdisciplinary experience" in the curriculum, which essentially means that, for the most part, the field has depended on selected course offerings from conventional departments (Walker, 1958).

Emerging fields struggling for legitimacy over the last two decades have raised similar questions about intellectual rigor, as well as brought to the forefront disputes about the influence of political commitments on teaching and scholarship. Their processes also highlight the problematic nature of assessing new kinds of scholarly contributions.

For example, what is known today as ethnic studies began as Black studies in the 1960s, and became Afro-American studies alongside the then-developing field of Chicano studies. Significantly, the period was characterized both by abundant resources for universities and by a climate of considerable campus unrest. Lauded by proponents early on for their potential to transform the curriculum, the various ethnic studies were to serve both additive and corrective functions for a curriculum which previously either had excluded knowledge based on cultural diversity or had painted nonwhite experience and attributes in negative terms (Dressel, 1971; Brubacher and Rudy, 1976). Since the inception of ethnic studies programs, opponents have criticized its scholars for being "merely political" and not intellectually rigorous (Cruse, 1969, p. 5). Opponents have also raised the issue of academic viability: "[I]s ethnicity a proper organizing principle for scholarly pursuits or is that subject matter more appropriately treated in existing disciplines?" (Bell, 1977). Furthermore, critics' questions remain whether or not ethnic studies has stimulated new intellectual questions and/or a distinctive scholarship. While one scholar (Professor McGee from San Francisco State) has claimed that "ethnic studies scholarship has grown in quantum leaps," other scholars still hold perceptions of it as "rap and rhetoric." Into the 1980s, ethnic studies programs became likely targets for consolidation, if not elimination, particularly as universities experienced budget cuts and sought to retrench (*Chronicle of Higher Education*, April 25, 1984). By the 1990s, one structural strategy was to combine various ethnic studies units, as Stanford University sought to do in an unprecedented program entitled Comparative Studies in Race and Ethnicity. Not surprisingly, some of the constituent groups (most visibly Afro-American studies) worried that this consolidation would be a step backward rather than an organizational achievement.

As in the case of ethnic studies, proponents of women's studies have attempted to provide additive and corrective functions to the curriculum. By the late 1970s, ample evidence suggested that a new academic area of feminist scholarship had emerged in several disciplines and was evident in initiatives for curricular change (e.g., Ruddick and Daniels, 1977; Lauter and Howe, 1978; Watkins, 1979; Fowlkes and McClure, 1983; Langland and Gove, 1981). However, women's studies and feminist scholarship faced decades of resistance and sustained scrutiny, amid accusations similar to those leveled against ethnic studies: that they lacked intellectual rigor and that their concerns for social change were "too political." The extent of early institutionalization of women's studies into the curriculum varied across campuses (Howe, 1975; Wood, 1979). As will become more apparent in later chapters of this book, the variation in success was due to several additional problems that have yet to be remedied. These include the accusation that women scholars are not only biased but promote their own self-interest by doing research on women (Sternhell, 1984). Further, an increasingly visible clashing between norms and subcultures have undermined the ostensible solidarity between feminist groups (Spender, 1981a).

In spite of a mixed record of organizational accomplishments, feminist scholars and their scholarship have made substantial advances in generating a new scholarship, albeit an uneven one, across the disciplines. The scholarship is distinctive in terms of its reshaping of intellectual priorities, both in the topics designated as worthy of research (Millman and Kanter, 1975; Jacklin, 1984) and in the types of inquiries pursued (Stanley and Wise, 1983; Spender, 1981a). Some scholars have claimed that a "gendered perspective" has transformative potential both within and beyond the disciplines to an extent that concepts of class and race/ethnicity have thus far had only limited success attaining (Stacey and Thorne, 1985). Even so, it may still be argued that feminist scholarship is too new to be able to judge its chances for long-term survival or growth as an intellectual and organizational presence throughout the 21st century. In short, it is a dramatic example of knowledge creation that, in the long run, may or may not ultimately be recognized as a legitimate and enduring academic field.

This brief overview of mainstream, marginal, and interdisciplinary fields suggests some commonality among emerging fields and their proponents as they seek to become established. The histories of these disciplines and fields demonstrate that faculty interests (be they intellectual, occupational, social, or political) play a primary role in the development and potential legitimacy of a field. Faculty interests have many dimensions, including the extent to which they seek to integrate a political orientation with scholarly work, differing hopes for their scholarship or teaching as a means to wider societal change, and varying aspirations for finding a viable professional path in a traditional university setting.

In addition to the salience of faculty interests in affecting new areas of study, a second factor is the nature of the intellectual content in an emerging field. Bell (1977) refers to this determinant as academic viability: whether a new field's central concept is a proper organizing principle or whether it may be more appropriately treated in the existing disciplinary structure. This raises a formidable challenge to establishing credibility in a new field. How can one be considered a specialist or expert in an emerging field, if at the same time respect is determined based upon evaluative criteria from those in established fields, who have a vested interest as gatekeepers of their disciplines?

Along with faculty interest and intellectual content, existing organizational and administrative arrangements also determine a field's place in the academic order. A university's prevailing academic management practices and available resources lead to a range of options for dealing with a new field, from granting full departmental status to ignoring a field altogether. Founding a new department normally entails the allocation of full-time, tenure-track faculty billets and degree-granting autonomy, while interdisciplinary programs have a lesser status, offering a degree or a certificate that may be pursued in conjunction with a degree in a traditional discipline. Still weaker footing is a loose arrangement of coursework strung together across existing departments as a concentration. An occasional interdisciplinary anomaly has persisted in departmental form—for example, the University of California at Santa Cruz's program in the history of consciousness, with their faculty also carrying that title (e.g., Professor of History of Consciousness). Yet the basic pattern for new academic knowledge suggests several types of organizational responses and several layers of forces at work that may shift with fluctuations in resources and periodic review of academic structures.

The Organizational Factors That Constrain or Permit Change

Organizational theorists have produced a vast literature on academic change in the past several decades, writings that suggest some answers to the question that the historical analyses left unanswered: What in the organizational context of universities either constrains or promotes change, and specifically, knowledge change?

The dominant approach among organizational theorists has been an attempt to isolate factors that are determinative in organizational change. Within this general orientation, Scott (1981) identifies three distinct views of organizations that can be applied to postsecondary institutions: rational, natural, and open systems. Understood as rational systems, universities are seen as establishing a purposeful formal structure in order to pursue goals such as knowledge production, teaching, and credentialing of students. From the natural systems perspective, universities are held together more informally through shared interests in preserving themselves and their mission. Seen as open systems, universities reflect ever-changing interests that are strongly determined by the external environment. In the past several decades, organizational research on academic change has been dominated by open systems approaches that underscore the determinative role of environmental forces in redefining academic missions, structures, and resources.

Although few and far between, specific empirical studies have identified some structural characteristics that may facilitate or impede academic change.

Factors that are considered to enhance the likelihood of new fields becoming established are a decentralized organizational structure (Blau, 1973), available material or slack resources (Hefferlin, 1969), the presence of demands from student clientele (Ross, 1976), and a subunit's ability to achieve intellectual consensus and thereby be perceived as having a well-articulated point of view (Pfeffer, 1981a, 1981b).

Other features of organizations have been explored for their role as obstacles to the establishment of new fields, including the departmental reward system (Dressel, Johnson, Marcus, 1970; Mayhew and Ford, 1971), a sectarian institutional mission (Ben-David, 1972), a lack of a critical mass of students (Hodgkinson, 1970), and a lack of a critical mass of faculty (Roy, 1979; Blau, 1973; Scott, 1979).

Oriented toward an analysis of differences that occur across colleges and universities, these studies make important substantive and methodological contributions by linking numerous organizational factors with the successful emergence of particular fields. A conclusion of "multiple causation" is clearly articulated by Hefferlin (1969, p. 189): "[A] whole network of factors—attitudes, procedures, mechanisms, pressures—appear to be involved. [And] a constellation of several factors tends to be present in different kinds of change. Colleges and universities, like other organizations, are systemic by nature. To alter their operations significantly requires effort on several fronts at several levels and by several means."

Following Hefferlin's conclusion, recent studies by organizational theorists reflect a distinctive turn toward producing more interpretive understandings of postsecondary institutions (Gumport, 1988). Based on the premise that reality is socially constructed, attention is focused on the interactive dynamics between organizational participants and their ability to establish shared meanings. The implications of this view for understanding academic change in general—and the establishment of new knowledge in particular—have not yet been adequately explored. Although interest in the subjective understandings of the organizational actors has a long tradition in phenomenology, the approach has not been developed to examine the specific social conditions in which knowledge creators develop and successfully establish new ideas.

The Views of Sociologists of Science

The analytical perspectives put forth by sociologists of science fall somewhere between two very different conceptions of knowledge. At one extreme, one traditional group of scholars in the philosophy of science has argued that knowledge (more specifically, science) develops autonomously as a natural unfolding of ideas, reflecting a cumulative growth and according to its own inner logic and cognitive antecedents (among others, Popper, 1935, and Lakatos, 1971, both cited in Elguea, 1984). At the other extreme, sociologists of knowledge have focused on the relationship between knowledge and society. Claiming that all knowledge is political, these sociologists view knowledge as a reflection—or rather, a reproduction—of the prevailing socioeconomic order, as well as an instrument through which the dominant forces in society maintain their hegemony (e.g., Apple, 1982; Young, 1971; Mannheim, 1936; Pusey and Young, 1979; Bowles and Gintis, 1976; Bernstein, 1982). In my mind, neither extreme is satisfactory for analyzing how academic knowledge changes and how new academic knowledge arises, for they downplay the potential for change to be derived from the social relations among knowledge producers and their individual interests.

As distinct from the sociology of knowledge, conceptualizations from the sociology of science provide an alternative framework for studying how and why a field has emerged. This perspective calls for an examination of the development of scientific thought as it occurs in its social context. This line of inquiry also assumes that knowledge may be shaped by the social origins of and influences on the knowledge producers. Since knowledge—in their terminology, science—is a cultural activity and thereby amenable to sociological analysis, an investigation should include not only the activities of scientists, the cognitive structures they produce, develop, and alter, but also their social relations (Whitley, 1974; King, 1980).

This approach to knowledge emergence and development as both a cognitive and social process is founded in a tradition of inquiry which itself has undergone dramatic developments in the last several decades. Prior to Kuhn's landmark contribution (1962), knowledge growth was conceptualized as an ongoing social process involving a social system, whereby scientists engaged in "a particular sort of behavior" (Storer, 1966), exchanging, producing, and disseminating ideas according to certain shared norms (Merton, 1942, 1945, and 1957). Underlying these conceptualizations was a positivistic orientation toward knowledge, assuming a linear advancement of scientific ideas. The intellectual enterprise progressed cumulatively and provided occasions for the ongoing social relations and disputes in science (Merton, 1957).

Kuhn's perspective deviated from the prevailing one by bridging the emphasis on the social system of science with the substantive content of the intellectual enterprise. Kuhn's theoretical contribution was to suggest that the sociological categories are not external to the cognitive sphere but are related to it, and thereby he brought the social and the cognitive together as not only influential but interdependent forces in knowledge development. Kuhn contributed by offering a different theoretical orientation as to how and why knowledge develops, and the implications of his work mark a distinctive shift in how and on what levels to investigate its development. This breakthrough in turn stimulated inquiry into the reasons for variations in the development of different fields. It also encouraged the further formulation of categories to describe cognitive—or intellectual—phenomena and social structures in science. Kuhnian concepts such as scientific community, paradigms, consensus, normal science, and incommensurability became dominant constructs, redefining the foundation for further theoretical and empirical advances, including the notions of "branching" into specialties (Mulkay and Edge, 1973), network models, and "mapping" a field with sociometric measures (Farkas, 1974; Elkana et al., 1978).

In the Kuhnian tradition, Crane (1969, 1972, 1980) investigated knowledge development in a variety of fields, asking whether scientific communities and communication patterns among them affect the development of knowledge; that is, the accumulation and acceptance of ideas. Crane's approach is to examine "cognitive cultures" (also known as research areas, or invisible colleges) as having both intellectual (her term is *cognitive*) and social influences, and both intellectual and social outcomes. Critical assumptions for this type of investigation include that it is possible to measure knowledge growth (for example, by number of publications per year), to define its boundaries (that is, by demarcating one research area from another), and to define membership and to trace knowledge growth empirically (for example, through patterns of authorship and coauthorship, and through patterns of citations).

Again, the thrust of such research is to combine traditional social indicators (e.g., professional association activities, involvement in scholarly journals) with cognitive categories (e.g., topics of research, nature of objects studied, methods and principles of inquiry). Other related studies have explored how scholars are motivated by a reward system of reputation among peers (Hagstrom, 1965), and interact in social circles (Kadushin, 1966, 1968) or networks (Price, 1965; Mullins, 1973). Into the 1970s, research along these lines burgeoned, as scholars sought to elaborate and refine these theoretical and methodological advancements in the sociology of science (for example, Law, 1973; Lewis, 1980; Lindsey, 1978; Griffith and Mullins, 1972; Spiegel-Rosing and Price, 1977; Hill, 1974; Duncan, 1974; Worboys, 1976).

The fundamental conceptual anchor for this line of work is that cognitive and social aspects of scientific development are interrelated and cannot be analyzed in isolation from one another. As such, it provides a theoretical framework for investigating intellectual and organizational influences in knowledge production. The approach links several important elements, including individual and group judgments concerning the interpretation of results and problem solutions, and the development of ideas, as well as such features as the journal structure of a science, the educational stratification system, the patterns of citations, and social networks in a field (Whitley, 1974).

According to this British orientation to the sociological study of science, the critical conceptual leverage for understanding both the cognitive and social structures of science is to identify the differing degrees of institutionalization at different levels, for these differences in degrees of cognitive and social institutionalization play out in the development of all fields. The concept of institutionalization is useful because it makes explicit that knowledge development is always in process at several levels, with interdependent influences and outcomes. At any point in time, institutionalization applies to both the macrolevel of science development in society and the microlevel as the work of scientists progresses in any particular field. According to Weingart (1974) and Whitley (1974), the institutionalization process of science represents the mechanisms through which external societal influences are translated into cognitive developments and these, in turn, are translated back into society (Weingart, 1974, p. 56).

So, as these theorists began to suggest, a major limitation of some traditions within sociology of science both prior to and since Kuhn is that knowledge development (i.e., science) was viewed as a closed system. Examples of this perspective include ethnographies of laboratory life. Referred to as "black boxism" (Whitley, 1972), this approach has been criticized for emphasizing the intrainstitutional factors affecting knowledge development at the neglect of broader contextual influences. As some critics stated boldly: "[S]ociologists of science are almost exclusively concerned with the visible inputs and outputs of the science system. . . . [They] are preoccupied with the producers in a way that takes little account of what is being produced, why it is being produced, or what it is being produced for" (Mok and Westerdiep, 1974, p. 210). From this perspective, traditional sociology of science neglected the significance of the wider historical context, specifically, "deeper changes in . . . experience and expression" (Nelson, 1974).

In a similar spirit, Nelson's proposal for a historical and comparative sociological study of science leads to a type of cultural analysis, where science is viewed as a cultural activity or product. This further reinforces the presumption that there is a connection between metaphysical ideas in a science and the dominant ideas and images within a particular society. While a cultural analysis at such a macrolevel is beyond the scope of my study, Nelson's view does direct attention to the potential significance of political influences that lie in the changing social setting outside the university, thereby coming full circle to the basic sociology of knowledge interest in the impact of wider social conditions on ideas.

Further evidence from higher education research supports this expanded focus of inquiry. Citing the relevance of factors external to the academy,
Hefferlin (1969) identified how the impetus for academic reform often comes
from beyond the walls of any particular campus. In fact, his conclusions clearly
imply that external factors may also influence the emergence of new fields of
knowledge. These may consist of factors from social movements, to admitting
different kinds of students, to changes in the labor market. In concluding that
both sources and constraints for academic reform are primarily external to the
academic system, Hefferlin reasoned that initiatives for reform lay in individuals' reactions to changing societal conditions, including changes in knowledge,
values, and events. While acknowledging that internal factors in an organization do affect the longevity of change, Hefferlin puts more weight on the external: "[T]he most powerful and influential conditions tend to be those outside
of academic life and academic institutions." The origin of academic reform,
then, simply stated, is that "outsiders initiate; institutions react" (p. 142).

The outsiders to which Hefferlin refers are advocates of change. Hefferlin
dichotomizes these origins a bit simplistically: either they lie within universities themselves, in "the spontaneous innovations of creative professors and
imaginative administrators" or are largely "imposed of necessity on reluctant
academics by outside forces and groups" (p. 142). His insight can substantiate
the likelihood that scholars themselves may actually mediate those wider forces
through their scholarly interests and political orientations.

Merton (1969) elaborates on precisely this notion. Of special relevance to
my study is his description of the sociopolitical milieu and the different interests and perspectives that correspond with different structural positions of insiders and outsiders. Outsiders, according to Merton, have "special
perspectives and insights" because they have been "systematically frustrated by
the social system" (p. 121). Their experience leads them to "inquire into problems relevant to the distinct values and interests which they share with members of their group" (p. 107). Outsiders are likely to be sensitized to aspects of
social life that are taken for granted by insiders. Merton's observations are especially relevant to this study if we consider women as outsiders and academic
women as having a mix of insider and outsider status, which is accompanied by
distinctive perspectives and insights that may be particularly generative for
new knowledge.

The implication that can be drawn from both this literature and from the
"black-boxism" criticism is that we need to incorporate an understanding of
factors beyond or "external" to the academic system because they are clearly influential in the development of new knowledge. The exemplary work of Mok
and Westerdiep (1974) represents a significant line of inquiry in this regard, for
they study how the research interests, motivations, and careers of scholars were

shaped, over time, by social and political influences outside the academic order. In their study of biologists, they state their expanded focus at the outset: "Our starting point was that, as biologists become politically oriented, or 'concerned,' they tend to derive their research topics from external sources. On a behavioral level, one could say that as scientists become politically oriented, that is show concern and responsibility for the application of their products to benefit society as a whole, they not only tend to take part in societal action, but also tend to view their science itself as a means to reach these larger goals" (1974, p. 211).

If we follow their lead and look beyond the academic order, the political climate of the past several decades has been a rich source for a plurality of political concerns: civil rights, women's environmental issues, nuclear disarmament, rights of sexual minorities and the disabled, and so on. To the extent that academics may be motivated by political concerns, these external influences are likely to affect both intellectual and organizational aspects of their academic career trajectories.

In summary, the sociological study of science is a third research literature that informs this study. Abandoning a purely cumulative view of knowledge growth, sociologists of science have made major inroads through analyzing knowledge development as an ongoing social process, a process that takes place at cognitive and social levels, through varying patterns of communicating ideas, sharing common research interests, and engaging in scientific activity with similar understandings of the dominant paradigms and norms. Whereas the interdependence between intellectual and organizational dynamics has been the main contribution of this research tradition, the significance of political influences outside the academy suggests a promising supplementary line of analysis to be pursued by sociologists and higher education researchers alike.

CRITIQUE OF PRIOR CONCEPTUALIZATIONS

The literature reviewed thus far—by historians of higher education, organizational theorists, and sociologists of science—identifies a wide range of factors that may influence the emergence of new scholarly interests. Yet in my opinion, the understanding derived from each of these important lines of inquiry nevertheless has limitations if one seeks a comprehensive account of emerging scholarly interests alongside the social conditions that facilitate knowledge creation. I offer several dimensions of critique.

First, the analytical strategy of most of the aforementioned literature is isolating factors that could be a cause or antecedent instead of studying the processes of knowledge creation itself.

Second, little attention has been given to the dialectical tensions between the world of the disciplines and the day-to-day organizational processes of universities, the two primary academic contexts within which new scholarly interests are pursued. Furthermore, neither political interests nor wider societal currents have been systematically incorporated into an inquiry that focuses on the development of a new field of study.

Third, the literature has not viewed the individual scholar as both being influenced by the multiple levels of context and actively recreating them. Prevailing research conceptualizations do not reflect the contemporary awareness in the academy that academic knowledge is authored and that authors have social locations that necessarily inform their knowledge work (Geertz, 1983a, 1983b, 1988).

Fourth, for the most part, empirical studies have not examined differences in perceptions and experiences among people who work in the same disciplines or institutions. In spite of their similar locations, it is worthwhile to inquire into whether individuals offer differing accounts of the academic barriers and supports they have encountered.

Finally, the literature has not yet illuminated the epistemological anchors of the struggle for legitimacy across the disciplines. These include coherence of dominant paradigms, centrality of theory, the extent to which disciplinary legacies acknowledge or actively seek to incorporate contemporary societal trends, and foundational disciplinary premises about how knowledge is acquired and validated.

Taken together, these deficiencies point to the need for an exploratory study that explicitly links organizational, intellectual, and political contexts, all of which give rise to intellectual obstacles and opportunities around which scholars begin to imagine the possibilities for working in new academic directions. Such an approach to investigating knowledge creation requires an interpretive framework that incorporates the ways in which the structural realities of academia are subjectively experienced by the knowledge creators themselves.

A PROPOSAL FOR AN ALTERNATIVE FRAMEWORK

While the sociology of science provides initial conceptual and empirical justification for the significance of intellectual, organizational, and political dimensions, I have constructed a framework that also draws on theoretical developments in the sociology of organizations (Clark, 1983, 1984; Pfeffer, 1981a) and the sociology of culture (Schein, 1985). This broader framework preserves the analytical and functional distinctions between different levels of context but also addresses their interdependence, as well as the role of individuals' choices in mediating that interdependence.

My framework rests on two basic assumptions, as substantiated by Clark in his landmark contribution, *The Higher Education System* (1983). First, knowledge is the central academic substance and "the invisible material around which action takes place" (Clark, 1983, 12–13). "Bundles of knowledge" are the basic organizing principle of academic activities (Clark, 1983, p. 16). Over time, universities may revise their categories of knowledge and thereby determine the existence of new areas of expertise. Building on Meyer (1977), Clark (1983) has observed: "As educational institutions in general evolve, they develop categories of knowledge and thereby determine that certain types of knowledge exist and are authoritative. They also define categories of persons privileged to possess the bodies of knowledge and to exercise the authority that comes from knowledge. Educational structures, in effect, are a theory of knowledge, in that they help define what currently counts as knowledge" (p. 26).

Second, academic activities including knowledge creation occur within two primary contexts: the discipline and the academic organization, each of which is subsumed under the broader contexts of the academic profession and the national higher education system. Clark (1984) conceptualizes that these two academic contexts both connect and fragment each other: "The discipline links parts of one [institution] with similar parts in others but it also thereby fragments each institution" (pp. 30–31). Clark envisions that the two "lines of membership"—in the discipline and in the institution—constitute the master matrix of higher education.

Following Clark's conceptual division, the parameters for my study are the disciplines and the universities within which scholars pursue their knowledge work. To focus the analysis, I give primary analytical attention to the disciplines. I also attend to powerful influences external to the academy (such as the women's movement) and the extent to which such politics are reported as salient. These research foci are selected not because they are the only factors involved in the emergence of new knowledge, but because they frame the foundations of the academic order within which knowledge work is pursued. My analysis will suggest that the interdependence between these influences defines the intellectual and organizational possibilities of each academic generation, including the subjects they deem are worthy of scholarly pursuit.

Each academic context contains elements that function as possible supports and barriers to scholarly interests. Each context is constituted by a dominant paradigm, a set of explicit and tacit understandings that comprise a constellation of beliefs, values, and techniques that are shared by a community (Brown, 1978). My study is unique in that it investigates the content and function of both disciplinary paradigms (Kuhn, 1962) and organizational paradigms (Pfeffer, 1981a) as they interact to shape new knowledge. While my focus will be on scholars' experiences and perceptions, the academic contexts are relevant insofar as they provide a range of opportunities and constraints for their particular academic pursuits. My framework is composed of three main axes.

Disciplinary Paradigms

The emergence of new scholarship may be attributed, in part, to its intellectual heritage: the ideas developed in prior works, the receptivity to work on potential unresolved research problems, the established disciplinary criteria for defining and judging problem relevance, and the sort of ideal explanations or interpretations that have been conventionally accepted as valid (Whitley, 1974).

To the extent that "scientists share a common attitude concerning [a field's] aims, methods and explanation ideals," a field is said to have a high level of paradigm development (Whitley, 1974, p. 71). The higher the level of paradigm development, the more likely a scientist or scholar is to perceive the intellectual order as having coherence and consensus, and the less likely that a field will be permeated by innovation. Economics, for example, may have the most highly developed paradigm of the social sciences (Lodahl and Gordon, 1972; Pfeffer, 1981a) and thus far has been one of the least open to feminist perspectives (Langland and Gove, 1981).

Since Kuhn (1962), both theoretical and empirical work in sociology have explored how paradigms function in disciplines as disciplinary ideology (Hagstrom, 1965), belief systems (Clark, 1983), and cultural paradigms (Schein, 1985). It should be noted that the concept of paradigm has been challenged because of its ambiguity (Masterman, 1970), its alleged inferior applicability to the social sciences as compared to the physical sciences, and its greater accuracy in describing specializations within disciplines rather than entire disciplines (Kuhn, 1972, postscript). However, the concept of paradigm is a useful heuristic. When considered broadly, the concept may be a useful shorthand to characterize two major aspects of disciplinary contexts (Benson, 1983, pp. 36–38). First, each discipline has an intellectual stance, which includes phenomena of interest, preferable methods of inquiry, and modes of explanation. Second, each discipline has a way of life, which includes the social relations produced from a shared sense of commitment, identity, and boundaries. Both dimensions are united and reflected in the dominant discourse and working assumptions of the disciplinary community.

In the case of analyzing the emergence of feminist scholarly interests, as in any investigation of how scholars' experiences vary across disciplinary contexts, it is important to describe the line of thought in each discipline prior to the new work. For each discipline one might ask: What were the distinctive problems or issues that set the stage for the conceptual schemata and epistemological assumptions of this new work? How were problems generated and how did they come to be formulated? What were related theoretical and/or empirical advances that may have spurred on the new work (Blume, 1977)? Might an established field have been at a juncture that made it open to critique or challenges? Further specification of paradigmatic features in a discipline would include the subject matter's proximity to societal issues, the prominence of theory in the discipline, and the extent of empiricist assumptions or critique of such assumptions (Stacey and Thorne, 1985).

Organizational Paradigms

Just as dominant paradigms differ across disciplines, different organizational paradigms hold sway at different universities. Some researchers have attempted to investigate the viability of paradigm as a useful concept for examining organizational differences. This line of inquiry characterizes organizations as having values and priorities (Pfeffer, Salancik and Leblebici, 1976), consensus on norms for autonomy and collegiality (Adkinson, 1979), shared history and traditions (Brown, 1978), shared definitions of boundaries for inclusion and exclusion of members (Pfeffer, 1981a) and shared systems of belief (Pfeffer, 1981a; Clark, 1983).

While these features of organizational life may be important, in my study the crucial factor underlying their organizational differences is their prestige orientation: whether a university is oriented toward the national prestige hierarchy and attracting faculty with disciplinary fame or whether the university is more oriented toward teaching, student interests, and enrollment-driven financial structures. Each orientation moves to the foreground in the university responses to emerging academic fields. In the case of women's studies, organizational receptivity varied. The research universities that were more prestige-oriented evidenced a conservative, wait-and-see approach in order to discern the scholarly respectability and vitality of feminist scholarship. In contrast, the comprehensive state universities were more concerned with boosting student enrollments and therefore quicker to meet student interest in course offerings within the new field.

With these differences in mind, in selecting the sample of scholars for this study, I deliberately drew from a range of universities. Ladd and Lipset (1972) found that faculty at elite, research-oriented institutions are significantly more liberal-Left than their colleagues at less prestigious institutions. However, Wood (1979) found that low-prestige institutions have been more likely to adopt women's studies programs. If this is so, different challenges present themselves to academic women at each type of university. As local organizational arrangements convey to their faculty substantively and symbolically what academic work is valued, women in different settings may perceive discrepancies between the knowledge work they want to pursue and the university rewards they are likely to receive for it.

The Relevance of External Politics

To the extent that scholars have political orientations, external political influences are likely to affect the scholarly interests they pursue (Mok and Westerdiep, 1974). The converse is also the case. Academic freedom enables a wide range of motivations and activities vis-à-vis politics. The potential for political motivations to shape a faculty member's knowledge work has been a neglected topic of inquiry. It seems reasonable that political commitments may be extended into, or a catalyst for, the pursuit of new research questions (such as bringing to light the role of minorities or the working class in particular historical eras) or for the use of methodologies that write previously neglected accounts into the historical record. Moreover, special status or recognition may be conferred by their political allies on scholars who are politically oriented for carrying out a movement's professed aims of consciousness-raising and other knowledge transformations. So, in addition to being potentially influenced by a wider political climate, scholars must also be seen as active agents who work in their disciplines and their universities. In this sense they may be considered at arm's length from a movement and part of the institution. Thus, we need to inquire into what was underlying their choice of topics to study and how they conceptualize and articulate the significance of their knowledge work.

My analytical perspective attributes more agency to scholars than do conventional approaches to the professional and disciplinary socialization of faculty (e.g., Ladd and Lipset, 1972, p. 1,095). Moreover, my framework explores how influences from several contexts interact to affect the individual scholar, a phenomenon which has remained obscure through 40 years of research studies on academic careers (Finkelstein, 1984).

Initial evidence from the late 1960s into the 1980s points out that explicitly feminist strategies were directed at transforming the dominant disciplinary and organizational paradigms (Fowlkes and McClure, 1983). That they accomplished some of these goals while accruing varying degrees of disciplinary and university legitimacy is remarkable. My analysis will account for these variations within the confluence of forces operating on universities, on the disciplines, and on the scholars themselves. My framework will also make explicit some of the variation in how the scholars traversed the disciplinary and university contexts at the same time that their scholarly work in turn shaped the contexts where their contributions came to reside.

Evidence on feminist scholarship thus far also raises the possibility that the patterns of influence actually depart significantly from those proposed by sociologists of science. The conventional understanding of how intellectual content develops is that social-structural aspects of academic work directly facilitate the formulation of new ideas and the acceptance of new intellectual departures (Lemaine et al., 1976, p. 17). Although this may be true, the development of feminist scholarship suggests a different set of dynamics: nonsupportive academic contexts and organizational invisibility may actually have functioned to stimulate new research interests that reflected concerns about omission, oppression, and the need to articulate alternative understandings of reality. In short, feminist scholarly interests may have been strengthened by an inhospitable context—at least in the early years.

Moreover, if organizational invisibility has been a common experience, one implication may be that proponents of new scholarship self-consciously form alternative channels in order to gain autonomy within disciplinary and institutional contexts. Simultaneously, and with some ambivalence, others may try to make inroads into the existing academic structures as reflected in mainstreaming practices. Thus a tension can erupt between those who pursue separation and those who pursue integration, the former striving to develop a distinctive disciplinary ideology including "feminist theory" and "feminist methodology." Whether separatists feared cooptation by the larger academic order or they desired to forge a new, truly interdisciplinary path, the question of whether or not to develop an autonomous entity to reflect the new scholarship became a potentially divisive factor among academic women.

Indeed, this dilemma may have been central to the intellectual and career choices of feminist scholars as they pursued their work in a variety of academic settings. Whether feminist scholars saw themselves as pursuing a new paradigm that would transform—if not replace—extant modes has been significant. First, their strategies within disciplinary and institutional contexts may have reflected different views on the potential for change in academia. In seeking to promote a new area of academic inquiry, some feminist scholars may have attempted to establish or emulate the structures and norms of established disciplines. Other scholars may have sought legitimacy while simultaneously posing challenges to the disciplines, thereby raising the question of whether or not it is possible to redefine established norms and rules within academia. So, my analysis of their accounts will add to our understanding of the range of transformative aims that have existed among feminist scholars.

In addition to differences in their visions for change, advocates of particular strategies may have held different beliefs about how change in academia actually takes place (Bowles and Klein, 1983, p. 2). Those who engaged in integration efforts, for example, may have assumed that persuasion through conventional channels is the way to contribute most directly to institutional and disciplinary change, whereas proponents of autonomous women's studies programs may have sought to gain control over their own reward system, which could serve as a necessary base from which to establish the legitimacy of their scholarship on its own terms and in its own right. Each path has entailed risks, as proponents of each acknowledge: mainstreaming efforts may result in dilution or cooptation by the very frameworks that feminist scholars seek to transform, while separatist efforts may result in marginal status or invisibility. My analysis of the retrospective accounts of the scholars themselves contributes to our understanding of each of these dynamics, and together, how they played out in their knowledge work.

2

Academic Feminism: Antecedents, Initiatives, and Unresolved Issues

While first-wave feminism was considered to culminate in women's right to vote (1890–1920), "second-wave" feminism refers to the movement that culminated in feminist scholarship (1968–75). In examining the wider social conditions that gave rise to second-wave feminism and its emergence in the academy, the political agenda of the late 1960s women's liberation movement figures centrally. Not only did it provide women with a way of making sense of their life experience, it also gave them a vocabulary to talk with one another, a sense of urgency for action, and a basis for solidarity to pursue their interests within academic settings. In this sense, energy from a wider political agenda provided a catalyst for women to analyze the organizational and intellectual milieux of organizations and disciplines.

Thus the emergence of academic feminism and its teaching arm, women's studies, can be traced back to important antecedents at three interdependent levels: the wider political movement, organizational preconditions that led to visibility in the professions and on campuses, and intellectual openings that enabled women to develop a semiautonomous scholarly agenda. This chapter examines the conditions at each of these levels: the political, the organizational, and the intellectual.

POLITICAL CATALYSTS

Several social movements thrived during the 1960s, most prominently the civil rights movement, the student movement, and by the late 1960s the women's movement. In retrospect, reform in the curriculum, changes in organizations, and transformations in the disciplines may be seen as responses to demands that were vocalized by movement members who were active on campuses. Specifically, the history of women's studies as an academic specialty grows directly out of women's mixed experiences with the Left, which set the tone for women's liberation and which included marching for civil rights, protesting the war in Vietnam, and participating in student uprisings on campuses. Many women became disillusioned with the sexism, oppression, and exploitation of the Left, which some later renamed "male radicalism." Many of these women were white, middle-class young adults who would later become students in graduate schools.

In conjunction with personal awakenings for many women activists, this period was marked by two significant events occurring on the national level: the establishment of the federal Commission on the Status of Women in 1961, and the inclusion of sex discrimination in Title VII of the 1964 Civil Rights Act. Central to the women's movement was a growing consciousness of the need for social change, most prominently the need to understand and improve women's position in society.

As early as 1965, women in the academy made efforts to reconcile political commitments from the women's movement with their own experiences. Early women academics (whether as young faculty, graduate students, or undergraduates) turned to the few existing texts at the time: Simone de Beauvoir's *The Second Sex* (1953, although published in France in 1949) and Betty Friedan's *The Feminine Mystique* (1963). Other popular writings appeared on their reading lists over the next few years, including Kate Millet's *Sexual Politics* (1970), Shulamith Firestone's *The Dialectic of Sex: The Case for Feminist Revolution* (1970), Dorothy Dinnerstein's *The Mermaid and the Minotaur* (1976), and Juliet Mitchell's *Women's Estate* (1973).

Several articles first appeared in mimeographed form, such as those that became "Notes from the First Year" (June 1968). Two widely read works were "The Politics of Housework" (Mainard, 1970) and "The Myth of the Vaginal Orgasm" (Koedt, 1971). At the same time, manifestoes were produced by the Feminists, the New York Radical Feminists, the Westchester Radical Feminists, and the Redstockings. By 1971, an editorial in "Notes from the Third Year" observed a shift in women's liberation writings toward a more in-depth and sophisticated analysis: "This year has seen fewer manifestoes and more work on specific issues such as prostitution, women's literature, rape, and lesbianism. It has been a period of intensive rather than extensive analysis" (Koedt et al., 1971, p. 300).

A number of feminist journals and newspapers also began publishing articles that became widely circulated, including four in 1970: "Notes from the

Second Year" (New York), "Off Our Backs" (Washington, D.C.), "Ain't I a Woman?" (Iowa City, IA), "It Ain't Me, Babe" (Berkeley, CA) and in 1974, *Quest* (New York), a feminist theoretical quarterly.

To these lists were added the original contributions of the first generation of feminist scholars, including Natalie Davis in history and Alice Rossi in sociology. The proliferation of "underground publications" consisted of pamphlets, monographs, and papers, most of which were homemade and distributed throughout informal local networks of feminists. Freeman (1973a) observed the intensity at the time: "The resurgence of feminism (in the 1960s) tapped a major source of female energy. . . . [M]ost of the movement is proliferating underground. It often seems mired in introspection, but it is in fact creating a vast reservoir of conscious feminist sentiment which only awaits opportunity for action" (p. 792).

Jessie Bernard (1987) has referred to this period of the late 1960s as the Feminist Enlightenment, likening feminists to the male philosophers of the French Enlightenment. She states: "Like them, these women wrote, discussed, published. The stream of books, pamphlets, articles, monographs . . . has been spectacular. The effect of these words, shaped and sharpened by their increasing mastery of research—itself one of the most important arrows in the feminist quiver—was like the storming of the Bastille or the 'shot heard round the world.' Academia will never be the same again" (p. xxii).

While the women's movement provided a basis for solidarity in a shared commitment to change the status of women, disagreement was ever-present about what changes were desired and what strategies were appropriate—even among a relatively homogeneous group of white middle-class young women. The emerging feminist discourse became marked by deep differences on such fundamental questions as the nature and causes of women's subordination, the functions of the state, and what constitutes human—especially female—nature. These resulted in the emergence of different ideological strains of feminism and groups of women who advocated more or less distinct political philosophies: liberal feminism, classical Marxist feminism, radical feminism, socialist feminism, and lesbian separatism (Jaggar, 1983). Socialist feminist perspectives are especially relevant because their debates have been prominent in feminist academic circles. (See, for example, Rowbotham, 1973; Barrett, 1980; and Eisenstein's influential anthology, 1974.) It was not until later, in the 1970s, that women of color began to interject race as a prominent line of critique.

In spite of fundamental differences in political philosophies, the women's movement inspired the formation of a national organization to promote legal reforms and improve the status of women. In June of 1966 the National Organization for Women (NOW) was formed by 28 women, each paying five dollars to join. Friedan coined the name. By October of that same year, over 300 women and men were charter members.

The momentum of the women's movement in those years had relevance for women in the academy in a number of ways. At the most basic level, it provided a sense both of shared oppression and of open possibilities (Rosenberg, 1982). At a more complex level, the political themes heightened the tensions and ambiguities faced by those women academics who were politically inclined.

Two themes in particular proved most relevant: undoing the artificial dichotomies between the personal and the political, and similarly, between the political and the intellectual. As personal, political, intellectual, and academic aspirations became intermingled, feminist scholars faced many opportunities to resolve creatively a wide range of perplexing questions: What is the responsibility of scholarship to the movement? What about the choice to work in an academic setting? Does the movement need theory at all (Fildes, 1983)? Is self-disclosure a necessary or even an appropriate teaching technique? Should political and academic interests even be connected?

Thus, on a profound level, the women's movement provided a new challenge for academic women who were motivated to raise new questions out of their life experiences. The potential link between the academic and the personal led them to question their experiences as women and the relationship between those experiences and the traditional canons of knowledge as well as the culture at large. As Rosaldo and Lamphere (1974) stated: "[W]e are searching for ways to think about ourselves. . . . Along with many women today, we are trying to understand our position and to change it. . . . What once seemed necessary and natural has begun to look arbitrary and unwarranted. What once could be assumed, ignored, or tacitly acknowledged now seems problematic and difficult to explain" (p. 1).

A similar sentiment is expressed throughout many introductory passages of books and monographs by women scholars of that era. For example, Spender (1981a) echoes the realization that women have been "left out of codified knowledge" (p. 2). Daniels (1975), in a reference to the influence of Millet's book on her own thinking, realizes that "women offer a unique contribution to our knowledge of the world because of their underdog position" (p. 342). And Benston (1982) suggests that, as scholars, feminists must work with an explicit commitment to end oppression and to that end "the feminist critique of the various disciplines is the attempt to fashion intellectual tools that are freer from the distortions of present male scholarship" (pp. 49–50).

In sum, the initial emergence of feminist scholarship reflects this strong connection between demands for inclusion, critiques of existing knowledge, and motivations to revise the status quo. Key themes that grew out of the Left, the antiwar and the women's movement are: the importance of challenging and questioning authority, the centrality of personal experience, and the need to "define a reality which resonates to us" (Rich, 1979).

ORGANIZATIONAL INITIATIVES

In the early 1970s, universities were populated by women who had begun graduate school in the mid-to-late 1960s, and who were asserting a discourse of women's rights, including the right to be free of discrimination, to be included, to be heard, and to choose. As women students and later, for those who became faculty, they sought to establish a visible organizational presence. Universities typically responded with additive solutions: new courses and, eventually, programs; new positions albeit often not tenure-track; and new organizational forms—such as women's centers and women's student associations—that stabilized an expanding network. Of course campuses responded in varying ways, as did the disciplinary associations that these women came to populate. In response to the range of opportunities and constraints that arose in these arenas, three spheres of organizational activity provided fertile conditions: informal networks, professional associations, and campus environments.

Informal networks of local academics furthered the momentum of women as a group with shared interests. Meetings of small groups provided forums for discussion, consciousness-raising, presentations, communication, and support on practical, political, intellectual, and emotional levels. The potential for exchange was unlimited, not only for expressing feelings and lending support, but later as cross-disciplinary study groups formed to examine differences in intellectual perspectives. Collaborative enterprises shared both scholarly and political interests across the conventional academic hierarchies of rank and status (students as distinct from faculty as distinct from staff, and within faculty ranks) as well as across universities in a similar geographic region.

Little research has been done to examine the spread of these informal networks, although there is some documentation. One such group, the Bay Area Women's Research Group, was founded in Berkeley in the mid-1970s. Prior to that period, dozens of other informal groups were formed with a mix of social and intellectual purposes. Of course, sometimes gatherings did not have an explicit purpose. Their longevity and proliferation is a testament to the potential of informal association as the sustenance of grassroots movements. In retrospect, a critical line of inquiry would be the longitudinal study of such groups: who were the initial members; whether they were in academia; if so, in what disciplines; how the membership has changed over time; what they envisioned accomplishing; and how a political agenda fared in groups that came to be dominated by academic women from higher-prestige research universities.

In addition to informal networks within and across campuses at a local level, the emergence of professional women's groups is another arena where academic women attempted to make significant inroads, and encountered resistance as well as support. The formation of caucuses in the disciplinary professional associations has been traced to 1968–69, when women united in reaction to the discrimination and sexism that they experienced (Klotzburger, 1973). In that year, women's groups were formally organized in the Modern Language Association, political science, and philosophy; in 1970 they appeared in sociology, anthropology, and history; and in 1971 they emerged in psychology, mathematics, physics, chemistry, and philosophy of education. By 1971 women's groups had formed in 33 professional associations: 17 had both advisory and activist caucuses; 12 had only advisory commissions with "more moderate tendencies"; and four had only activist groups. By 1980 there were more than 80 commissions, caucuses, and committees on women inside professional associations and about a half dozen new professional associations of or about women (Howe and Lauter, 1980).

The organization of women's groups in disciplinary associations was linked to the emergence of conferences of, for, and about women, organized by women. For example, a preliminary review of historical documentation on the Berkshire Conference on the History of Women raises some interesting questions. It is not clear who were the initial participants although it is clear that the first annual meeting attracted women from history as well as additional disciplines. The expansion of the group over its first 15 years is significant: from the first meeting at Rutgers in 1973 with a four-page program, to the third meeting in 1976 with a 22–page program and 73 sessions, to the sixth meeting at Smith in 1984 where the theme was "Reassessing Our Past: Women's History after 15 Years" with a 30–page program, 141 sessions, and about 1,000 people in attendance.

Another key aspect of professional association among academic women is access to publication, which was especially problematic for those producing work that departed markedly from the topics and methods that appeared in mainstream disciplinary journals. Early efforts to establish alternative publication channels can be traced to 1969, when NOW formed KNOW, Inc., in Pittsburgh as a publishing house directed toward the dissemination of serious feminist writing (Schramm, 1979). Among its groundbreaking publications were the Female Studies series, the early issues consisting of course outlines and bibliographies for the rapidly expanding women's studies curriculum.

In December of 1970, Florence Howe, then chair of the MLA Commission on the Status of Women, established a "clearinghouse" for information in the emerging field. Feminist Press was founded in Baltimore in that year by Howe and Lauter and moved to New York in 1972.

By 1972 three cross-disciplinary feminist journals had been founded: *Women's Studies* and *Feminist Studies* were for "scholarly articles," and the *Women's Studies Newsletter* (published by the Feminist Press) was to be "a forum for the women's studies movement." In the fall of 1975, *Signs: A Journal of Women, Culture, and Society* was founded. Published by the University of Chicago Press, over the next 15 years, *Signs* was housed at prestigious institutions such as Barnard College, Stanford University, and Duke University. In 1979 another key journal, *Feminist Review*, a British journal, was launched as a vehicle to unite academic theory and political practice, and as a forum for dialogue, discussion, and criticism of the work in progress and the current debates in women's studies.

The significance of the emergence of separate feminist journals for feminist scholars cannot be underestimated; but it is both a blessing and a disadvantage, for it has created a dilemma for some academic women who, upon promotion, are judged for their publications. By directing their work into feminist channels of publishing, these scholars get their work to feminist audiences whose agenda vary in the mix between scholarship and politics. At the same time, however, their feminist scholarly perspectives are not represented in the disciplinary journals, where advances in the disciplines are most commonly published and which carry more prestige vis-à-vis peer review from colleagues in traditional departments (Spender, 1981b).

Similar to establishing alternative feminist publications, another significant arena of professional activity has been the establishment of women's studies conferences. The first national conference was held in November of 1971 in Pittsburgh, followed by a second conference in May of 1973 in Sacramento. These initial meetings were characterized by internal dissent as ideological factions within the growing community of scholars and teachers were self-defined. Over the next few years, these internal conflicts were surmounted by a shared commitment to use their energy and intellectual creativity for organizing on the national level. In January of 1977 in San Francisco, the National Women's Studies Association (NWSA) was founded, according to the constitution's preamble, to promote and sustain the educational strategy of a breakthrough in consciousness and knowledge in every educational setting at every educational level. By the fall of 1984, the NWSA membership was still growing by 10 to 20 percent each year, in spite of the concurrent conservative national trend in education (*NWSA Newsletter* 2, no. 4). During those years of expansion, a tension remained between the ideological factions of the membership and erupted into heated conflict over divergent interests and allegiances that were based not only on the debate between academics and politics but also on sexuality, class, and race differences.

Women's Studies Programs

Nationally, the most prominent organizational manifestation of academic women's feminist agenda was the founding and growth of women's studies programs. It is important to distinguish between an academic program of women's studies from other efforts to establish a feminist presence on campus; for instance, in a women's center and other extracurricular services for students. Over the past several decades, women's studies programs across the nation have been characterized by a wide assortment of courses, programs and degrees, and instructors, suggesting mixed organizational responses to the subject matter, to the students who sought coursework in women's studies, and the faculty who taught in the program.

The first women's studies course, according to Florence Howe, was taught in 1965 at the Free University in Seattle. In 1966 a course was taught at the University of Chicago by Naomi Weinstein and another at Barnard College by Annette Baxter. The proliferation of courses offered around the country over the next 15 years is astounding: from 17 courses in 1969, to 110 courses in 1970, to over 4,600 courses offered in the next four years, to approximately 2,500 courses offered in the academic year 1973–74, to 30,000 courses in the United States by 1980 (Howe, 1975; Howe, 1980). Most courses were introductory and considered interdisciplinary.

The expansion of women's studies programs across the nation similarly burgeoned during the 1970s. The first officially established program was at San Diego State in 1970, although other early programs were established at Portland State University (Oregon), Sacramento State (California), and the University of Washington (Boxer, 1982). By 1971 there were at least 17 formal programs, by 1978 there were 151, and in 1980 an estimated 500 degree programs (Howe and Lauter, 1980). Most programs were interdisciplinary, meaning that they created entirely new courses or combined courses that were offered from several departments, such as literature, language, sociology, anthropology, history, political science, philosophy, biology, psychology, and economics.

While some campuses offered just a handful of courses or fewer, others came to establish a certificate in women's studies or a minor that supplemented the traditional undergraduate major, and several campuses offered more fully institutionalized programs. By the fall of 1984, the NWSA Program Directory listed 247 institutions granting B.A.'s in women's studies—among them such elite schools as Barnard, UC Berkeley, Cornell, the University of Michigan, the University of Pennsylvania, and UCLA. At the graduate level, 55 institutions offered master's degrees and 21 offered doctorates (Ph.D.s).

By the 1986–87 academic year, an increasing number of job announcements called for academic expertise in women's studies. Some positions were for directors of women's studies programs, often senior-level appointments, where the advertisement specified that "candidates must have a substantial scholarly record in women's studies and in a discipline with departmental status" in that particular institution, for example at Ohio State University and Pennsylvania State University. There were also openings for full-time, tenure-track positions in women's studies. Oberlin College, for instance, called for someone "with a Ph.D. in an established discipline and evidence of scholarly achievement in women's studies." The qualified candidate would hold a full-time position in women's studies, yet have a joint appointment for the purpose of retreat rights, should the program be dissolved. Around that time, the University of California at Berkeley also made the same arrangement for a new director of women's studies, a position initially filled by a well-respected historian. Vacancy announcements also pointed to two types of less secure alternatives for people with expertise in women's studies: lecturer positions (e.g., San Diego State University) and visiting professorships in women's studies (e.g., University of Cincinnati and Rutgers).

A few observations are worth noting about this dramatic expansion of women's studies on campuses over a relatively short period of time—20 years. First, Howe (1978) and others have observed that the simple addition of courses was not necessarily indicative of social change; she referred to the "add women and stir" method of social change—an approach which postsecondary institutions have found more practical, and perhaps more palatable, than transforming existing structures.

Second, the geographic expansion of women's studies followed the women's movement up the West Coast from San Diego to Seattle, and down from New England to New Jersey, extending over to Cornell, Buffalo, and Pittsburgh (Howe and Ahlum, 1973). In the course of this expansion, some variation occurred between the elite institutions, who were slower to innovate, and the less elite (and often public) institutions, which generally developed large-scale programs. According to Howe (1975), a disturbing practice emerged at the University of California, Berkeley, which stole faculty from other institutions in order to establish its own program. While perhaps noteworthy because directors were few in number, the practice has become commonplace among research universities seeking to develop new programs, and it has been known to even enhance the prestige of the person who was recruited.

Third, the proliferation of courses and programs reveals inconsistencies in the labels for and within the new field. They included women's studies, feminist studies, gender studies, and female studies, in addition to courses on sex roles and courses in masculinity and femininity (Stimpson, 1975). Strong arguments have been made by proponents of particular favorites, and objections have even been raised regarding the use of women's studies at all (Bell and Rosenhan, 1981), as well as to the distinction between women's studies and feminist studies (Evans, 1982; Degler in Langland and Gove, 1981). Showalter (1971) observed that this range of definitions of women's studies gives some indication of the controversy surrounding its function in the university and in society.

In addition to the expansion of courses, programs, and degrees, the emergence of women's studies on campuses across the nation points to the organizational significance of tenure-line faculty positions and the criteria by which those are allocated. Committing faculty lines exclusively to women's studies rather than to a traditional department is a precondition necessary to establishing women's studies as a department. Whether or not women's studies should even seek departmental status is itself another point of disagreement within women's studies programs and among academic women. Goodman (1984) observed that only a handful of colleges have granted women's studies full-fledged departmental status, which entails a budget, tenured positions and some control by the department's own faculty. For the most part, Goodman noted, about 90 percent of the courses offered in women's studies continue to be taught by faculty members attached to traditional departments.

The structural arrangement of de facto joint appointments created at least two significant problems for the faculty in those positions. First, such faculty have encountered a strain in their commitments, for they do knowledge work inside the world of disciplinary expectations as well as in the world of women's studies and feminist scholarship (Howe and Ahlum, 1973). A second and related problem has been in these scholars' reviews for promotion and tenure.

Even if there is not a joint appointment, those who do feminist scholarship from a traditional departmental location are vulnerable. In a well-publicized appeal of a denial for tenure in the mid-1980s—a case of a full-time tenure-track sociologist located in a sociology department and doing feminist work—a top administrator in the University of California system complained that he was left no choice but to dismiss the testimony of outside experts in the peer review process. In his words: "It has become clear that there is an academic network of 'progressive' social scientists who will fervently support any member of this club. . . . This makes even the interpretation of outside evaluations very difficult. . . . Supporters of these politically committed women . . . are by definition politically motivated, by definition invalid. . . . Critics of these women, on the other hand, are motivated only by a disinterested respect for scholarship" (*Ms.*, October 1984, p. 97).

Among the many issues raised by this statement, it conveys how some academic leaders presume feminist scholarship and its supporters to be inherently political, and dismiss them accordingly. An alternative interpretation is that the promotion of feminist scholarship and women's studies suggests new academic priorities, some of which threaten "old disciplinary masters [male]" who would be displaced. It is for this reason, Benson (1972) explains, that academic peer review itself is inherently problematic: "women's studies . . . is not considered by some academicians to be quite 'legitimate' as part of a college curriculum. In response to this one might say simply that the definition of 'legitimacy' is itself political, that the notion of 'legitimacy' is a strategy to keep the in-people in and the out-people out" (p. 283).

Under such discussions have run some very strong currents about the legitimacy of the knowledge as well as the people and academic units associated with it, for commitments to faculty lines raise the related question of appropriate organizational designations. There is an ongoing question of whether or not women's studies is deserving of departmental status or should even have degree-granting status at the undergraduate level. In response to the question of departmental status for women's studies, the faculty at one elite institution originally answered with a definitive "no." A 1974 report of the Committee on the Status of Women in the Faculty of Arts and Sciences at Harvard stated:

We have . . . not seen fit to recommend the creation of a new department devoted to "women's studies" and predisposed, most likely, to fill its ranks with women. There are many subjects of special interest to women or focused in some special way on the history or the psychology of women or on the fictional representation of women which surely ought to be studied at the university level, but none of these is likely to prosper in isolation from the study of humankind. . . . We suggest, instead, that courses dealing with these and similar subjects ought to be initiated in departments where they are relevant.

Times change, however. At a November 1986 meeting, 200 Harvard faculty voted their nearly unanimous approval to establish women's studies as a degree-granting program. When asked why Harvard waited so long, the chairman of the Women's Studies Committee explained: "Harvard faces a double exigency: it's an intellectual leader, but it also has a responsibility not to be faddish. In this case, it has not been the leader, but Harvard has adopted the concentration after a prudent waiting period to see if it was a genuine field of scholarly inquiry" (Nelson, 1987). The one dissenting voice at this faculty meeting called the program "a foolish and almost pitiful surrender to feminism" (*Harvard Magazine*, January/February 1987).

It is revealing that the proponents of women's studies at Harvard at that stage in the process had anticipated and specifically addressed this concern about politics in their proposal. They stated that the women's studies program is not intended to "foster a 'dogmatic' or 'ideological' approach. It is certain that women's studies is a critical discipline—but one which must not confuse criticism with dogma." By establishing a formal concentration, they argued, Harvard would allow its students to "assess judiciously the ongoing debates and discourses within this vital field . . . without undue impediments" (pp. 2–3, proposal presented to the Faculty of Arts and Sciences, November 18, 1986).

This acceptance of women's studies at Harvard 12 years after its initial rejection there illustrates the possibility for organizational change as well as for academics to change their minds. However, the appropriate organizational form for women's studies is still deliberated, and solutions vary by campus setting depending upon local configurations of supporters, legacies, and resources. For women's studies proponents, the issue of departmental status is more than a question of organizational convenience. It raises the deeper question of whether or not women's studies constitutes an autonomous scholarly agenda that can be deemed a discipline and a viable area of expertise that can anchor an academic career. Ambivalence on these issues surfaces among women's studies proponents and opponents alike. The preference for one particular organizational form of women's studies or another is intimately linked with one's assessment of the intellectual content of feminist scholarship and the potential of the transformative aims it professes. Those in favor of disciplinary status (Coyner, 1980, for example) do not consider it necessary to demonstrate that the field has a distinct or unique methodology, a requirement in the eyes of many in the traditional disciplines.

Before considering the intellectual content of the new field, one final organizational feature of its position on campuses deserves to be noted—the development of centers for research on women—for these centers contribute to the scholarly status of feminist research. In September 1979, a national listing identified 20 such centers, most of which were affiliated with major universities and colleges, including Stanford, Wellesley, Columbia, Cornell, and UC Berkeley as well as UCLA, Ohio State, Rutgers, CUNY, and the universities of Wisconsin, Arizona, Kansas, and Michigan. By 1981, 28 research centers had formed a coalition, the National Council for Research on Women. The council's president, Mariam Chamberlain, reported that the organization had 50 members in 1986.

A critical aspect of women's research centers' establishment and maintenance has been foundation support. Chamberlain, who was then a program officer at the Ford Foundation, characterized 1971 as a pivotal period for the development of guidelines for women's studies and of a budget for it; she reflected on that as a time when they were all trying to decide what the field was. By November of 1971 a meeting of about a dozen visible feminist academic women on the East Coast was held at the Ford Foundation, to which the president of Ford was invited. By the end of the meeting, which he found intellectually engaging, the president decided to set aside half a million dollars to establish fellowship programs in women's studies. By 1986 the foundation had contributed over five million dollars to support the institutionalization of women's research programs. In those years, the Carnegie Corporation was also a visible contributor toward similar ends.

In spite of foundation support in the early years, sustaining a base of funding for women's research centers remained a major concern for the council. Chamberlain pointed out that the money does not come from membership dues (which by the mid-1980s were set at $100 per year per organization, generating a total of $5,000 per year). Concern about funding for women's research centers was periodically publicized. For example, in July 1984, *The Chronicle of Higher Education* (July 25, 1984, p. 5) reported widespread concern over the potential diminishing support for research on women; as a response and under Chamberlain's leadership, the council formed a commission to investigate.

Through the end of the decade and into the 1990s, several women's research centers changed their formal name to the more inclusive research on gender, not simply women. The national council's name remained, however, and the council extended its reach as a clearinghouse for information and as a resource network with expertise from research to policy, with national as well as global initiatives. In addition to continuing the valuable directory of women's research centers, the council lists funding opportunities for visiting scholars, faculty and students, and publishes occasional reports that aim to support the interests of women's research in academic settings. For example, a 1993 report sought to defuse the backlash against political correctness and refute the myth that teaching about gender, sexual orientation, and race suppressed intellectual freedom. By the end of the century, the council was thriving, with over 90 women's research centers in its membership, and listed expertise in over four dozen topics from affirmative action and sexual harassment, to economic literacy and legal issues, to aging and employment.

Locating research on women and women's studies within the academy entailed a tremendous collective effort in a wide range of campus organizations and professional associations. Acknowledging these advances, we can also understand that there has been much variation in the organizational conditions for feminist scholarship. The range of conditions and distinct campus circumstances suggests the need for further inquiry into how these academic women have been engaged in an active organizational struggle for legitimacy, how they have affected change over time through their networks, how their own intellectual and organizational expectations have shifted, and the extent to which they were committed to or identified with the organizational units in which they were located.

INTELLECTUAL ADVANCES

Within the political catalysts and organizational initiatives associated with women's studies, the ideas themselves comprise the core of the intellectual content of what came to be known as feminist scholarship. A substantial body of knowledge has emerged, including new research questions, topics to be studied, and methodologies to be explored. For some academic women, the work of feminist scholarship was a direct translation of their political commitment to social change. Others were drawn to the ideas because those seemed to be the next intellectually interesting questions to pursue. Still others fall into categories unidentified and little understood by empirical studies to date.

That women's studies has survived this long is a tribute to its idea power, claims one practitioner/scholar (Schramm, 1979). While many of the intellectual departures of the new scholarship are distinctive in their fusion between feminism and academia, the intellectual substance reflects a diversity of scholarly interests, disciplinary perspectives, theoretical commitments and pluralistic methodologies. In this sense a singular label, such as "feminist scholarship," suggests some commonality but does not capture the wide range of work and scholarly aspirations associated with it.

In the 1970s, emerging feminist scholarship was lauded by some for its ability to rejuvenate the humanities and enliven other disciplines as well. According to Lauter and Howe (1978), the impact across the disciplines had been "reinvigorating": "Feminist historians . . . have questioned the accuracy and usefulness of the standard period divisions of history—indeed the concept of periodicity. Feminist psychologists have raised questions about the empirical generalizations on achievement motivation, to cite one instance. Feminist art historians have destroyed the basis for the old saw 'why are there no great women painters?' There are and were" (p. 3).

Such additive work grew directly out of women's demands for inclusion and voice. Yet deeper shifts in intellectual traditions served as preconditions for feminist scholarly contributions. Two developments in the wider intellectual climate were most crucial: the increasing legitimacy of subjectivity in the construction of knowledge and the critique of ideology (Smith, 1979). Together these two currents had garnered popularity throughout the 1960s, especially among those who read radical theory and those who sought to link their life experience with academic knowledge.

In the late 1960s, a renewed interest in the work of Marcuse and Horkheimer surfaced. A central theme in that interest was the idea of critique as "oppositional thinking" as an activity of unveiling or "debunking." Two senses of critique were popular at the time. One was concerned with uncovering the conditions of our knowledge, of our perceptions of reality, a line of reasoning that had roots in Kant. A second sense of critique identified the constraints on knowledge derived from human-imposed structures and latent social conditions. Habermas has described these two themes in his conception of theory, which he casts as reconstruction and criticism. In the former, it is assumed that knowledge is possible if the conditions of knowledge are right. In contrast, critique as criticism assumes that conditions of false or distorted consciousness may result from hidden structures of social action; and therefore self-reflection will bring about liberation from constraints, especially for classes of oppressed individuals.

While both senses of critique resonated with the 1960s' sensibility of questioning authority, it appears that for the most part early feminist scholars drew upon this second sense of critique. In fact, one emerging stream of feminist discourse has built on this notion of critique by challenging whether empiricism is even an appropriate mode of knowledge. Grounded in a newly developing feminist epistemology, this approach suggests that knowers are inextricably situated in a specific sociohistorical location. From this position, truth and objectivity are impossible. Yet, rather than implying relativism, this line of argument suggests that a standpoint may yield more accurate knowledge due to the subjugated position of the knower. (For example, see Harding, 1986.)

Other intellectual traditions provided early academic feminists with theoretical support for raising questions about the significance of subjective and ideological aspects of education and about the production and transmission of knowledge per se. Noting the inherently political nature of education as one of those institutions or structures needing to be critiqued, the reproduction literature of Althusser, Bernstein, Bowles, and Gintis put forth some of this discourse (MacDonald, 1980). Also, Paolo Freire has conceptualized education as a vehicle for developing critical consciousness, a model founded in his assumption that education is never a neutral activity.

Moreover, in the 1970s, widespread debates about the production of knowledge and the functions of knowledge fit nicely into the resurgence of academic interest in Marxism. Much of the Marxist-feminist debate of the time was rather abstract. But it was valuable because it provided a springboard for the development of feminist experience and theory; it also provided some direction for new topics to be studied, for example, domestic labor, housework, comparable worth in economics, and in social history, history from below.

Feminist scholars could also draw from a Marxist intellectual tradition in terms of its implications for methodology: No research is carried out in a vacuum; it necessarily has a historical location. Several feminist scholars have theorized about developing feminist methodology so that it is more consistent with feminist notions of nature and with the values of interpersonal relationships (Oakley, 1981; McRobbie, 1982; Stanley and Wise, 1983).

At the same time, the wider intellectual climate provided formidable resistance to early feminist scholarship for its radical intellectual roots. Taylor (1966) characterized the intellectual resistance to the development of Marxism within philosophy, where certain schools of thought have been accepted whereas others were not acknowledged or were dismissed "as literally meaningless or at best confused" (p. 231). Marxism, he explained, was faced with resistance from a strong empiricist movement. In much the same way, we could analyze the intellectual trends in this country that ran counter to feminist concepts and methods in varying degrees, such as logical positivism and empiricism, which dominated the sciences and mainstream social sciences. Such traditional intellectual approaches have notions about human nature, reality, the bases of human knowledge, and social change that run directly counter to feminist scholarly premises that are grounded in a social constructivist framework.

In addition to these dynamics in the wider intellectual climate, within the parameters of traditional disciplines, women scholars made rigorous efforts to find openings that enabled them to pursue feminist ideas. Bowles and Klein (1983) describe the task of the "disciplinary feminist scholar" as formidable because she not only has to be knowledgeable about the structure and ideas of the discipline, but she must "take apart brick by brick the ideas of her forefathers"; she never can work "free from the patriarchal belief system," in contrast to "women's studies scholars who have more freedom" from the confines of a single disciplinary world.

By the mid-1980s, several anthologies were published that assessed the impact of feminist scholarship in the disciplines, the most notable among them Dale Spender's *Men's Studies Modified* (1981), Langland and Gove's *A Feminist Perspective in the Academy: The Difference It Makes* (1981), Fowlkes and McClure's *Feminist Visions: Toward a Transformation of the Liberal Arts Curriculum* (1983), and DuBois et al.'s *Feminist Scholarship: Kindling in the Groves of Academe* (1985). In the 1990s, further works tracked the progress (e.g., Anderson et al., 1997) as well as the dissension across generations of feminists (e.g., Looser and Kaplan, 1997).

Stacey and Thorne (1985) were among the first to examine the specific differences among the disciplines in terms of their receptivity to critical feminist perspectives. They encouraged further speculation on what features of a discipline are most relevant—perhaps the weakness or absence of a dominant paradigm, the centrality of theory, the basic epistemological assumptions of a field, or the extent to which a discipline focuses on changes in the wider society. Over time, many feminist scholars have sought to identify these features as well as others, as they accounted for the development of the new scholarship in their fields: for example Bernard (1973) for sociology, Lauter and Howe (1978) for literature, Atkinson (1984 lecture) and Shapiro (1982) for anthropology.

The development of women as a scholarly topic in one field (anthropology) at one institution (Stanford University) can best indicate the sort of documentation that most directly addresses this question. In the introduction to their 1974 classic Rosaldo and Lamphere explain that in 1973 a collective of women graduate students organized the first undergraduate course in their discipline, "Women in Cross-Cultural Perspective." Their aim was to ask "what anthropologists might have to say about women and, conversely, how an interest in women might provide a new perspective" in anthropology. Noting the deficiency and distortion in anthropological accounts of women's experiences, they were motivated to re-examine "the ways in which we think about ourselves" in order to broaden the discipline's conceptions of "human social life." They also had a self-consciousness about their attempts as a first generation that would be followed by more sophisticated thinking.

Such self-conscious descriptions of perceptions and intentions are commonly found in the early work of feminist scholars, especially for those within traditional disciplines. In some cases the aims both to do political work and to transform the discipline are made quite explicit. For instance, a paper entitled "The Politics of Gender Research" was presented by a scholar who explained (and defended) her explicit political motivation:

[M]y research . . . has been perceived as political, and correctly so, because it has explicitly challenged the prevailing assumptions about gender held by both psychologists and laypersons alike. Thus . . . the research not only generates and tests empirical hypotheses, but it also attempts to shift the dominant paradigm within psychology. . . . Simultaneously, as part of a feminist analysis that advocates social change, the research also attempts to persuade the layperson. . . . In the realm of science, such an attempt to transform perception is known as paradigm-shifting; in the realm of politics, it is known as consciousness-raising. The difference between the two is less than most people suppose.

Thus, her own awareness of this mix of political and intellectual motivations and interests was central.

The notion of paradigm-shifting requires further exploration. Among feminist scholars themselves, opinions differ considerably as to whether it is accurate or even appropriate to view their work as paradigm-shifting. Strathern (1987), an anthropologist, has suggested that it is not possible to be aware of paradigm shifts before they occur. This implies that some feminist scholars who are self-acclaimed paradigm-shifters may wear the label in order to gain the high prestige often granted to scholars who engage in paradigm-shifting activities.

In sum, the development of feminist scholarly content has departed from conservative disciplinary currents through building upon legacies that permitted openings for their distinctive critical and transformative interests. A general constellation of feminist scholarly premises may be stated as follows. First, feminist scholarship conceives of knowledge as useful, even central, to the process of social change. Second, gender is a basic category of analysis. (For an example in history, see Scott, 1986.) Third, women's experience is valued and often at times taken as a starting point. Fourth, prior to feminist scholarship, the development of knowledge in the disciplines was based on male experience. Lastly, the scholarship reflects ongoing self-awareness and self-criticism of its theory and method. Through these essential beliefs, the intellectual, organizational, and political influences on feminist scholars found a convergence.

UNRESOLVED ISSUES

Since the late 1980s, marked differences, divisions, and sharp criticism among feminist scholars as well as among women's studies proponents have become prominent both within universities and within professional associations across the country. Although these dynamics have not been systematically chronicled, the general thrust is remarkable. Academic women have turned their critique to focus on one another and on one another's academic work and have done so on a number of grounds, including these: for not being political enough or being too political, for neglecting either their own racial or class privilege or both, for being ignorant of or prejudiced toward sexual differences, and for being ego-driven or coopted by their institutions in word and deed.

Given this heightened conflict, it is instructive to look back at the mix of enthusiasm and wonder articulated among academic women regarding the prospect of feminist scholarship. As one example, reflecting upon the potential fusion between feminism and academia, the well-known scholar Catherine MacKinnon commented on the exciting opportunity to her academic sisters in 1987:

I have never been asked to speak on such a utopian subject. It calls for a real depth of critique and a real flight of the imagination, and, somewhere in between these two, some reflection on our experience as women. It really asks for an investigation into the relationship between women's lives and the process of the creation of what matters as knowledge and of what comes to be counted as knowledge. . . . It also calls for an inquiry into the relationship between social reality and thinking. And it requires some further thought [about] the way things are and what is not yet permitted to be. (1987)

MacKinnon's remarks reflect the genuine sense of novelty, and perhaps some naiveté, felt by these women in undertaking this ambitious enterprise. And, as the women in this book express, that sense of unlimited possibilities on several levels provided both impetus and sustenance as they made their way into the academy.

As alluded to earlier in this chapter, the development of feminist scholarship has been marked by the absence of a unifying ideology even in its very preconditions. The most salient and potentially divisive issues that surfaced in the academy focused on questions of ends as well as means, goals as well as how to advance the feminist scholarly enterprise. These disputes involved an intermingling of theoretical and practical concerns that would be played out in extensive deliberations over appropriate structures and strategies.

Politically, the omission of a race and class critique by second wave feminist scholars was the decisive blow that delegitimated the contributions of that generation of Pathfinders (Looser and Kaplan, 1997). Yet other ongoing sources of fragmentation have persisted since the late 1970s, the primary one being the autonomy versus integration debate. The core disagreement there is whether to establish an autonomous enterprise and separate location for women's studies or to strive for integration in the disciplines. Institutionally, the question is this: Should there be a women's studies program (or department) in order to develop a visible identity and power base or should the work of feminist scholarship be incorporated into existing departmental structures? On the one hand, establishment of a separate entity risks "ghettoization." Yet mainstreaming with the aim of transforming (or gender-balancing) the curriculum risks assimilation and dilution (Bowles and Klein, 1983). Up to the late 1980s, the trend was for institutions to grant autonomous status to women's studies as a teaching program (which requires little funding and brings little prestige) before they undertook mainstreaming projects, and then when they did set about mainstreaming, campuses were running both sets of parallel efforts. (Examples of this pattern include Stanford, San Francisco State, and UCLA.) In the name of "curriculum transformation," such short-term projects became even more visible on campuses across the country in the next decade.

On the disciplinary level, tension between autonomy and integration aims and strategies has also been long-standing. One direction has been to establish feminist scholarly perspectives as a separate discipline. The other direction has been to make a frontal assault on the discipline as a whole, attempting to transform its prescriptions for what counts as knowledge, what topics are worthy subjects of scholarship, and how inquiry is to be constructed and verified, in other words, attempting to affect the entire canon. Within the disciplines there is evidence of some transformative achievements. Increasingly, subfields have emerged in some disciplines, such as women's history, sociological study of sex roles, and feminist ethics, thereby making feminist contributions more visible. It is important to note that the emergence of a subfield does not reveal the extent of efforts to dramatically change the discipline. For example, feminist ethics is not the sum total of efforts to modify the content and manner of philosophical inquiry. In this sense it is difficult to assess the extent to which these subfields are indicators of disciplinary legitimacy at all. Like women's studies programs, autonomous subfields may indicate that feminist perspectives have found a niche. But whether the niche is a corner in the basement or a penthouse suite remains to be seen. In a way, subfields are by definition marginalized. Like women's studies programs, a subfield may be seen as a conventional disciplinary response to new scholarship during a waiting period. But in the case of feminist scholarship, one cannot help but wonder if it is a way to relegate to the margins faculty with those interests, thereby keeping the disciplinary canon intact.

Many feminist scholars envision disciplinary legitimacy as moving beyond women as subject matter or a collection of topics, to constructing a lens through which the entire canon is critiqued and then reconstructed. Preliminary efforts towards this kind of impact have been attempted by some feminist scholars in history, sociology, and philosophy, although it is unclear to what extent far-reaching transformations can be achieved in each discipline. Perhaps one of the most successful cases of challenging a canon has taken place within literary criticism, where those in the discipline seem to agree that feminist literary criticism is something in which both men and women students as well as faculty need to be at least conversant. But even in that case, it must be asked whether feminist criticism has become simply a recognized subfield or whether it has shaken and transformed the canon in a more fundamental sense.

The tensions between efforts for autonomy or integration are intertwined with important theoretical questions about why some disciplines are more receptive to feminist contributions than others. One set of questions concerns the extent to which a disciplinary canon might be gendered. This kind of critique entails the analytic project of asking how particular canons have explicitly and implicitly excluded women. (For example, see Grimshaw's (1986) chapter on "The 'Maleness' of Philosophy.") A second set of questions considers the extent to which one's experience as a woman might be the basis for a female, feminine, or feminist voice. The aim in this case is constructive, to explore the potential for a feminist epistemology, a feminist ethics, a feminist methodology, and so forth. In other words, each type of project is framed according to whether the objective is to construct an autonomous feminist scholarly discourse or to integrate feminist work into disciplinary agendas. Presentation to a feminist scholarly audience generally calls for more interdisciplinary, political, and practical awareness whereas a disciplinary audience requires some further translation into specialized theoretical concerns.

Feminist scholars themselves have recognized that portraying autonomy and integration efforts as mutually exclusive forces those involved to take sides, which as we have seen has been detrimental to the enterprise itself. Seeing the two alternatives as incompatible may cause needless tension, according to some observers (McIntosh and Minnich, 1984). A large proportion of the academic women I interviewed expressed the view that both projects are important and should be pursued respectively by those working primarily in women's studies or primarily in their disciplines. Although such a two-pronged approach may be a short-term solution, the reality of the academic reward structure and the scarcity of resources (especially time) generates pressure to prioritize. Trying to contribute to both scholarly endeavors causes strain, especially for the individual faculty member herself, who may be located within an existing discipline where she is likely to meet expectations and rewards that see her feminist scholarly interests as peripheral.

Over the past few decades, these various tensions have surfaced in many circles—among men and women academics, among academic women generally, among women working in the same disciplines, among feminist scholars, especially those in existing disciplines as opposed to those in women's studies—even introspectively, within individual feminist scholars. The manner and extent to which one's scholarly life is touched by each issue depends upon one's intellectual and institutional location as well as deeply personal aims and life experiences. For some academic women, as is the case for those I interviewed, the knowledge work itself became the primary arena for their attempts to resolve these issues.

3

Investigating Knowledge Creation

THE RATIONALE FOR THE DESIGN

This study is grounded in an exploratory research design for analyzing knowledge creation, both the processes and the conditions within which academic women worked. Since my objective is to describe and analyze how a core group of women perceived constraints or opportunities for their ideas to develop, the phenomenological analysis takes into account both the discipline and university contexts. Variation in these contexts emerged as a key determinant of these women's possibilities for linking their experiences as women with their academic work.

The data are drawn from a core group of interviews with 35 women faculty. (For further details on the research design and methods, see the appendix.) Semistructured interviews were used to elicit reflective autobiographical accounts of the evolution of each scholar's intellectual interests and career choices. Scholars were asked to describe how they were influenced by their contexts and how they responded to them. My primary informants were selected from a wider population of women who currently work as full-time faculty within 10 postsecondary institutions, ranging from high-prestige research universities to state comprehensive universities, all within one metropolitan area. The close geographical proximity of these academic women allowed me to explore the extent to which cross-fertilization of ideas, politics, and support was channeled through informal local networks over time.

Women faculty working in two types of locations were selected. First, I drew a stratified random sample of women faculty whose primary location was currently in their home discipline (i.e., same department as Ph.D. training): 27 scholars, nine each with Ph.D.s in the corresponding disciplines of history, sociology, and philosophy. In addition to this core group, I interviewed 10 women scholars who were currently located in women's studies positions. (I subsequently omitted two of them from the data analysis as they did not have Ph.D.s.) The purpose of this design was to yield a wide range of orientations to feminist scholarship. Some women in traditional disciplines have neither interest in, nor knowledge of, new feminist scholarly discourse; others have been at the cutting edge of feminist work within their disciplines. And as would be expected, those with a primary affiliation to women's studies are intimately involved in the teaching of women's studies and the construction of feminist scholarship. Such a range of perspectives provides some interesting insights about the development of the new field and the ways in which people with similar disciplinary training may end up in different institutional and intellectual locations.

The rationale for selecting these three disciplines—history, sociology, and philosophy—is twofold: (1) these disciplines are more likely to be affected by external influences than sciences such as mathematics, physics, chemistry, and astronomy (Hagstrom, 1965, citing Mannheim, 1936); and (2) evidence indicates varying intellectual and organizational responses by these fields toward feminist scholarship, history being the most receptive (Spender, 1981a; Fowlkes and McClure, 1983; Langland and Gove, 1981; Stacey and Thorne, 1985; Wood, 1979), and philosophy the least.

THE CORE SAMPLE AND THE INTERVIEW DATA

As a framework for examining the processes by which my informants came to develop their intellectual careers within various institutional and organizational settings, my analysis of the interviews is organized according to cohorts of women who attended graduate school during the same period. My sample consists of 35 women who entered graduate school between 1956 and 1980. Given the dramatic social changes that occurred during those two and a half decades of United States history, these academic women fall into groupings that may be considered academic generations. Women from each generation faced different social conditions as well as different intellectual resources in their disciplines. Their having undertaken graduate study before feminist scholarship, as pioneers of it, or after it, entailed a distinctly different set of academic possibilities for each generation. Based on the year in which they began their Ph.D. programs, the women I interviewed are grouped as follows: those who entered graduate school before 1964, whom I consider to be the Forerunners to feminist scholarship; the Pathfinders, who entered between 1964 and 1972 and initially developed feminist scholarship; and the Pathtakers, who began their graduate training after 1972. The following table displays the distribution of the sample by generation, designating the disciplinary location at the time of my interviews with them.

The Sample: Disciplinary Location for Each Academic Generation

	Forerunners	Pathfinders	Pathtakers	Total
History	3	5	1	9
Sociology	1	5	3	9
Philosophy	1	5	3	9
Women's Studies	1	5*	2	8
Total	6	20	9	35

I interviewed two additonal women located in women's studies programs but omitted them from the analysis because they did not have Ph.D.s.

The mean age for each generation and by academic location is also informative. As expected, the Pathfinders are a middle generation in relation to the Forerunners and Pathtakers.

Mean Age: By Generation and by Academic Location

Generation	Age
Forerunners	49
Pathfinders	43
Pathtakers	37

Location	Age
History	45
Sociology	42
Philosophy	39
Women's Studies	43

Through autobiographical accounts by women academics of their intellectual and career history choices, the interviews trace the evolution of their scholarly interests, from graduate school to their current academic positions. Their academic career histories are analyzed as a process of choice and adaptation in which scholars mediate among existing organizational and intellectual parameters that both determine what counts as legitimate knowledge and shape opportunities for new research. Throughout the analysis, I sought to understand how these academic women were influenced by and in turn acted upon their most immediate contexts. All of the interviews were framed by a common set of guiding questions and unfolded in a semistructured approach that left room for the interviewee to elaborate and even digress.

THE ANALYSIS BY GENERATION

Two aspects of this generational analysis must be noted at the outset. First, the choice of the specific years as dividing lines is somewhat arbitrary. Clearly, some women were at more politicized campuses before 1964, for example. Yet in this particular study, the patterns seemed to correspond to groupings according to these years. Second, I selected the year in which they entered graduate school instead of the year they finished. I did so because the early years of graduate school are more likely to have students in a cohort, engaged in coursework together for example, as opposed to the later years, when students tend to do work more on their own. The early years of graduate school are also a period when students take extensive coursework, thus are more explicitly socialized into the expectations of the discipline.

My analysis reflects the opportunities and constraints that were present for each group of academic women: the Forerunners, the Pathfinders, and the Pathtakers. Each generation went through a variety of processes to sort through their experiences. Their concerns included whether or not to pursue the Ph.D., how to deal with being in academia, what career opportunities were available, how political orientations may be relevant to academic work, what intellectual work they hoped to contribute, and so on. In spite of the diversity within each group—that is, diversity of ambitions and outcomes—several distinct patterns emerge.

The patterns suggest two interrelated story lines. One is the story of how women penetrated academia during dramatically different periods of sociohistorical positioning for women. While the process of becoming established in academia is noteworthy, my interest is to explore more deeply, to draw out the other story of creating knowledge. So, I look at the patterns through which some of these women became innovators in the academy, creatively formulating new knowledge within existing organizational and intellectual constraints.

In analyzing knowledge creation, I present a portrait of these three generations of academic women as historically situated within periods of an emerging feminist scholarly discourse. The Pathfinders created the first fusion between feminism and scholarship. The early years may reflect attempts that were relatively crude intellectually, even though they were daring ones in personal terms. As feminist scholarship evolved in the 1970s, the Pathfinders produced an increasingly visible and well-articulated feminist scholarly agenda. This agenda became anchored in a growing body of knowledge and a new way of seeing, and provided an already existing paradigm for the third generation of women—the Pathtakers—who then had the luxury of choosing to pursue it or not. The Forerunners by contrast had begun their graduate training at a time when woman-ness did not appear to have any relevance to scholarly concerns.

Viewed from this perspective, the three academic generations of women may be seen as preparadigmatic scholars, paradigm developers, and those working within a paradigm. The Pathfinders were people who, with few antecedent intellectual resources, actually produced a feminist perspective in the academy. In the context of few available resources either within graduate school or in early academic appointments, how was feminist scholarship generated? How and where did those creators of this new knowledge get the sense that this would be a fruitful path to follow? Did they have a sense that these ideas could eventuate in a discourse that would challenge the disciplines and the organizations that housed them?

Guided by these questions, the analysis traces the competing interests in the lives of the knowledge creators, focusing on the generation of Pathfinders. Those feminist scholars who emerged from the Pathfinders generation had great ambivalence about being in academia to begin with. Many of them reported having had (and still having) doubts about whether or not they wanted to be in graduate school, to be scholars, to be located within academia.

Yet what emerged out of this ambivalence is striking: given their various political commitments and intellectual interests, having few intellectual models to draw upon, the Pathfinders nevertheless found new ways to be scholars and to create a new field. By examining the contradictions that they experienced, we learn how they negotiated the competing interests around them to pursue their ideas and ultimately to advance their careers.

In summary, the focus of this analysis is on both generative conditions and processes. The analysis locates each group of academic women within their historical situations vis-à-vis national politics as well as in relation to an emerging feminist discourse. It suggests the dynamic sense in which several kinds of pressures and opportunities intersect. This intersection gives rise not only to individual academic careers, but also to generations of potential knowledge creators to come.

Each Generation in Context

Before discussing each academic generation, I briefly describe each cohort and its location in particular sociohistorical circumstances external to the academy, for as we have seen, the wider political environment was a crucial context in which academic women formulated their ideas, hopes, and dreams.

The decade leading up to 1964 was characterized by a low level of dissension on American campuses. According to Lipset (1976), "[I]t was a low ebb in student and other forms of radicalism. . . . Liberal and left student groups either passed away or existed in tiny memberships and small agendas" (p. 185). At that time, women who went to graduate school for Ph.D.s were generally motivated out of a love of learning. They liked going to school and were successful at it, without giving a lot of thought to what they would do next. Yet these women were pioneers by virtue of their gender alone; they were exceptions and exceptional. The problem for women, if a problem was even perceived, was how to be both a woman and an academic. A common view was that an academic woman would not finish the doctorate, or if she did finish, upon completion would simply get married and thereby forego her career.

One woman in my study with a B.A. from a prestigious women's college explained the advice she received as she prepared her application to an Ivy League graduate school: "The professor told me that when I send in my photograph with the application, not to make it too pretty because then they will assume I'll marry, but not to make it too ugly because they won't want me around. I remember thinking that this was amazing advice. That these people actually made these kinds of predictions for you!" Another informant characterized the milieu at Harvard: "They had a quota on women then. They assumed you weren't going to make your mark no matter how good you were." Contrary to this received wisdom, these women found a niche, even though their experiences tended to reflect the reality that, by virtue of their femaleness, they were pushed to the margins of academic life.

By 1964 and with the passage of the Civil Rights Act, early signs appeared of a major shift that would politicize academia significantly and alter societal expectations for women. Student radicalism rapidly became the dominant theme on campuses around the country. Riots and demonstrations made visible the passion and turmoil generated among overlapping movements: free speech, student rights, civil rights, and anti-Vietnam War protests. It was a time of "general revolt against oppressive, artificial, previously unquestioned ways of living" (Zinn, 1980, p. 526).

This great unrest also involved questioning the purposes, processes, and content of higher education. Faculty too were involved in this radicalism; and at one institution in this study, the faculty went on strike and eventually unionized. Against this backdrop of upheaval, the modern women's movement germinated. It captured the attention and galvanized the energy of many women, some of whom had been active in the Left but had become disillusioned with its devaluation of women and others who became newly politicized, gaining a consciousness that women's experiences matter and that women's capabilities are equal to men's.

Women who entered graduate school between 1964 and 1972, the Pathfinders, thus made their way through academic channels in these turbu-

lent times, when it may have seemed more important to be political than academic. There were actually many ways for a student to be considered
legitimately political. The context emphasized social responsibility and permitted anger and passion as driving forces to "at least do something." As one
informant suggested, "It was political involvement in the sense of social injustice. We were beginning to shift to seeing it more as a system and less as what
can I as a person do to help."

The idea of going to graduate school to do scholarship—to think about
ideas in an ivory tower—seemed inadequate. At the same time, in the late
1960s, many women received fellowships to go to graduate school and subsequently enrolled without being oriented to the demands of the labor market.
These two factors meant that these graduate students did not feel insecure in
their academic futures, nor were they bringing with them conventional academic aspirations. Their resulting detachment may have allowed them to pursue risky intellectual ventures.

Although somewhat constrained organizationally because they were graduate students, Pathfinders made conscious, as well as unconscious, attempts to
find a way to do academic work that would take into account their political interests. The women's movement outside of the academy gave these Pathfinders
a language and political agenda that could be translated into their academic
work. For some women, a central question became how to be both political
and academic. For others, the question soon crystallized into how to be feminist and academic.

By 1972 women were entering graduate school with a very different outlook
from that of the cohort only a few years ahead of them. Women entering graduate school after 1972 more easily came to adopt—without having to invent—a feminist perspective if they chose to. Both feminism and the presence
of women had become more established in academia, thereby creating two
possibilities for the Pathtakers. A new academic profile allowed them to continue and even intensify the feminism from the Pathfinders' generation. Yet it
also permitted some women to be academic women without feeling a pressure
to be feminist.

Also by 1972 "both activism and radical sentiments on campus [had] de-
clined considerably" (Lipset, 1976, p. 198). This was "a different political era"
in which concerns were turned more toward economic uncertainty because of
a depressed labor market (Lipset, 1976, p. xxxii). Nineteen sixties' visions of
utopia receded, but women's issues and feminist activities remained. For
women, discrimination and equal rights were pressing issues. Sisterhood was
becoming more institutionalized in women's networks. Affirmative action leg-
islation (Title IX) was passed. Affirmative action was an encouraging sign that

the nation, at least on the surface, was beginning to apply institutional reme-
dies to some of the problems identified by the earlier generation.

Women graduate students of this era were less compelled to assume a critical
posture than the generation before them and were therefore able to pursue
their individual scholarly careers without making their gender primary and
without the overwhelming urgency to change the system or resolve social injustice. Whether by conscious choice or unconscious inclination, these
Pathtakers had a new set of possibilities—to develop scholarly agendas and careers aside from their gendered experience of disciplinary or university settings.

Against the backdrop of national politics, women of each academic generation developed into knowledge creators. Although chronologically the middle
generation, the Pathfinders are the focus for the first part of my analysis (chapter 4), for they effected the initial fusion of feminism with academic and scholarly discourses. Following an examination of their breakthroughs from the
disciplinary perspectives (chapter 5), my analysis then traces the scholarly development of the Pathtakers and Forerunners (presented in chapter 6).

4

The Pathfinders' Breakthroughs

To portray the generation of Pathfinders, my analysis considers the major stages in their intellectual biographies and career histories. A chronological approach best captures how the Pathfinders came to create what came to be thought of as feminist scholarship, whether they did so within their home disciplines or within a separate location known as women's studies.

The Pathfinders ultimately made significant intellectual contributions that must be seen in the light of their early career development, for they came to create new knowledge through a distinctive lack of identification with the traditional academic career. This detachment from conventional academic aspirations perhaps enabled them to undertake such risky intellectual ventures.

STARTING POINTS: GOING TO GRADUATE SCHOOL

The generation of Pathfinders entered graduate school during a period of campus unrest. In their stories about how they ended up in graduate school, two interrelated themes emerge. First, these women perceived their career options as limited. Second, the highly politicized social climate they inhabited called into question the worth of a scholarly career. For the majority of the Pathfinders, these two themes converge in a pervasive ambivalence about being in academia, a striking finding given the tremendous excitement they would come to generate in their feminist scholarly pursuits.

Career Options for Women

Most women in this generation went to graduate school because they lacked any other clear alternative. As one historian in my study suggested, graduate school was a safe option. She had anticipated both liking it and succeeding at it. "Graduate school [seemed like] a safe thing to do. It was like going on with your education, and that is something I could do. . . . I was sure I could do it. I knew I could do history. . . . What else is there that you can do in the world? Well, I had tried to do this social reform-type job for a year, but that didn't feel right."

Many of her peers expressed similar views. For these women, who strongly desired to be independent, graduate school seemed like the natural next step. As she put it, "Something in me always knew I had to be self-supporting. And I just didn't see a place for me anywhere else. So, I backed into graduate school." The intention to be self-supporting was actually affirmed by most of the other women of this generation. Given this need to find some kind of employment, graduate school seemed preferable to other kinds of jobs that were stereotypically female. For example, another historian explained that she worked full time as a secretary for a year, after obtaining a bachelor's degree in history. Having liked history, "I then backed into graduate school, thinking it was preferable to doing clerical work. . . . But I didn't think too much about what I'd do afterward." It is noteworthy that both of these women described themselves as having "backed into" graduate school.

One of the sociologists reinforced this experience of wanting to flee from secretarial work. At the same time, she did not perceive herself as having an academic career:

I see it as really accidental, somehow relating to discrimination in this society. Back then, women with B.A.s, if they didn't have teaching degrees, were hired to be basically secretaries. Many of the women I knew went off to New York City to be typists and receptionists. I had no clerical skills, had no interest in acquiring them and I did real well in my major and somewhere along the line I guess the faculty really gave me a lot of feedback that I was really talented at it. . . . (Since) my husband was in the service in Washington, I applied to grad school there. That was better than having a rotten job. But I really had very little perception of becoming a career person. I just sort of fell into it.

Backing into graduate school in a rather short-sighted manner gives the impression that there were few options available at that time. Some women did at least briefly consider law or business. They then dismissed those as viable options. As these three Pathfinders recall,

I think partly I went to graduate school because there weren't any other options. I wanted to do something in the world. . . . When I came to think about law school . . . it didn't seem like a real option for me. Nor was business school, like students do now. I didn't think about that.

I wasn't clear what I wanted to do and there was no one to guide me with information on careers. I considered law school but was told that women were treated badly. So I thought why would I want to do that. . . . At the same time it hadn't occurred to me that the same kind of thing happened in academia. If I had opened my eyes and looked around I would've seen that all of my [professors] were male.

I didn't know what to do with my life. . . . I was certainly programmed and was going to prove I could be something. I wanted to go to law school. There was no question. I took the law aptitude test and I did very well, but I had no money and also, I didn't know any lawyers and I talked to a few people and they said, well, you'd be a clerk—law clerk—there are no women [lawyers] in 1964 and so I had no role models.

Graduate school at least had a few token role models, so it seemed like a possibility. But for the majority of those in this generation, not much forethought was involved. As one woman describes, the very idea of obtaining a Ph.D. arose unexpectedly. She was initially attracted to it because it was a way to remove herself geographically from her family. In her words,

So, then I decided I had to leave and I told my parents I was coming to California. I only knew one person here and I had no plans. They talked me into seeing a friend of my father's who was at Harvard who also had some interesting jobs. Of course, I didn't tell them the truth about his jobs. For reasons I'll never know, I think he just wanted to get me out of his office and said whatever came to his mind, . . . "Oh, I think you'd be a great sociologist. . . . Get your Ph.D." I will admit I didn't know what it was, but I said I didn't know much about it. [Since he knew someone] in Social Relations, he [got] me a reading list.

She described how she took this reading list and went to the library daily, sitting "with a clock, I timed myself to sit for five hours at a time without moving. It was a solitary world" in which she was actually very much intellectually engaged. In her words, "I just read. . . . It was interesting. I had never been challenged before and I had nobody to talk to. . . . I also didn't know what a sociologist did or does or [anything about] being an academic. I thought, why not? So I took the GRE and the advanced sociology GRE which you had to take . . . and I got this perfect score. . . . Who else had such an uncluttered brain?"

This sociologist, like most of her peers, went on to graduate school without actually imagining herself becoming an academic or picturing what an academic career would look like. As she stated simply, "I didn't have anything better to do."

So, for the majority of Pathfinders, going to graduate school was something they "fell into," for they perceived no other attractive options. In contrast to the present-day emphasis on more rational or at least self-conscious planning, the accidental nature of these "decisions" is striking.

One would imagine that those entering graduate school are likely to consider the Ph.D. program as preparation for a career in college teaching or research, especially for those entering high-prestige universities. But some Pathfinders ended up in graduate school despite inclinations that would suggest a Ph.D. program would be inappropriate. Consider the mismatch between a Ph.D. program in history at a high-prestige university and this woman, who entered it feeling confident that she wanted to teach at the elementary or secondary level:

I certainly had a sense that I wanted to be in teaching, probably a junior high or high school teacher. And this may have been affected by my being a woman. Once I got into graduate school, I got nervous. I was treated very much as my male cohort was, and I got nervous about being different. How come they were going on to a university career and I was still talking about kids ages 11 to 13, you know, teaching on the junior high school level. I couldn't understand that difference. . . . My surroundings started to push me forward into essentially what was a male career pattern, which was go for everything, as far as you can, as fast as you can. I just got caught up in it. . . . There were several moments when I stopped and said, "But I don't think this is what I want to do." But I couldn't resist it. It was simply there and I followed.

This historian got swept up by the compelling stream of the academic trajectory without having intended to do so. Her story resonates with those of many of her colleagues in this generation of Pathfinders, who did not anticipate that going to graduate school would ultimately lead to participation in a fast-track, high-prestige career, let alone a genuinely innovative project. It is almost as if these women ended up creating this major scholarly innovation in spite of themselves.

In addition to being intensely ambivalent about going to graduate school, these women were launched on an academic trajectory that was by no means smooth and enticing. In fact, it often involved major compromises. Some of their experiences were marked by painful periods of self-doubt and uncertainty. This historian confesses feeling that she did not fit in with the other history graduate students, who happened to be men: "Nobody ever said to me, 'What do you really want and what are your values?' That was never part of the process. [Oftentimes] there was a question of my values being in direct conflict with this trajectory. I got slapped down and I was very well aware of that. I could see that happening. I cried. I wept. I said it was unfair, and I changed."

Many women of this generation characterize going to graduate school as having a huge "emotional cost," as this woman suggested. Generally speaking, the Pathfinders reported that going to graduate school involved a loss of naiveté. As one reflected, "I've always thought that there was a misapprehension there, sort of like—and the metaphor that always comes to mind is making out was so much fun, I figured sex would be as much fun, only more so, and that undergraduate school was so much fun, and I thought graduate school would be, too. I was wrong on both counts. Nothing, nothing matches that early thrill."

The actual experience of going to graduate school was not something many women considered beforehand. It seems that external pressures were most compelling; for example, the desire to postpone marriage or the motivation to obtain credentials. Somewhere between the "push and pull" of different pressures, a sociologist made her decision:

When I think back on it, there was sort of a combination of calculation and naiveté. . . . I was engaged to be married. . . . That was a legitimate way to postpone making any decisions about getting married. I think it was both a push and a pull, which was that I love sociology, and I thought graduate school in sociology would be great fun, and I really actively didn't want to get married, and I certainly didn't want to get married without a career. . . . I was doing well in school, so it was something I knew how to do well. I think even then I was aware that women pretty much needed as many credentials as they could get from the best place they could get them, but I didn't have other clear alternatives.

Some of the Pathfinders may have weighed various considerations. Yet when it came right down to it, going to graduate school "was really a flip of the coin," as another sociologist recalls: "Looking back you forget how fragile are these turning points in one's life and how easily it could have gone another way. . . . It was a choice between social work, Peace Corps, or sociology. I applied for all of these. . . . I tried to combine a stint in the Peace Corps with a master's thesis. In the end, I decided I wanted to learn about how societies worked and I could write about it."

Financial support, which is usually a major concern, made graduate school a more attractive option, as fellowships were plentiful and extended through all the years of a graduate program. A woman in literature identified the offer of financial support as an important consideration: "[Graduate school] was not planned. I was really much more on the road to be a journalist, but I think I was drawn into it partly because what I liked to do best was read and write. In college I had spent so [little] time studying that I decided I wanted to read for a couple of years. . . . I was astounded that somebody would pay me to do that. . . .

It started paying me to read and write, so somehow, even though it had not been my intention, I got sort of hooked into the whole academic thing."

The same was true for this sociologist: "They gave me a lot of money. . . . I was funded from the minute I walked in the door. . . . It wasn't so much that I had a self-conscious identity as a graduate student in sociology, or even a sociologist, but it seemed that it was an opportunity to continue to do something I enjoyed. I was fully funded, and I didn't have other clear alternatives."

And for this anthropologist, who had funding from the National Science Foundation (NSF): "I didn't know if I even wanted to go to graduate school, but I was offered a NSF scholarship. You couldn't postpone or turn those down if you ever wanted to get another NSF. So that sort of made the decision for me."

While ambivalence was pervasive for most Pathfinders, in a few instances they reported wanting to get a Ph.D., to "teach somewhere and be a researcher or scholar." But even the few with such clear ambitions admitted that "the practical realities of that were slow to come to me."

A philosopher reported that she had to overcome several practical obstacles to fulfill her ambition to continue with academic training, and the challenge of it was perhaps part of the attraction for her. Not only was financial support essential, but her advisor was working against her. She had started out in premed, "where women were not supposed to be—that's the only reason I was there; I had to do the hardest thing." By her junior year she was an honor student in philosophy: "I was the cream of the crop." In spite of having gone through "an intense traditional philosophy program," she did not get into any graduate schools the first time she applied because, as she later discovered, her advisor ("who was entrenched in the analytic tradition") had written a damaging letter of recommendation about her undergraduate thesis. In any case, her determination prevailed:

When I didn't get into graduate school, I thought I *am* going to go to graduate school and I'm going to get in. This is my attitude. First, I had to get a job and I worked . . . while I was trying to get in. . . . [I] came home one day from this steno pool where I . . . typed card catalogue cards for eight hours a day without stop. I was called on the carpet for showing too much initiative when I wanted to xerox card sets. It was deadening. I cried all the time. My mind was dying. . . . [Soon] I got a call from the head of the department at _____ University offering me a four-year NDEA . . . scholarship. I took a plane, I took all the money I had, and went.

Having her sights set clearly on an academic career was unusual among the generation of Pathfinders, as we have seen. Yet her character reveals another trait that is common among the Pathfinders: a certain readiness and determination that would eventually serve as a primary resource for generating new intellectual work.

Her perseverance in getting into graduate school also exemplifies how, among the Pathfinders, different temperaments and predispositions play certain roles. These include, in their own terms, "troublemaker but a nice troublemaker," "critic," "rabble-rouser," "hell-raiser," and "raving radical." At the other extreme, some Pathfinders describe themselves as being "subtle," "discrete," "not belligerent," "incredibly naive," and "a watcher rather than a doer." Their self-concepts again underscore a variety in the ways in which Pathfinders came to graduate school. Even those who came "backing into it" and perceiving limited career options would soon be drawn into an exciting intellectual, political, and emotional venture.

Political Interests

Whether or not they perceived any career options, some of the Pathfinders entered graduate school already highly politicized. Their orientation to leftist politics was a prominent theme in their ambitions and in their day-to-day lives. Indeed, for many of these women, their political concerns heightened their ambivalence about an academic career. Politicized Pathfinders decided to go to graduate school with one of two motivations: they viewed graduate school as a good temporary location for someone with a political agenda or they saw a graduate program as a good place to work out a radicalized intellectual agenda.

At one extreme, political values were such strong motivators that it wasn't really a conscious choice to go into academia. Even though this woman is currently a tenured professor at a high-prestige university, she was so immersed in the leftist movement that she never became immersed in the plan of going to graduate school:

It sounds strange, but I didn't think about it. My identity really lived with the movement. It was more of a practical thing. I was in academia because of a lack of anything else to do. . . . In some ways, I think I assumed that being in graduate school felt to me like a way of treading water until something more interesting happened. . . . I didn't have any illusions that academia could especially serve any of those [political] interests. My own intellectual interests were always shaped more by the movement. I think I sort of half hoped that there would be some sort of journal or whatever that I could be associated with. I think it was characteristic of a lot of people who were involved in the movement in the late sixties. We sort of assumed that there would be jobs for us and we really did not think about it very much..

Further along on her academic career path and now having tenure, she finds herself still not identifying with either the academic or the scholarly role. Academia, she asserts, "has always seemed more intellectually arid to me." Her ideas are "very much tied to the movement agenda." In a sense, she has always been "in academia but not of it."

On the other hand, being grounded in the movement did not necessarily preclude feeling comfortable becoming a scholar. Another woman wanted to continue studying philosophy and found a graduate program in a department that was highly politicized, a perfect match for her own political orientation: "When I was an undergraduate, the department was liberal and the place I went to graduate school was radical. The old faculty were old line, socialist liberal and the young faculty were hippies. . . . I found the university with the same values and intellectual interests as I had. I particularly found that in the philosophy department, which tended to be liberal to radical, politically. . . . And I wanted to be a philosopher."

So, for this woman, going to graduate school was a comfortable and natural next step where her politics and intellectual interests could coexist, if not merge. As one might guess, the fusion of the two would not ultimately be as easy as she imagined.

For the most part, their explicit political commitments caused Pathfinders to be more skeptical about entering graduate school. As this African American woman explained:

I grew up in a poor family 50 miles from Atlanta, Georgia, in the 1960s. I went to a segregated high school. From that background I was not ready to go on to be an armchair sociologist! As an undergraduate I was at a black university and the whole educational experience was tailored to meet Black needs. The emphasis was on black cultural enrichment, and it was geared toward issues related to blackness. The ultimate question was what can we do to make this situation better. . . . I always knew I wanted to teach on some level, but I didn't want to do graduate work in sociology. I'm very practice-oriented. And the discipline looks down on applications to the real world. I always felt that theories had value in that they give you ideas about how to look at things in order to make things better for people.

After college, she got a master's degree in social work. "I've always had an agenda for social change. And in 1968 that was validated in social work. I even had a minor in community organization. The main issues were poverty and racial equality. . . . I got a social work position doing continuing education courses in social policy and health care. It was on soft money, NIMH funded. When the funding was not renewed, I went on to get my Ph.D."

She felt an ongoing separation between academia and "the real world" throughout graduate school. This was not just because of having experienced racism. As she explained, "I saw white women get opportunities that neither black men nor black women could get. I believe the first thing [people] see when they see me is my black face, and that shapes how they will interact with me. . . . At least once a week, I'm mistaken for a secretary!"

She felt a deep disdain for how theory is used by conventional sociologists: "Sociological theory like Merton has value for organizing their thoughts, but they must apply those theories to what's happening in their lives and the real world." Her reservations have not lessened over the years, even with her considerable academic success.

Like these three women, most of the highly politicized Pathfinders went to graduate school seeking a comfortable location where they could still have their political agenda. Yet some of their peers entered graduate school precisely in order to resolve a major intellectual tension in their lives. For those in some kind of internal intellectual, personal, and political crisis, the years in graduate school became a crucial formative period during which they found new ways to be scholars and to do scholarship. Within this group, those who started out with a more radical intellectual agenda essentially never reconciled their politics with conventional disciplinary demands, and they ended up with academic appointments as faculty in women's studies programs.

For example, one historian decided to go to graduate school in order to work out her own radical intellectual agenda. Raised in an intellectual family that was "steeped in Communism, Marxism, and history," she was passionately involved in politics from the time she was a child. Her worldview became shaken when she was introduced to feminist ideas. Finding herself at "a crucial intellectual juncture," she went to graduate school in order to reconcile the contradiction between Marxism and feminism:

I made my application to come . . . as a graduate student . . . to dissolve the hyphen between Marxism and feminism, and I had so much invested in that emotionally. . . . It turned my life upside down. I either had to jump into it or pull away from it completely. . . . I was so immersed in my own intellectual crisis . . . that I didn't really pay much attention to anything else. . . . And I had a full scholarship. . . . I didn't come out of a traditional academic background. . . . So I didn't really give a damn. I never have.

This woman experienced the intellectual crisis on so many levels that a Ph.D. program seemed like the perfect opportunity in which to resolve the conflict. Her experience suggests that some of the deepest intellectual, emotional, and political dimensions of turmoil can be extremely fruitful ground for developing new scholarship. In this case, the intensity of the crisis brought her to graduate school with an explicit intellectual agenda.

Another Pathfinder described how she chose graduate school to work out "what I've since described as my public/private split."

I grew up in a very political family. I was moved by my father's sense of social consciousness and social responsibility. . . . I was very politically active as an undergraduate. Then I went to Paris and I discovered art and literature. . . . Literature was taught to be cut off from life. It had nothing to do with the social world; it was just this gorgeous artifact. So politics was the outer world, as opposed to the private, domestic, interrelational and literary spheres. I couldn't figure out how to bring those worlds together. I went to graduate school . . . thinking about how one brings together the private and the public, because I am a very private person, but I also am a public person. Feminism taught me to feel that split to some extent . . . and to integrate that. . . . Feminist literary criticism helped me to bring literature back into the world where I intuitively knew it was, but had been taught that it wasn't.

Once again, resolving some deeply felt tension that is experienced simultaneously as intellectual, personal, and political became a motivation for going to graduate school.

Another highly politicized Pathfinder decided to go to graduate school to work out a critical intellectual agenda. Her motivation was consciously to apply her political concerns to critiquing systems of academic thought. Clearly, her approach deviated from a traditional conception of graduate training, and she had no intention of pursuing an academic career.

As she explained in detail, this Pathfinder ultimately ended up in women's studies. Having been brought up with years of Catholic education, her graduation from high school triggered long-standing conflicts about leaving her faith and going on to college in a "non-Catholic location, the world was one or the other." Trying to reconcile her faith with her intellectual interests, and both of these with her growing political consciousness, she chose to go to graduate school in order to critique "biology as a cultural practice." As she describes it:

Up until my mid 20s I spent a tremendous amount of time trying to hold it together intellectually. It was full of tension and contradiction, which isn't altogether a bad thing. . . . I left the Church in a very deliberate way. It was partly out of growing involvement in the Vietnam antiwar movement. . . . When I found myself in graduate school in biology, it was almost by chance. . . . I had always found natural science . . . compelling; I loved it. But it was also in contradiction with other things I also loved. In college I really majored jointly in philosophy, biology, and English. I very easily could have ended up in graduate school in any of those three. . . . I was really interested . . . in biology as a cultural practice, the complicated ways in which biology mediates political belief. . . . I became more and more interested in cultural and political issues.

Most of the Pathfinders who linked going to graduate school with being highly politicized expressed a variety of self-conscious political concerns that underlay their ambivalence about going to graduate school. The idea of being a traditional academic seemed to contradict some of the underpinnings of their political worldviews.

Only one Pathfinder reported never having felt internally conflicted. Her politics took a priority:

When I think back on it, [graduate school] was easy in the sense that I didn't think I'd get through it at all. I didn't have a stake in getting a doctorate, and I didn't expect to get through it. I chose a place where for me there were no mentors, and that was fine. I just wanted to be left alone to do the work. It was important work that needed to be done. . . . I was always interested in departures from traditional academia, and that's the stake I've had in women's studies, to what extent will it depart from the dominant ways, methods and assumptions of academia. . . . I have constantly found a conflict in the sense that if . . . there is a choice between my political convictions and academia, [the latter] can go to hell. . . . It's not an internal conflict, but it's a conflict with the system.

So, the contradiction she experienced was not an internal one of ambivalence. Rather it was between herself and a system which she chose to reject instead of compromise with. Like the two other politicized Pathfinders with radical intellectual agendas, this scholar ended up happily in women's studies, essentially never reconciling her political interests with traditional disciplinary demands.

In summary, the majority of Pathfinders decided to go to graduate school while experiencing some combination of ambivalence about academia and a self-awareness that they had political and intellectual issues to work through. It may have been precisely their detachment from conventional academic purposes that became the distinctive foundation for the significant intellectual contributions they went on to make.

POLITICAL ORIENTATIONS

The content of feminist scholarship emerged directly out of the Pathfinders' political orientations. Rather than their political outlooks subtly shaping their academic understandings, Pathfinders consciously sought to apply their politics to their academic work. As one might imagine, they experienced an ongoing conflict between their political and academic commitments. In an attempt to resolve this conflict, Pathfinders devised new ways to merge the two sets of concerns and to translate interests from one domain to the other.

With the unprecedented historical circumstances of campus unrest and widespread anti-Vietnam protests, academic women of this generation report having been highly politicized either early on or later in their careers. As one informant suggested, "You couldn't escape the new Left. We were all in one thing or another." Some acquired a political consciousness before graduate school, whereas others came to it during or just after.

Guided by a political, and ultimately a feminist, consciousness, many of the Pathfinders have long histories as activists, especially those who ended up in women's studies. Their political orientations took different forms while in graduate school. Most significantly, for some, having political concerns resulted in rethinking the worth of doing scholarship.

One historian explains her drive to integrate politics and scholarship:

I was still focused on the question of politics. In my master's essay I focused on could you be a radical and an intellectual. I was asking that question because I was thinking about myself in those terms. . . . I was totally bored, bored with male politicos, bored with leftists in general. . . . I was asking myself what am I doing in graduate school, moving from doing the social reform work back to the university.

I had these romantic fantasies of going off to live on the land, and getting away from it all, perhaps getting all my friends to move with me to Vermont and we could run a coffee house and a bookstore in the middle of nowhere. . . . I also wanted to do all this organizing. I had values and all. And yet I really loved doing research. And I felt this split between them. I didn't know if I'd end up being an administrator or what. I also had this idea that you could do political work by going out and teaching in a community college or something.

Trying to reconcile these contradictions was an ongoing inner dialogue for this historian and for many of her peers.

Yet integrating the two sets of concerns was not the aim of every Pathfinder. Either politics or scholarship might be the dominant vehicle, with the other set of concerns downplayed. This approach was one strategy for feeling less internal conflict. A sociologist recalled how political concerns dominated her thinking at that time:

I felt I was a voice for the voiceless, and I felt that I had something to say, because there was this whole reality that was left out of sociology. Here was sociology allegedly explaining the social world, and the social world I lived in had just been ignored and overlooked, and so it gave me an energy. . . . I think it's because I didn't really even then think of myself as a scholar. I thought of myself as an advocate, but I didn't think of myself as a scholar, so I didn't self-consciously try to integrate that. It was just very much a part of my existence and who I was.

It is especially noteworthy that her taking on a "voice for the voiceless" resulted in her explicit critique of her discipline, as well as "an energy" that perhaps exceeded that of her more conventional sociology graduate student peers.

Advocacy was not a comfortable stance for all the Pathfinders, however. A philosopher admitted having reservations about even being politically active, let alone having an advocacy voice in her academic work. When asked how she would characterize her political involvement, she responded:

Never to the extent that I was actually in any sort of situation that I could have been arrested or put out of school. I'd attend rallies sometimes. I would certainly attend lectures on certain instances when certain people would come onto campus. I never sat on the steps when [the police were] carrying them off. It's interesting, I can remember as an undergraduate, when some classmates were arrested. It didn't happen a whole lot, but on one instance when it did happen, I would accept who did it without any judgment, because I didn't see myself as having the courage to do it at that point.

Yet, even in her role as a political bystander, she came to question whether or not she was justified to pursue a career as a philosopher and, within philosophy, what subfield would be acceptable.

The truth is, when I came to _____, I began to think about what kinds of justifications are there for doing this. I'd seen analytic philosophers when students would ask them, "What kind of a moral justification do you have for talking about [this] . . . when people were dying in Vietnam?" [They would] say things like "That's not relevant to me." I thought that was not acceptable. I thought, "What is acceptable if I'm interested in this? Is there any sort of justification? Shouldn't I at least be doing moral philosophy? Shouldn't I be doing political philosophy? Shouldn't I be doing something that obviously dovetails into the chaos of our society?"

After much thought, this philosopher did come up with an understanding of her role as a scholar that justified her remaining in philosophy and specializing in esthetics. She accomplished this by conceptualizing esthetics as a necessary precondition, almost a first-order set of concerns, before one could even tackle the other subfields that appeared most relevant to contemporary political issues. As she describes the resolution: "I thought, you have to continue doing research and reading about some of these things and writing about some of these things. I came to the conclusion that fundamentally you can't even begin to expect people to ask moral and political questions . . . if they don't get some esthetic sense to begin with."

Not all of the Pathfinders expressed ideological uncertainty. Some had purely pragmatic considerations. Consider the historian who was politically active in demonstrations, yet reluctant to put herself in a vulnerable position because she was worried about being deported.

I was involved in protesting the Vietnam war. I demonstrated. I did not get arrested because I was afraid since I was not a U.S. citizen at the time. I went to organizational meetings and was on the [campus] student rights steering committee, which consisted of students and rebellious faculty. Once I moved to [another graduate school], that was not the kind of place where any kind of protest got under way; it was an extremely conservative place. . . . In my first year there only 10 people showed up for a protest. And they didn't even have any signs. When I saw there were TV cameras for local news coverage, I ran to the bookstore and bought poster paper and markers and quickly made signs so it would look better.

She explained that on a personal level, "I had no tension between my political convictions and academia." But there were other pragmatic concerns that restricted her activities. The simple issue of time was a major consideration, as she indicated: "The only tension was that one doesn't have enough time to do everything. We worked hard in the history department. . . . Even though it was a conservative place . . . , I never feared for my career. And I don't think anyone would have dared to tell me that my career was in jeopardy because of my political . . . outlook."

Other Pathfinders expressed the frustration of not having enough time "to do both." Yet a few of them felt even more constrained by the milieu of the graduate student culture on their particular campuses. A sociologist described this at a large public institution: "A lot of us in graduate school were against the war. And many undergrads were active in the antiwar movement. But we weren't active like the undergrads. We had a different mission. We gave them psychic support, that's it. . . . We were focused on our own goals."

Their "different mission" may have been just trying to survive graduate school, which she saw as an enterprise separate from political action and which required a narrowing of her interests to academic concerns.

Several Pathfinders stated that graduate school was an overwhelming task in itself. Another sociologist expressed that her aim was to "just finish" and "survive" in spite of the fact that she had been politically active before then.

I had been involved in a way in civil rights . . . not in an organized way but growing up in Jackson. . . . I simply had done some things. I had tomatoes thrown at me . . . when I was in high school I just remember walking into Walgreen's drugstore and they had pulled all the countertop seats off the stools, and there were these blacks in the booths back there. . . . I just repelled the tomatoes [went and sat with them]. . . . I just did it. . . . In college I wasn't involved. . . . In college I was just trying to survive. . . . My strategy was to just finish.

This woman apparently was politically oriented, but she made the choice not to act it out. Another shade in the political spectrum was the absence of political involvement, although that was rare among the Pathfinders during graduate school. An historian describes that she "left her political group" in order to "stick to academics":

When I look back, I see myself as someone who got into college and became extremely political (1960) and then got derailed by some of the other movements of the early sixties which were beginning. . . . I left my political group and I went through things that I now look at and say, "Why did I do that?" . . . I stuck to academics . . . as much as I possibly could. I was fairly conventional. . . . But then, I was in graduate school, and that was not part of the culture of graduate students. . . . Undergraduates but not graduates, so I didn't get involved in any of that.

These variations in political activities among the Pathfinders suggests that the kinds of feminist scholarship they were soon to create would also vary. Only some saw politics and scholarship as needing to be fused, whereas still fewer at that time saw politics and scholarship as inseparable. Of course both orientations provided fertile soil for the feminist scholarly interests that were about to emerge.

Regardless of the form and extent of their political orientation, a common theme for many of the Pathfinders is evident. Most of them clearly did not identify with the role of a traditional scholar or with an academic career path. From that stance they could become critics, not only of campus-wide and departmental policies, but of their disciplines as well.

FEMINIST AWAKENINGS

The intellectual directions these women ultimately took were also crucially shaped by powerful feminist awakenings. For the majority of Pathfinders, the question of how to be political and academic became reformulated as how to be feminist and academic. Some informants were more explicit about this than others. One, who was an especially articulate and astute observer, suggested that by virtue of being female, women in this generation were feminists by their very presence in graduate school, whether they knew it or not, and whether they acknowledged it or not. She observes: "I sort of feel in that period we were all feminists, and I should probably say that when I hear [them] today say, I'm not a feminist, . . . I always want to say, yes, you are, you just don't know it. Yes, they were. I think I was probably more to the left politically than they were. I think they were . . . it would be fair to describe . . . more cultural radicals than political radicals. But yes, every woman [there] shared those feminist beliefs . . . maybe not in that conscious a way." Most of the Pathfinders, however, were not only conscious of their emerging feminism but they actively attempted to integrate it into their lives as graduate students.

However, the roots of the Pathfinders' feminism are traceable back to the wider culture. Only later did they find a way to fuse the ideas from the women's movement with their scholarship. Prior to their innovative intellectual work, their early feminist awakenings often resulted in confrontational activities on their campuses for the purpose of improving the situation of women. These initial efforts were significant precursors to feminist scholarship because they established agenda-setting networks of women on campuses. Such networks took shape within departments, across student-faculty-staff ranks, and across departments, as well as extending beyond the academy and into the local community.

The remainder of this chapter traces these two significant patterns: (1) that feminist awakenings had nonacademic sources, especially in literature from the women's movement; and (2) that Pathfinders applied their new-found consciousness to form networks for exploring a mix of ideas and experiences.

Sources of Feminist Awakenings

The dramatic moment of awakening to feminism was easily and specifically remembered by many of the women I interviewed. Typical is the flash of insight described by this graduate student who, at the time, was hurrying to finish a book on a reserve reading list for an anthropology class. As she remembers it,

I was standing up in the crowded dingy library and the book was due in two minutes . . . because the library was closing. . . . I remember reading [this] statement that the culture is based on the exchange of money, words, and women. I remember the moment I read that. . . . I read that and I simultaneously felt, how brilliant. To get economy, language, and kinship in one sentence, but I also felt a certain tinge of outrage—are women just like money? . . . I didn't have anything to make me go further with it, but I can look back and see that feminism resonated with doubts I'd had about things early on in my education.

Her story illustrates the unexpected quality and suddenness sometimes experienced in a feminist awakening.

While only some of the Pathfinders shared this experience of a dramatic shift, two other aspects of the experience were shared by many others: a moment of validation for what had previously been an unarticulated and private experience and a sense of not knowing where the revelation would take them or "how to go further with it." For all the Pathfinders this validation became stronger as they realized that feminist awakenings, however personal, were occurring on a collective level.

Although most Pathfinders acquired a feminist consciousness while in graduate school, the sources for their revelations were for the most part nonacademic. Popular literature from the women's movement was the most common first encounter with feminist thinking. The most frequently mentioned works were *The Second Sex, The Feminine Mystique,* and *Sisterhood Is Powerful,* as well as a variety of articles and pamphlets that were reproduced and widely circulated across social circles.

Although she cannot remember the exact year, one historian recalls that her awakening occurred while she was reading one of these books:

I can't remember when it was, but I know it came without any warning. . . . Sometimes I get overwhelmed when I think of that [incident]. It was when I started to read *The Second Sex*. . . . It didn't take more than a page and a half. I read a page and a half and I put it down. I thought, I cannot believe it. The peculiar power of that book is that instead of taking on the conservative ideas which I already knew, it took on what I considered the avant-garde and have accepted. It demolished everything that I felt was on the forefront. In five minutes it demolished it all. The power of that just overwhelmed me. I just saw the world differently from morning to night.

Her experience led her to talk to other women to see if they had similar experiences with that book: "I talked to my friends. People who were starting to read it. And I would say, "What happened to you when you read that book?" And they would say, "My life changed." In one week. Incredible when I think about it. I just can't believe it. . . . Then maybe two years later I read other feminist books, . . . and it changed my life in a much deeper way."

It was also not uncommon that there was a time lag of several years, especially in the mid-1960s, between reading one or two perspective-changing books. The pattern seems to be that by the later 1960s these women began reading everything they could get their hands on. A sociologist describes the wide range of movement literature that she was able to find:

I remember reading *Sisterhood Is Powerful*, and I remember reading a lot of what you might call ephemeral literature, you know, sort of pamphlets and leaflets, and I remember the Redstockings of New York, for example. And I have a very first copy sort of on newsprint-type paper of the Boston Women's Health Collective's *Our Bodies, Our Selves*. . . . I was in a women's group and I know we talked about the article on the myth of the vaginal orgasm. And I seem to remember Andrea Dworkin's writings . . . Chrysalis, and *Off Our Backs*, and others. . . . [There] was such a period of proliferation of women's journals and magazines and newspapers. . . . So, I was reading more of the things that eventually became collected in anthologies like *Sisterhood Is Powerful*, and I probably read most of those as articles, as part of the alternative press, I guess they call it.

Some of the women recalled that this literature was hard to find. "I was always going to hunt for these things," remembered one woman. Accessibility varied depending on geographic location, with New York, Boston, and the San Francisco Bay Area having the widest range of publications. It was not uncommon for interviewees to state proudly that they still had these books. As one said: "I could take you to my other office. I still have every one. You name any book that came out on women and I bought it and read it. They're some of the few books I haven't given away. I'm always getting rid of them, but I haven't been able to give away my women's books."

Of course, not every woman read so widely. Nor would they all include these books on their bookshelves in their university offices. A few women reflected on being touched by the women's movement literature "on a personal level," as one historian described. "I read the newspapers. I read a couple of books on my own. *The Second Sex* for example. But it wasn't in bulk or systematic." It is noteworthy that this scholar eventually did read more systematically, but not until 1980; she was a late bloomer who then began to do very original work in women's history.

The movement literature not only planted seeds of women-oriented and feminist thought, but it also named and perhaps encouraged much of the militancy that has come to be associated with that period. As an historian explains,

I was reading Simone de Beauvoir for the first time, and I was reading mimeographed articles that became "Notes from the First Year." I read Kate Millet's book in that year. And what I remember most is *Loving Other Women* and the article on the vaginal orgasm.... It was mind-blowing. Just frightening [because] I found myself getting much more militant and assertive, really angry about a lot of stuff. Especially after reading de Beauvoir and Millet. I was struck particularly by Millet's anger, and the idea that you had to reread everything, and that you could just turn everything around.

For this scholar, Millet's work especially was associated with a constructive kind of anger. It enabled her to "see the world differently," and she marks that book as the beginning of her experience with feminist theory, then called "radical politics and radical feminism." She remembered that the book was invaluable in providing an explanation for "things that were upsetting me":

For example, the job situation, that I was being treated differently than the men I worked with who were less competent.... It helped explain things that had been bothering me in categorical terms, in political terms. And the contradictions about sexuality, particularly the unhappiness I had had in some relationships with men.... There were those that were boring and those that were problematic, the ones that were problematic were because there was this category male, and it had to do with that. It wasn't so much that there was this category female yet, as there was this category male.... And that was interesting to me.

The increased anger was flavored with intellectual engagement, revealed in her comment, "that was interesting to me." It is not surprising that, simultaneously, she then started reading more "feminist theory," began to lead a separatist lifestyle, and switched her academic focus from urban history to women's history.

A few Pathfinders went through a similar awakening, yet with the opposite result. Rather than becoming female-identified, they became male-identified. This was especially true of those who experienced these revelations in the early 1960s, before there were other women they could talk to. For instance, one scholar in literature explains how this shift occurred for her as a graduate student:

In 1961–62 I read *The Second Sex*. That was my first formal contact with feminism as a movement and [thinking about] the situation of women. Three years later when I was in graduate school I was rereading French novels, and I started thinking about "the woman question" because there were some magnificent women characters, particularly in Stendahl, characters who were ambitious and powerful and often extraordinarily independent who live in a world of men, but are independent. . . . This was the mid-sixties so there was nobody around to talk with then. . . . Women like myself were considered exceptional by the culture that surrounded us. And we were exceptional in the sense that we were very independent and very involved in our intellectual lives. It tended to alienate us from other women. I was extremely male-identified in those days, because of the men I knew. They were thinking about the things I was thinking about and lots of women weren't—not all women weren't but the majority of them . . . so it tended to set you apart from other women. It was a time that was very separate for women.

A similar kind of awakening occurred for another Pathfinder, although she was not immersed in graduate student culture. She was more of a loner and married at the time. It is not surprising that Friedan's book spoke to her particular situation. In her words, "Feminism was coming into my life around 1967 or 68 through the back door. I was married to this doctor. . . . I didn't like my life that much and I was so struck by his power and role in the community as a physician; and I saw that it was not unrelated to his being male. . . . After I read Betty Friedan's book, I began to hear these issues in my own life. . . . It certainly affected me. . . . There was a readiness for all of it. . . . It affected me powerfully, but I wasn't drawn to other women."

In summary, for all of these women, reading the movement literature was very powerful, even transformative of the way that they saw themselves, saw their life experiences, and viewed other women in society. As a philosopher comments: "I was struggling inside myself . . . to overcome the notion that women had always been subordinate. That was theoretically and conceptually and emotionally a revolution in thought for me and opened up a lot of new space inside of myself."

For many Pathfinders then, a feminist awakening was a major shift that occurred on many levels simultaneously and which made them consider, perhaps
for the first time, the relevance of their woman-ness. In the larger frame, the intensity of these feminist awakenings suggests how inseparable are the intellectual, personal, and political dimensions of knowledge. Over time, the feminist
ideas appearing in literature from the women's movement grew increasingly sophisticated: from early manifestos proclaiming that women should not be oppressed, to more refined analyses of the mechanisms that maintain women's
subordinate status. The ideas that prevailed in the popular literature, as well as
other perspectives, would soon emerge in the scholarly thinking and early writings of academic women and would dominate feminist discourse through the
late-1970s.

Forming Networks for Change

One of the precursors to pursuing feminist scholarly interests was the recognition that one's discipline and one's campus warranted critical attention.
Armed with feminist consciousness and a vocabulary from the wider women's
liberation movement, many Pathfinders reinterpreted their academic contexts
to see them in need of change, change that would require collective effort.

In their recollections of applying feminist revelations to their academic surroundings, the majority of Pathfinders expressed feeling validation: "What
had been a private feeling for me I now see is a real problem." They found their
concerns were legitimate. A sociologist stated her new perspective succinctly:
"It's a male world around here and there is no room for the likes of me. The feeling was not one of discovery but one of gaining cultural legitimacy for a private
feeling."

This sociologist characterized herself as being "ready for feminism when it
happened." She recalls the first time "I became aware that I was really committed to women. It was 1963–64 and the American Sociological Association was
publishing want ads that "discriminated against women" because they specified that only men should apply. As she explained:

I wrote to the secretary of the association and he wrote back a letter basically saying that
employers could specify anything they wanted. This was before civil rights and he was
correct legally. One faculty member in the department saw my letter. I posted it on the
bulletin board. It caused a great uproar among the male faculty who would stop me and
argue with me. They'd say, "Well, you couldn't teach at Princeton anyway; it's all male."
I'd say, "There were men teaching at my women's college, what's the difference?" . . .
Washington had just passed a civil rights law. . . . So, I went to the law library and
looked it up and sent a letter to the association saying I would ask the Attorney General
to impound all the journals coming in because they violated the law. I got no response

but that immediately stopped. The advertising never appeared after that and I was never given any formal acknowledgement. Obviously, it was something that happened in a closed door meeting where they informally agreed that they better not do this.

This incident made her realize that her anger and activist inclinations could make a difference, even if she did not get validation from her department for her concerns.

In a similar spirit, many Pathfinders commented on the power of organizing as a group of women. They recalled a real excitement when they organized a "women's liberation meeting" or "women's caucus meeting." The participants were diverse, blurring boundaries between women in different catego- ries—graduate students and nongraduate students, wives of graduate students, and the few women faculty at the time.

One woman vividly recollected her first meeting of the women's liberation group during her first year in graduate school:

I physically remember sitting at this long, thin table in this incredibly Baroque room in the graduate school. . . . I remember sitting there 15 minutes into it and just feeling this relief wash over me, that I wasn't crazy, and that all these other women who I knew to be smart and intelligent and interesting and wonderful, were feeling all the same feelings I was feeling, that it wasn't individual. I mean, it was . . . I sort of get goosebumps telling you about it now. . . . It was an epiphany to hear all these women that I looked up to, ad- mired, and liked, I'd been sitting in seminars with them and I knew they were perfectly smart. We just talked about real power, and I remember a lot of tears, and I remember real powerful emotions.

This meeting was "really a turning point," as the group ended up becoming highly significant for her. She had been having a difficult time relating to fac- ulty and peers, mostly male. First "I thought it was me, and now I see it was be- cause I was a woman." Things became "easier at one level because I didn't think it was personal anymore, but they were harder on another level because I did think it was political. I now had a sort of ideology that made sense out of these experiences, and it fucking enraged me."

It is worth noting that during the interview, she paused to comment rather self-consciously on the wording of her response to me: "The word 'fuck' hardly ever crosses my lips now . . . because I'm sort of a well-integrated member of the academy. Yet . . . when I talk about this I can feel how stirred up I get just talk- ing about it and remembering it."

Like many of the Pathfinders, she recalled several incidents when she was enraged at being treated differently. For example, she remembered: "A faculty person came up to me once and sort of pushed me against a wall and said, 'If they ever hire a woman in this place because of you, I'm quitting the next day.'"

She was also systematically excluded from social activities in the department: "There were informal things that faculty do that show students that they're valued and esteemed—like you get invited out to meet visiting faculty who they're trying to recruit, and . . . you get invited to parties and all those sorts of things. . . . Or to get somebody's reading list represents so much time, by having gone through all this drek just to give you the cream, to be the recipient of an enormous amount of intelligence and hard work of other people."

She felt confident that she was "a pretty good student," but she "was getting no recognition." So she tried to talk to the department chair about this pattern: "And, I will never forget I went into [his office and] listed a set of sort of seemingly small incidents, but each one of them added up to a pattern. And he came out from behind his desk . . . and he put his hand on my knee, and said, 'But you're so pretty. Why are you having trouble in graduate school?' It was sort of like, wait a minute, you know, feminism told me this might happen." The result was that she became, in her words, "even more actively hostile and aggressive."

I describe her experience in detail because it typifies the inhospitable organizational contexts experienced by the majority of Pathfinders. However, most Pathfinders channeled their anger into feminist networks. The result was that, if they felt alienated in one arena, at least they did not feel marginal in women's groups. The more typical pattern for the women in my sample was to do collective work with other feminists in the academic context. For example, a sociologist describes how she and her academic friends were "all in various women's groups shifting from one collective to another." She recalled "giving women's liberation talks . . . as representatives of Bread and Roses." Saying nothing about being sociology graduate students, they once gave a talk to a large undergraduate class at Harvard. The insights they gained from doing this were both intellectual and political. As she explains: "We discovered that there were other places to learn besides the classroom. We [realized] that we could do it together; . . . it gave us a glimmer of different kinds of relationships that we would ultimately try to create in women's studies. . . . It was our utopia."

She indicated that it was a powerful learning experience in other respects as well. Not only were they empowered by their collective voice ("We learned to be uppity!"), but they also "learned the shortcomings of traditional knowledge." At the same time, these women were encouraged to pursue critical intellectual perspectives by leftist faculty in their sociology department. In fact, several professors were so consistently supportive of their critical perspectives that the students were unaware that they were specializing in areas that were marginal to the discipline, until they went out on the job market.

Another pattern was that women graduate students—and women faculty if there were any—would "get together and share horror stories over lunch," as one woman described it, "to overcome anomie basically." Over time, they began to organize politically, consciously sharing valuable information and planning strategies for improving both the intellectual and organizational dimensions of their academic lives. Often their discussions would culminate in a well-orchestrated confrontation with departmental faculty in order to have their complaints heard. The complaints ranged from policy decisions (e.g., having a fixed admissions quota for women) to sexism (e.g., women were being ignored or neglected in advising) to curriculum reform (e.g., biology courses should be organized around social issues to reveal the politics of science). The results of such collective efforts were generally twofold: women gained the experience of bringing their ideas to the forefront and male colleagues stopped and took notice.

Some women's groups were formed with the initial motivation of seeking to validate members' emotional responses to their graduate school experiences. Some groups also formed with a specific agenda to change university policy. For example, while writing her dissertation (as "a faculty wife, God forbid that unbelievable status!"), one Pathfinder "joined with some other feminists to work against the nepotism regulation at the university." Out of this experience they developed a "women's liberation group," which in turn influenced their teaching once they got positions after graduate school.

At some time during graduate school or during her first academic appointment, each Pathfinder in my study had witnessed women coming together to reflect on their institutional experiences and, for virtually all of the Pathfinders, this was a major turning point. One woman, then a new instructor, explains how she initiated a "women's caucus" in her sociology department:

I guess it happened more orally. Talking with other women grad students in the department, about 20 percent of us in the department were women, and a good number of us were dropping out. . . . And I did notice a lot of the women my age and slightly younger were drifting out. And it was because of that that I held a meeting . . . in my apartment. . . . At this meeting I asked, "Do we have something in common as women in our department?" There were no women faculty to speak of in the department. . . . It looked as if there was some structural barrier. We were in the pipeline, but could we get aboard? That was the question. Obviously all of us were wondering. . . . As we went around the room, people said they were having a writer's block, having difficulty in the library, one thing and another, but not one of them gender-related. At the end of the evening, I felt, well, we gave it a try. I called the meeting to an end, and no one left for three hours afterward; they turned to the person next to them and could say privately what they couldn't say publicly. And so we held another meeting and a little more came out.

Neither the organizer nor the participants anticipated the significance of this women's caucus when it first met. The fact that it would continue to meet regularly for the next eight years is evidence of its important function.

What is striking is that the meetings became a forum for exploring new ideas. Pathfinders used them as a place not only to reflect on their experiences as women, but also to begin to reconsider their disciplines. As they began to apply some of their interests as women and feminists to the discipline, their fresh perspective generated long hours of discussion during which they would formulate questions they had not considered before: "[I]t turned into a wonderful group in which we began to really talk about ideas, and reconceiving sociology; for example, what was social class, what was social mobility, and why is it determined by the male occupations, what does that mean about the work women do, how should it be conceived, also sociology of organizations, sociology of family, sociology of networks, whose networks—we began to really reconceive the whole thing. And it was intellectually an extraordinary experience."

The emerging feminist scholarly questions focused on assumptions that were embedded in the central concepts of sociological theory and methods. In the course of my interviews, many sociologists told me how exciting it had been to participate in this group, having been in it at one time, either as a graduate student or as a faculty member.

Other Pathfinders had similar experiences on their respective campuses. Many emerging networks also drew people from a variety of disciplines, which was beneficial for someone located in philosophy, for example, who might have been the only woman or feminist in the department. And local groups in the metropolitan area drew people together from many campuses.

The growth and increased visibility of these informal networks marks the merging of political, feminist, and intellectual concerns. On one level, these networks may have been the first intellectual community these women had in graduate school. On another level, the networks were the first opportunity for academic women to engage in critical and imaginative dialogue about reconceptualizing a discipline, to think about the potential for a discipline that placed women at the center of inquiry or the potential for a truly interdisciplinary field.

The informal networks remained an invaluable resource and forum for galvanizing energy and inspiring organizational and intellectual innovation among Pathfinders. Simeone (1987) commented on the dramatic impact of these networks across the country, concluding that they were a major reason academic women became innovative. She states:

These networks are not a reaction and a second-best alternative to women's exclusion from male networks, but rather speak to the positive valuing by women of each other's work, experience, and support. In fact there are some who would argue that these networks constitute the most vital development within the recent history of American higher education, and that this shift in centrality has opened institutions and disciplines to new and exciting dimensions in scholarship, curriculum, methodology, and practice. (p. 99)

The data from my study confirm Simeone's opinion that these networks have dramatically influenced the creation of new knowledge. They created a new space for feminist scholarly questions to be formulated and discussed. The networks provided an intellectual community, a channel for exchange that stimulated and inspired this generation of women in a way that would not have been possible among their traditional disciplinary colleagues. Feminist scholarship emerged out of precisely this intersection of creative tension among women's interests, disciplinary ideas, and various political orientations.

INTELLECTUAL CONTRIBUTIONS

Given the starting points of the Pathfinders, it is not surprising that they would aim to create new knowledge that some deem "innovative." Simeone (1987) characterizes the role of an innovator for academic women as one of challenging societal expectations for women: "Being an innovator requires, by definition, that one challenge the status quo and battle active or passive resistance to get one's ideas to the forefront. One must be prepared for, or even relish, the spotlight and have confidence in one's abilities and one's work. None of these behaviors are consistent with the traditional female role" (p. 53).

Charting new intellectual directions is, however, consistent with the scholarly role. And scholarly innovation is often given high prestige. Yet when the scholar is female and the scholarship is feminist, tensions result. The ways in which reconciling those tensions may generate a new scholarly discourse and create knowledge are worthy of examination.

Simply stated, the overall tension is between scholarship and feminism. In fact, several people I interviewed suggested that "feminist scholarship" has, in some sense, been perceived to be a contradiction in terms. There is some truth to this observation. On the one hand, disciplinary concerns protect the canon and maintain standards of rigor. On the other, many politically rooted ideas arouse interest for further exploration. In the process of mediating these competing concerns, scholars created a feminist intellectual agenda. And, by identifying a new genre of questions for academic inquiry, they expanded what counted as scholarly discourse.

All of the Pathfinders reported having wrestled with tension. Some did so with a rebellious pride that they were perhaps doing something forbidden, challenging and pushing disciplinary boundaries, and ultimately finding new paths for their own scholarship. Those who were most tied to feminist ideology were the most inclined to set out on this course.

Most of the Pathfinders in my study, however, found themselves generating feminist scholarly work within the context of conventional disciplinary demands, whereas fewer took women' studies positions. The former group reflects two-thirds of the Pathfinders, who ended up taking faculty positions within departments of sociology, history, and philosophy. The analysis in the remainder of this chapter focuses on the general patterns for creating feminist scholarship across these disciplines. Then, in chapter 5, the analysis explores the way in which different disciplinary settings influenced the Pathfinders' intellectual biographies.

Generating Feminist Questions

The thread that unifies the Pathfinders' intellectual contributions was their purposeful effort to reconcile divergent political and academic commitments. Although the individuals' backgrounds and campus experiences varied widely, these women came to generate feminist questions in one of three distinct patterns.

Some women were guided primarily by their political commitments. Since these women subordinated their academic work to their political concerns, this first group was the least likely to develop new forms of scholarship that were considered legitimate. A second group of women were guided primarily by academic commitments. Only due to organizational opportunities did they come to generate and pursue a feminist intellectual agenda. A third pattern saw politics as present but subordinate to academic commitments. Primarily guided by academic commitments but also wanting to take their political interests seriously, these women found intellectually interesting ways to integrate feminism with academic sensibilities. These scholars developed a strategy of finding intellectual questions that no one had asked before, thereby establishing a new terrain of feminist scholarly discourse. I will discuss each of these three general patterns below.

Extending Political Concerns

The scholars who reconciled the tension between politics and academia by subordinating were few in number in this study. Although only a few Pathfinders followed this extreme, the analysis of their accounts reveals how they fit their academic work into their politics, an approach that was least likely to be recognized as within the parameters of existing scholarly contributions.

While many scholars in academia hope that their work will have an impact in some way, the extent to which that impact is preconceived and targeted to a specific arena is another matter. A few Pathfinders formulated their graduate studies in a way that leaned toward a political extreme and offered an explicitly political argument. Deeply committed to having contemporary political relevance and to working for social change, they ended up developing dissertation topics that grew out of their involvement in the anti-Vietnam War movement.

One sociologist developed a dissertation topic on Vietnam War veterans based on her opposition to the Vietnam War. She traced the development of her research interest from an influential course in graduate school, to an influential professor, and finally to a clear commitment to merge her politics with her academic work in a dissertation that would forcefully advocate social change.

Her first course in graduate school alerted her to the tremendous gap between academic theory and "the real world." Having "always had a structural view of things," she was introduced to symbolic interactionism in a course on the sociology of mental illness. She rejected this theoretical framework as "stupid, false—valid academically, yet meaningless in the real world," because it was at odds with structural determinism, which she knew on a deeper level to be "true and right."

While this course enabled her to clarify her discomfort with academia, it also made apparent the level of writing skills required for doctoral work. Writing papers was so enormously difficult for her that she picked courses "according to the ones that would let me talk." One of her professors was helpful because he validated her "for my kind of thinking . . . and my intellectual talents, which tended to be more creative." She respected him because he was "very unconventional, and . . . perhaps the most brilliant person I've ever met in a creative sense." From him she learned the difference between intellectual and academic, and she became more determined that she wouldn't do academic work unless it were grounded in politics.

Beginning with her dissertation, her political interests were primary. This professor encouraged her interest in the antiwar movement. She was very open about her activism, including acting as a coordinator of Vietnam summer; she says her phones were even tapped. She and her professor came up with the idea that she could do her dissertation on Vietnam veterans and the impact of the war on their consciousness. However, during the process of working out the logistics for sampling and data collection, she had a major conflict with her advisor that confirmed her sense that she did not want to be a conventional academic anyway.

In fact, her disdain for traditional scholarship has dominated her subsequent research choices. After graduate school, she decided to do research only in order to be useful, specifically "to help change the situation of women." One research project grew out of her concern for how women faculty on her campus were being treated by their students: "I was intrigued because it struck me that despite all the rhetoric of feminism, . . . these students weren't giving them the same respect." So she did some studies in which she interviewed all the faculty, and students interviewed students. She analyzed this in a paper which revealed "how these subtle dynamics were going on. . . . It was the truth. Every woman who read it said, 'Oh my God, it is true.'" Since her political interests were satisfied, she did not care whether or not she used standard methods (she mentioned parenthetically that she did not have a comparable male sample); nor did she care whether or not the paper ever got published.

Not only did her political concerns determine her selection of topics to research, but she maintains that she always aimed her research at a popular audience. For example, she decided to write a book that would help women make the decision whether or not to have children. "I didn't want it to be a narrow academic book. I wanted it to be a trade book." So she chose a trade publisher, and she decided not to have any footnotes, in order for it to be "written in a way that would be useful." Even the format of the book reinforces her self-image of always having "one foot out the door" of academia.

Selecting a research question with contemporary relevance is not unusual for a sociologist. What is unusual was her explicit purpose of directing her work primarily to an audience other than her sociology peers. In the one case, she did research for women faculty on campus; and in the second case, she wanted to make it accessible to a popular audience. Given her primary concern "to help women," she pushed herself out beyond the margins of what was considered conventional scholarship.

A second sociologist pursued academic work as part of her political agenda, but with results more intellectually challenging to the sociological canon. This sociologist directly translated her support of draft resistance into her academic work. The political climate of the time provided both a context in which she was able to articulate her antiwar commitments and the momentum for bringing a political concern into the academy. It was a "movement context for learning," in which she and her graduate student peers were both reading and writing political tracts. In her dissertation she used this emerging literature as well as sociological references on social movements: "It was important to know that there were people like Jo Freeman who published great stuff under her battle name. I got a certain pleasure to cite both things in my dissertation. . . . And I certainly cited them all over the place in my dissertation."

Not only did she formulate a dissertation topic on draft resistance, but she actually managed to merge her political organizing efforts with her research. And in the process she experienced "nothing but encouragement" from the faculty:

"What I was doing was totally unorthodox because I was just a draft organizer and I was studying at the same time. They—the faculty—said, 'Go for it.' "

In fact, her research project was government-funded through a National Science Foundation fellowship. During this time, a senior sociologist wrote letters to the funding agency on her behalf to continue getting the money: "He thought what I was doing was important, so he covered for me. He loved the irony of it." Her experience as an activist combined with support from sociology faculty enabled her to explore an unorthodox methodology as well. Conventional sociological methods are grounded in the aim to maximize objectivity and to separate the researcher from the subject of study. Instead of restricting her, she recalled, "[T]hey didn't do any of this nagging at me, about where's your objectivity. They helped me to think about what my stance was, what the dilemmas were. . . . They encouraged political engagement. They encouraged unorthodox methods. . . . We had very little statistics. . . . I was trying to sort out what I [was doing] that was unorthodox methodologically. I was a political activist observer."

Motivated by political interests, she formulated and attempted to legitimate a new research stance, one that validated engagement. "I was questioning the idea that the researcher can ever be detached from the subject of study." This work subsequently led her to raise feminist epistemological questions and to critique sociological methods from a feminist perspective.

Although she knew she was doing something new in her dissertation, she did not have a sense of how unorthodox it was for the discipline of sociology at the time. She recounted that she did feel part of the discipline, particularly because she was analyzing a social movement. But she "did not realize how weird we were until I went into the job market." As she suggested, perhaps the knowledge that members of her cohort would all get jobs "had something to do with our courage." Doing her doctoral work in a politicized department, while simultaneously doing political organizing, kept her insulated from the awareness that her work was "marginal to what I now know is Columbia sociology." It was in this context that she became committed to rethinking the prevailing epistemological assumptions in sociology.

Both of these sociologists made self-conscious and explicit commitments to find a way to extend their political—and later feminist—interests in their academic work. Especially in the case of the second sociologist, we can see how the tension between politics and academia may prompt questions that critique and potentially redefine what is incorporated into the sociological canon.

An anthropologist attempted to extend her already well-articulated feminist commitments into her research interests early in graduate school. Although this was unusual for Pathfinders in the early 1970s, she attributes the ease with which she was able to generate a feminist dissertation topic to being located in a "feminist bubble." Surrounded by outspoken feminist faculty and students, she and her peers often thought about anthropology and "what feminism can do for us." With the help of a young and open-minded committee, she developed a proposal that extended her "feminist proclivities" to the anthropology of religion: "I wrote a proposal to study the social division of religious knowledge. . . . I was really interested in the sexual division of knowledge. Basically I was saying that men and women have access to different kinds of knowledge and different specialties in healing, ritual, etc."

What at first seemed like a direct and smooth extension of her politics into her academic work took a surprising turn. Once she got into the field work, she did not find the subordination and devaluation of women that she had expected to see. "My informants couldn't care less about gender. I found nothing categorical, nothing like 'Women can't do this, women can't do that.' It was just not what I had come to expect." She found no clear gender asymmetry, or not in "the form that 1974-style feminism had mapped out." So she ended up writing a dissertation that did not include her feminist convictions. Over the next 10 years she continued to use these data in the same way for anthropology articles, while she channeled her feminist energy into her teaching.

The striking postscript to this case is that she continued to try to find ways to extend her feminism into her research, even when it felt difficult and not spontaneously appropriate to do so. After years of trying to put her feminism and scholarship together, a major breakthrough occurred. She realized that gender had been "so elusive" in her own material because it had taken a different form. "When I was looking at men and women and having my informants say it doesn't matter or denying any sort of categorical opposition, I couldn't handle it. But once I began to think about cultural forms and social practice, I then began to see that I was dealing with a culture where gender was downplayed as a cultural principle but had deep salience in social practice."

With a more sophisticated conception of gender, she came to see her data differently, as inescapably situated with a broader interpretive context, thereby resolving what for her had been a longstanding "constant tension." However, she pointed out, that deeper tension stays with her because she cannot clearly locate her feminism in this work that focused on gender. She mused:

"What's feminist about this? I've done quite a bit of work on gender but I cannot find in writing this book where my feminism is. It's not there on every page and that bothers me. . . . Right now what I'm writing is much more in the gender relations area and not on feminist politics in this country. It has been important for me to distinguish those two. Feminists need to start at home."

The ongoing tension as she labels it is between academic feminism and community feminism. On the one hand, she is interested in and "very committed" to her anthropological research. Yet she feels a strong "social and political responsibility to do something at home." The frustration occurs because academic life "tends to be an all-consuming thing. You find yourself sending checks instead of spending time."

In this way, these Pathfinders were aware that they tried to reconcile political commitments with academic interests. The two sociologists as well as the anthropologist were in some ways typical of the Pathfinders with strong political convictions in that they directly addressed their political beliefs while they were in academic settings, and they juxtaposed their politics with their research questions and their interpretations of data. In other words, their political commitments dominated their academic pursuits, whether as graduate students or as beginning faculty.

Finding Organizational Opportunities

Political commitments also informed scholarly commitments in another more obvious way, as local organizational opportunities opened for developing or teaching in women's studies programs. On some campuses, informal women's networks advocated forming women's studies programs, even though the new women faculty had little or no expertise and little reputable feminist literature available to draw upon. As these faculty created women's studies on their campuses, they were motivated to invent the intellectual content that would fill those programs and were enthusiastically spurred on by their students.

Some Pathfinders in my study spoke of being in situations where they wanted to establish women's studies courses and programs before they even had content to put in them. Usually few resources were available for such an ambitious undertaking. These women had each other ("students and other women faculty who were there, the few we could find who would support us") and their own internal drive. As one of the organizers of a program explains, she realized from the discussions in the women's caucus of the literature department that her own education was partial and incomplete: "I became very angry because here I had done this incredible degree that was supposed to be all about Western culture, and on my 60-author reading list there was not a single woman writer. I was very angry because this was purported to be this fine education, which in many ways it was, but it was an education about men writers."

On this particular campus, the efforts by women faculty and students had begun in 1973, and within three years a major in women's studies was established, but "of course there was no money." Reflecting on her personal involvement in this work, this organizer felt it "was a conscious decision to do something because I was excited about it and I thought it was important." She also indicated that the organizational opportunity to create women's studies was a way to bring together her political and scholarly interests and to alter her own scholarship towards researching women writers.

Organizational opportunities associated with the emergence of women's studies programs also drew in women to teach feminist courses. Having first pursued more conventional academic careers, these women became Pathfinders when they suddenly found organizational impetus for acquiring a feminist perspective. As more campuses began to recognize a need for someone with expertise in, for example, women's history, Pathfinders would find themselves drawn to acquire some familiarity in the emerging material. The initial motivation to do so may have been external, but teaching often led to further interest. Most typically, the women would first scan the nonacademic literature for its potential relevance as well as try to secure the few academic materials that were available. Then intellectual engagement from reading and talking with their students often led these faculty to develop their own materials and pursue their own research questions in the area.

Becoming motivated because of teaching openings was most often experienced by the historians in my sample. This may have been a matter of timing as in the early- to mid-1970s many campuses first established women's history courses to meet the changing interests of their student populations. The sociological counterpart to women's history was to teach courses on sex roles. Far less common, and not until the late 1970s, were philosophy courses oriented toward women, for instance Philosophy and the Sexes. Such courses reinforced and often kindled further interest in what was becoming established as new areas of expertise.

These teaching openings were located at institutions with varying levels of prestige, and the actual job opportunities also varied. Sometimes one course would be advertised either for a part-timer or as part of a full-time position. In other cases an entire position, usually nontenure track, would be created, such as an instructor in women's history. It is not surprising that lower-prestige institutions would hire someone without any graduate training in the designated area. The Pathfinders had the impression that, if you were a woman and you expressed willingness to teach about women, those were sufficient qualifications at the time.

One historian ended up in women's history having "never intended to do anything like this." A turning point for her occurred in 1970, when she graduated from a Ph.D. program. As she recounts the story, she was uncertain about going to commencement, "I was so ambivalent about the whole thing, all the years of what I had been through, that I couldn't decide whether or not I would get the degree formally." At the last minute, when she did decide to go, she was unable to find childcare for her one-year-old. Out of frustration over not being able to attend her own commencement alone, she made a big sign for the baby's back which read, "Why doesn't _____ University support childcare?" When she got to the podium, the baby was screaming and ruining the whole ceremony. The crowd's favorable response had a transformative effect on her and subsequently led her to a job: "The crowd just cheered—partly because I was morally right, and partly because this kid was so obviously inappropriate there. . . . When I came off the stage, I felt so great, that I turned to all these people around me and said, 'I want a job.' Some guy [nearby] said, 'There's a job at _____ State in women's studies,' so I got the name of the department chairman. This all was so unlike me. I was so shy. I had no self-confidence, but when I went through that ceremony in that way, it just happened." She continued:

When I came home I called up the chairman . . . and said, "I'm in women's history, and I'd like your job." . . . It was bullshit. I just went for it. . . . I had never read a book in women's history. . . . It was not my field and it was not my expertise. . . . I felt like these personal forces just pushed me into the job. If they had said it was a job in medieval history, I would have applied for that and told them I was a medievalist. I could have taken it on with the exact same commitment. I was just on a roll, and it happened to be women's history. And it happened to be _____ State, which was a very creative place.

Once she took the job, however, the fact that it was women's history became highly significant for her own career development. She realized that it tapped into "a very long-term desire which I had no place to express." She regards the desire as having "always been there in one form or another. It just needed some encouragement from outside forces."

While new organizational opportunities reflected an increasing demand for expertise in women's history, this historian's interest was reinforced by those around her. This first job was "what shoved me into the women's movement and women's history," and it became "the most meaningful thing that ever happened to me. I ran for it when it came." In retrospect she saw that she was encouraged to do women's history given that she was teaching in a "feminist environment." This was characterized by a tremendous amount of creativity and collective work: she used whatever materials she could find, especially work in art and literature; and students "just ran the show, teaching each other and the faculty."

At first she didn't do any research in the field, "I wouldn't have even known how to go about it." But soon after, it became the center of her scholarship: "I changed all my scholarship around. It meant a radical shift out of something I knew into something I didn't know." In her early research she used the historical skills she had acquired and applied them to new topics in her emerging field. Simultaneously, her exposure to feminist literary criticism caused her to question "the quite stringent rules of evidence" that historians are trained to apply: "Let's say you want to show the presence of independent women in a certain period. . . . Do you use statistical evidence? Is that relevant anymore? Or do you say the rules of evidence are entirely different? If I found three among 100,000, that's enough? Then you could do oral histories, and say look I found something. . . . Were you to find one feminist novel among 100, could you make a big deal of it? Historians would say that's not enough." So while struggling with the question of "Are we going to change those rules?" her inspiration to develop women's history continued.

Another historian had a similar experience of being drawn into women's history through a teaching opportunity. However, she was actively recruited for the position and needed to be persuaded that she was qualified to do it. Having had a background in Afro-American history, and having taught one course on Afro-American women's history, she was asked to teach a course called Sex and Power, to which she replied: "I don't know anything about sex and power. And they said, 'Oh, come on, you're a good teacher, and you can coteach this course with this other woman.' I didn't know anything about it. I just fell into it." She took the position and "stayed one chapter ahead of the students."

This job opening was the catalyst for a major turn in her intellectual interests. She went from having a little background in "Black women's history, but it wasn't even a field then," to being deeply transformed by feminist theory: "I was grappling with a lot, working it out with my students, experimenting with ideas, we were all grappling, our structures were unraveling." Since then she has gone on to teach regularly in women's studies and women's history and has produced widely respected scholarship in what has come to be known as feminist theory.

Organizational openings were also a catalyst for Pathfinders who were already in departmental faculty positions. In some cases a woman already in the department would be asked—or even told—by the department chair to teach a new course. A sociologist who works at a state university explained that she was told to teach a course in sex roles by her department chair: "I didn't know anything about it. It was simply assigned to me. . . . He said, 'You are the logical choice, you're a woman, you do it.' "

This mandate turned out to be a significant opportunity for her own intellectual development. As she stated: "It had a profound effect on me. It increased my awareness of my own gender position. It changed my career." She has come to see the area of sex roles research in sociology as being her "major orientation." In addition to regularly teaching a sex roles class, she reported reading feminist books for pleasure, including feminist versions of liberation theology. But she is not inclined to pursue research herself: "I read it for pleasure and it gets in my mindset somewhere and then into my class presentations. . . . Feminist scholarship is something I'd like to be doing, but since I've become a full professor, I have no desire to do research. To me it's a lot of work. I dread that stuff. Doing a study, getting the data, writing it up."

The opportunity to teach the sex roles class brought about an unexpected shift in her intellectual interests. Yet organizational constraints, primarily a heavy teaching load, reduce the likelihood that she will integrate her interests into pursuing research in this area. She indicated that if she does, she would definitely publish in women's studies: "People advised me not to get associated with the female ghetto on campus. But that is my home. And if I get with it and start to publish, I will publish in women's studies." Of her seven publications, three are in women's studies, including two articles in women's studies journals and a chapter on sex roles in a sociology textbook. Thus, although she does not currently contribute to a feminist research agenda, her intellectual interests have clearly broadened to a feminist perspective.

In this way, teaching openings drew some academic women into feminist thinking, and for some it ultimately reshaped their research agendas. Whether or not those interests developed into actual scholarship was, in part, determined by their institutional milieux and the structure of their job responsibilities. Those who remained in state universities after engaging in women's studies teaching opportunities tended to be less likely to produce feminist scholarship, even though they described themselves as very intellectually engaged by feminist scholarly ideas.

In summary, the organizational opportunities to teach in women's studies enabled academic women to share ideas and course material, and to plan initiatives on their campuses. Yet as women's studies programs got off the ground, a deeper conflict emerged within informal women's networks: between those who wanted a "regular academic program" and those who wanted "a feminist program," one that would directly challenge and critique the institutions and the academic canons within which they were situated. This tension produced dissension, which in some cases had positive consequences. As one participant recalled: "It wasn't an internal struggle that cut off the imagination. It encouraged us to think hard and share ideas."

In the course of my interviews, a majority of the Pathfinders reported having been involved with women's studies in one or more ways, teaching in programs, writing proposals to establish programs, suggesting ideas for courses, or persuading colleagues of women's studies' academic legitimacy. Over time, and especially at more prestigious institutions, Pathfinders were increasingly able to link up with the academic women's community and discussions of feminist scholarship without being required to teach or administer women's studies.

Identifying Unexplored Terrain

In addition to the two extremes, being guided primarily by political interests or by local organizational opportunities, a third pattern among the Pathfinders was evident in those who reported maintaining a primary scholarly commitment while simultaneously taking their political interests seriously. In the process of trying to integrate the two sets of concerns, these Pathfinders devised new ways of formulating feminist questions. The primary strategy was to identify unexplored terrain in their respective disciplines as well as to reframe the canon within their disciplines. In the process of rethinking disciplinary ideas, they created new domains and sought that they be considered as legitimate areas for further research.

One example of this process is the way in which an historian developed her research in family history. She explained that she always had been interested in social history. She pursued the questions that were most interesting intellectually, and "the women's part passed me by at first. It simply never occurred to me that women were part of that package." In fact, early in graduate school, a professor had suggested that she write on women, which she "took as an enormous insult, that I was pushed into that because I was a woman. So I ignored it." Even though she "managed to do her entire dissertation in family history without ever mentioning women," she identified a new area of research that became a precursor to extensive work in women's history.

Her dissertation topic illustrates the way she came to realize that her intellectual concerns could constitute an unexplored topic within history. Studying a kinship-organized revolution, she wanted to analyze how the kinship structures worked, rather than how the political revolution worked. Yet her colleagues were more interested in the more conventional questions of power: "I knew that if I couldn't translate it into political terms, it was marginal." Since they defined politics narrowly to mean the political history of kings and other leaders of nations, she had trouble making the domain of her interests understood: "That's the way [their] political questions were phrased. My papers were always about art and culture and relations and what's behind it. I never was told that's wrong but no one knew what to do with it. No one would advise me."

Trying to communicate resulted in frustration and efforts to shape her work to match their interests: "They would retranslate that into questions of power and ask political questions about that. I felt maybe I could answer these questions. Yet I felt I really ought to be a little smarter. . . . I tried to translate it into political terms, using political science models. I tried to fit things into that. But I didn't know what to do with my materials on dowries. I had to try to figure out what to do with dowries. What [could I] say about them politically?" Without knowing it at the time, and without encouragement or rewards from colleagues, she developed a thesis topic that can be considered prefeminist, thereby identifying a new area for future research.

However, this scholar's thesis was seen by the local powers that be as marginal rather than innovative, an assessment that left her questioning her own competence: "I felt I didn't understand the terms of the field." In retrospect, she saw that she had no way of saying there might be different terms because she knew of no precedent for doing so: "There was no model for that for me anywhere. I can't remember anybody I knew doing anything like this. . . . Obviously there were people [in history] like Natalie Davis at Berkeley who were working on this stuff, but I hadn't come across it."

She stayed the course in history nonetheless, but changed her focus within it. After graduate school, this historian began to do cutting-edge research in family history that paid primary attention to women. Reflecting on the reasons for this shift, she was not sure why the same subjects that she had first rejected as "dry" material she later found "tremendously exciting." She made sense of the turning point as an internal change, attributing it to a realization of her own emotional engagement with feminist materials: "I can't remember when they became interesting. I know it was emotional. . . . It was this kind of sudden sense of emotional involvement, which just connected me to material that I had once found dry. If you take the emotional excitement out of it, it's no more interesting than any other kind of history."

As we have seen, generating feminist topics for research was problematic when the process entailed identifying an interest that was not on the disciplinary agenda. In the case of this historian, there were no categories to describe her interests, so no one (herself included) was clear about the line of inquiry she was pursuing. Moreover, raising innovative questions while in graduate school may be a riskier undertaking than doing so at later stages of the academic career, when one is already employed in a faculty position.

Perceiving a risk of rejection by one's faculty while a graduate student is illustrated by the literary critic, who self-consciously moved outside the boundaries of her discipline when she changed her dissertation from "a very nice topic" in comparative literature to writing about women poets. Her interest in women poets had been sparked by a newly established Women in Literature course on her campus. Both she and her committee viewed her decision as a dramatic shift and a departure from pursuing scholarship in her field of study:

I said, "I'm not doing comparative literature scholarship." That's not what I wanted to do. . . . And they felt I was wasting my fine education. . . . They were angry. They thought I had gotten this great degree and I had this promising topic and I could get a fine job at a fine institution. . . . They resented it. . . . I was interested in the first topic, but I just didn't think it was important. I'm sure it would have been an interesting book. But it wasn't as interesting and it wasn't as important as writing about [these women].

To pursue her interest and develop it for a thesis, she "dug up people" for a new committee. She managed to locate a woman faculty member to chair it, who said she "didn't know anything about it" but "would support it because she had feminist interests" although she was not "doing feminist scholarship herself, [but] was a kind of voyeur of it." To round out the committee, she found "a very nice guy" and someone else "who just rubber-stamped anything." Pursuing dissertation work in this new area had meant that she clearly alienated the powerful faculty in her department.

In a way, what seemed a fundamental challenge to those faculty was in another way just conventional work in a different and emerging field. She wanted to add to the canon by legitimating women poets. She was attracted to the new topic because it was "wide open" and needed to be done. A "critic and rebel" by nature, this scholar wanted to do this "important work" on women because "nobody was writing about any of these women."

Another way that unexplored terrain may come to be recognized is when two scholars in different disciplines join forces and in so doing discover a new direction for scholarly inquiry. This occurred when a sociologist, with some background in sociolinguistics and strong feminist politics, recognized new terrain in an interesting footnote, which turned out to be a "wonderful wrinkle" in a "stale" book about family sociology. The footnote referred to a psychologist's work on the politics of touch. The sociologist describes her moment of insight about a new area of research: "I just suddenly saw this vision that hadn't quite come together, things that used to feel like separate strands. It just thrilled me because I saw that you could do micropolitics and feminism at the same time."

Through correspondence, the two scholars arranged to meet and "really it hit off." Out of their similar interests, they developed a bibliography on language and gender, which they developed into a book that "helped to found that field." The project required working across disciplines, which she characterized as "a different model of sharing" than how she had been socialized by her sociology department in graduate school.

In summary, feminist scholarly questions often arose when the scholar recognized a fruitful area of previously unidentified terrain. Whether or not and how she pursued the new way of seeing depended upon two sets of commitments: her intellectual conviction that the new topic has original scholarly value, and her serious intention to bring a politically informed perspective into academic understanding. In working to reconcile scholarly and political interests, these Pathfinders found their disciplinary contexts to provide fertile ground within which feminist questions could be raised and elaborated. The next chapter explores the different ways that the disciplines facilitated or constrained the efforts of these emerging scholars to create knowledge.

5

Knowledge Creation in the Disciplines: History, Sociology, and Philosophy

The discussion of the Pathfinders' starting points in chapter 4 illustrates the ways in which their ongoing feminist commitments influenced and were channeled into their intellectual contributions. Beyond that, the analysis suggests that their intellectual creativity was also stimulated to varying degrees by the process of trying to reconcile a deeply felt tension between their feminist interests and the scholarship in their disciplines.

Each discipline presented different opportunities for reconciling this tension. Pathfinders articulated unique intellectual problems that they saw to be both feminist and scholarly. That is, they wanted to extend feminist understandings that they derived from their personal and political experiences to the sense-making in their disciplines and to establish legitimacy for that work as within the boundaries of disciplinary significance. Each discipline also presented preconditions or opportunities in its canon to allow for the development of feminist thinking. In this chapter, I focus on the ways in which Pathfinders perceived and encountered opportunities for knowledge work in their disciplines.

Examining these scholars' intellectual biographies within their disciplinary locations reveals some variation in how Pathfinders created new knowledge. While they were able to take advantage of different intellectual resources that were hospitable to feminist ideas, they also were constrained in their efforts to develop feminist inquiry by the conventional parameters of their disciplines.

In some instances, paradoxically, disciplinary constraints seemed to spark more radical ambitions for feminist inquiry. In fact, Thorne and Stacey (1985) have suggested that those disciplines that were "thoroughly male-centered" provoked the most "dramatic analytical consequences" for feminist critique. In other words, the more "male-centered," that is, the more blatant the omission or distortion of women in the canon, they argue, the more pressing the need for feminist scholarship; and if ultimately successful, the more dramatic the results. My analysis of the Pathfinders in this study affirms Thorne and Stacey's suggestion: while history has offered the most openings for feminist ideas and expanded its subject matter to include women, philosophy offered the least fertile ground, but demonstrated potential for dramatic recon- ceptualizations of what counts as philosophy.

In practice, the canon and norms in each discipline function as a general kind of *gestalt* for its scholars and serve as a referent for their work whether they fully accept it or not. The analysis in this chapter considers history, sociology, and philosophy as if they were more or less distinctly bounded endeavors, in order to depict the dominant paradigms, or shared "beliefs about what are good questions to ask, what are proper developments of theory, [and] what are acceptable research methods" (Moulton, 1983, p. 152). The notion of "male-centered" disciplines is useful to identify a likely impetus for feminist critiques, but the unfortunate tendency of this terminology is to mischaracterize a discipline as monolithic and to overlook the interesting variation within it. While each discipline did have some male-centered characteristics, each also offered a complex set of openings or "cracks in the cement," to borrow MacKinnon's (1987) phrase. These cracks in the cement determined the extent to which a discipline offered opportunities for feminist re-visions.

My analysis examines the ways in which feminist scholars moved forward with their knowledge work in those contexts. By placing women at the center of inquiry, feminist scholars posed three kinds of challenges to what had historically been male-centered inquiry: in subject matter, in theory, and in method. These three dimensions constitute major contours of a disciplinary topography, and presented a landscape of obstacles and possibilities to be traversed by feminist scholars.

At the risk of oversimplifying, I sketch my argument briefly as follows: although Pathfinders may have attempted to contribute simultaneously on all three fronts—subject matter, theory, and method—one type of innovation tended to emerge as dominant in each discipline. Perhaps the most obvious way in which they tried to innovate was to expand each discipline's subject matter, as they did in history. Innovative efforts in sociology were oriented toward theory so that it more accurately reflected women's experiences, since sociology already at least superficially included women as subject matter. A third and more radical innovation took shape in philosophy, as the very proposition of inserting women into subject matter or theory necessitated a reorientation of philosophic method to nonuniversalistic—indeed, feminist—assumptions.

All of this knowledge work required intellectual and political resources that were evident in varying degrees. Feminists in history drew upon natural openings within their discipline, whereas feminists in philosophy turned outside their discipline and often considered leaving it altogether in order to maintain their feminist commitments. The accounts of those in sociology fall somewhere between these two extremes.

Although these women scholars did recognize that certain knowledge work would be considered legitimate and perhaps innovative, the distinct differences among the disciplines suggests that Pathfinders were determined to find a feminist way *regardless* of whether such an effort seemed promising for an academic career. In contrast to the discipline of history, which has recognized feminist inquiry early on as not only valid but intellectually exciting, the extreme inhospitability of philosophy dramatically illustrates that some Pathfinders persisted in the face of tremendous barriers with no promise of legitimacy, let alone prospect of rewards, for an original contribution.

HISTORY

In contrast to philosophy and sociology, history has been noted for being a prolific and fruitful site of feminist scholarly activity, a pattern confirmed by the informants in my study. Of all the Pathfinders, historians were the most likely to generate feminist research agendas and to develop them early in their careers. In searching for a way to integrate their feminist and historical interests, Pathfinders in history generated new knowledge in a most obvious way—by opening up a new subject area of women's history.

The success of this kind of contribution may be attributed, in large part, to the emergence of social history as a new field of historical inquiry. Social history signaled a change in notions of historical significance, expanding what counts as a worthy subject of historical inquiry and what counts as acceptable evidence. The expansion of acceptable subject matter and data sources provided natural openings for feminist scholarship to be deemed innovative. Social history marked a shift in the discipline to include the study of ordinary people, specifically the downtrodden and oppressed. By the late 1960s, this expanded subject matter for historical scholarship provided a clear opening for politically motivated questions about oppression based on sex and race. According to one observer, the emerging subfield of Black history also opened the door for scholars to study the status and experience of women. Further, these kinds of history were not captured and presented in the same way as the history of dominant groups. New kinds of data could be used for historical research; archival research and oral history were appropriate means for obtaining those data.

One Pathfinder remembered her recognition of this opening during graduate school in a course on the history of the family: "The material was there. It was about the family. So I was beginning to learn about social history, what you could look at. [O]f course it had no gender, no feminism, no women. But I was reading this stuff that began to make me realize that you could do this kind of thing."

Social history offered the generation of Pathfinders an opportunity to insert women into the canon and to elevate women from invisibility and marginality into historical significance. Since historical research was, for the most part, driven by empirical data, scholarship on women became a natural extension of the domain for inquiry. As one Pathfinder stated, somewhat as a matter of fact, "History . . . is defined by subjects, so you can put women in just like you can put pots and pans in. You can do anything that has a history." Historical research skills were thus extended to topics on women, serving both additive and corrective functions in the canon.

In this way, the inception of social history as well as the evidence-driven nature of historical inquiry facilitated the emergence of women's history as a variant of mainstream history. These facilitating conditions would suggest that, in the early 1970s, the emerging feminist scholarship met with an absence of constraints rather than an array of obstacles that necessitated deconstruction or systematic critique.

Nevertheless, the primary task for feminist historians in the early 1970s was an ambitious one. Even the most data-driven women's history was difficult. As one Pathfinder remembered, "It was damned hard to do because you didn't know where the sources were—they were so hard to find. You didn't know what the questions were. You didn't have the kind of definition by other people of what you should be looking for." So even though the discipline did not present outright resistance to research on women, the absence of essential resource materials was itself a major challenge. Again, the advent of social history had paved the way to justify such arduous data collection.

Due to the incremental nature of disciplinary change across universities, different Pathfinders learned of social history at different times. Those historians who attended graduate schools located in New York and the San Francisco Bay Area tended to be the first to sense that "the new social history" was gaining visibility and respectability. The realization was accompanied by excitement about the potential to use this intellectual juncture for developing feminist scholarship. As one historian recalled, "I don't know if it was my naiveté about how things worked, but at that moment in that place everything seemed possible. Everything was up for grabs. . . . Things were wide open. The new social history was the word, and women could fit in through social history, and through our politics, and through the social networks we were building. There was this sense of camaraderie that seemed limitless." The sense of possibility was twofold: scholars envisioned that they could make a new kind of scholarly contribution as well as find a legitimate place for feminist work in the discipline.

Most of the Pathfinders recognized the potential for a convergence of feminism and history during graduate school. A few Pathfinders in my study were already contributing intellectual work before the opportunity was clear. In reflecting on launching her career slightly before the wave, one historian reported some regret, feeling that she "should have done a dissertation on women," but she "was a little too early and had no women to talk to"; in choosing a topic she "just kind of latched on to the first thing I could think of, and it was a terrible mistake."

For three out of the study's seven Pathfinders in history, the time was ripe to study women for their dissertations. Choosing a dissertation topic on women reflected an attempt to satisfy both their feminist politics and their quest for establishing what would count as historically significant. For each of these Pathfinders, feminist motivations guided their scholarly choices. However, while some made self-conscious attempts to integrate feminist politics with historical inquiry, others were less conscious of their feminist interests as a driving force in their intellectual choices.

As an illustration of an historian who was less aware of her feminist agenda, a 19th-century historian initially described her selection of a dissertation topic on women as "more or less accidental." The topic originated out of a paper "I just happened to do in a seminar. I was not one of those people who was determined to do something in women's history and had to fight to do it. . . . I sort of slid into it." After finishing the dissertation, she went on to do another project on women and then "wound up doing a book on both." Her description of the evolution of these intellectual interests conveys no sense of having a prior feminist agenda or of struggling to legitimate a new kind of scholarly question. The fact that women in the 19th century even constituted a topic for a seminar paper, let alone an entire dissertation, is not something that she acknowledges as either a significant moment of recognition or an influential factor in the formation of her subsequent scholarly interests. She thought of herself as moving into women's history without ever intending to.

Yet when I asked about the driving force in her selection of research topics, she pinpointed "the women's movement, because that is where most of the intellectual vitality was at the moment, so that's what I was doing." Her primary motivation, then, had been to study what engaged her, the seed of which was located in the political climate beyond the academy. Like other feminist historians, she rather easily found a way to integrate her movement agenda with historical inquiry.

We see slight variation on this approach with a French historian, who expressed some self-conscious intent to study women because it resonated with her personal experience of going to a women's college. She had initially been drawn to French history because it was "the best and most exciting history" when a professor in graduate school suggested she study a topic on 17th-century French women. She explained that she "was immediately attracted to the idea. It appealed to me [because] I had come out of this women's college where there was this incessant discussion about being a woman. . . . There was a lot of consciousness and the issues were just being defined. When I carried these issues in my head and found there might be some historical dimensions to [them] as far back as the 17th century, it seemed very interesting."

In her mind, attending a women's college had predisposed her to "a feminist direction" even though "it was actually a prefeminist period." And the primary motivation for shifting to research on women lay in her desire to find a meaningful way to link her personal experiences with her scholarly interest in the subfield of French history.

In contrast to the professor who explored the moderately-stated feminist agendas of the 19th century and to the French historian, a specialist in American history directly sought to integrate her deep commitment to feminist politics with historical inquiry. Sparked by an increasing awareness that women had been "left out of the canon," the American historian recalled her early graduate school experience of writing "my first women's history paper."

Having come to graduate school already radicalized by feminist politics, she was "so hungry for anything about women." During her second year she got the idea to do a paper on women as part of a course on the United States between the Wars. She traced the idea for a paper with the encouragement of her professor, "an old guy, incredibly quirky":

We came up with the topic together. I was interested in women after suffrage because the only time you heard about women was with suffrage. So I wrote a historiographical essay. He gave me an A on it. And he said: "I want you to submit this to the *Journal of American History*; I'm on the editorial board, and you tell them I said so." It wasn't a great essay. . . . But at the time no women's history was being published. He wrote textbooks, and he said: "This will influence my textbooks. I never thought about these things, and I think other people should hear about this."

In her eyes, this paper thus marked the start of her career in women's history. She said, "I was putting together the politics and the scholarship and feeling like it had to be done." She considered writing this paper to be a "very radicalizing experience," and she remembered having "read all the literature that existed on women in the 19th century in 1971. And it was hard to find!" She developed her research directly out of her feminist convictions and received encouragement from a male professor who saw a strategic opening for it in the discipline.

This American historian subsequently became "committed to declaring myself as someone who does women's history." Her dissertation topic also originated out of a political conviction combined with intellectual curiosity. Her own realization that attention to women was lacking in the historical canon was later reinforced by her academic peers. She described it simply: "[Someone] had just written a book on prisons. There was nothing about women in it. I was living with some law students who asked me about . . . how did we get women's prisons. I said I didn't know. It seemed like a good topic and an important political question." When she asked her advisor about the topic, "he said he didn't know and didn't care." Rather than let this dissuade her, she arranged to work with another faculty member, who had "already sponsored one women's history dissertation yet knew nothing about the subject."

From her dissertation onward, this woman developed a mode of doing scholarship that was "clearly political." All of her articles "start out with the contemporary political issue and . . . end up with it too, and I do the history in between." Reflecting on the creative process, she conceived of herself as a pioneer. Like other Pathfinders, this American historian came to do women's history in relative isolation within her own department, only later discovering that other scholars were also writing in the emerging field of women's history:

I had this sense of being a pioneer. I didn't know at the same time that there were all these women out there writing all this women's history that was about to come out. I was totally thinking I was in isolation except for our little history department women's caucus that would meet for lunch and talk about their dissertations. So I knew you could do a dissertation on women. Millet had done her dissertation on women, and it became *Sexual Politics*. I knew you could do it, and I was beginning to move toward this commitment to doing it.

In this way, she began to recognize women's history as a possible field within which she was already a contributor.

While some historians came to women's history in graduate school, others shifted to it later in their careers. Even though by that time women's history had become more visible, their individual pioneering efforts still were characterized as a struggle to combine their historical inquiry with their feminist interests.

An economic historian, for example, came to women's history after graduate school with a sudden and unexpected intellectual engagement. Prior to this point, she reported having feminist politics that were not connected with her scholarship. A project in women's history raised the possibility of linking the two, which hooked her into women's history as well as economic history. The realization occurred when she "stumbled upon" a unique opportunity in the archives, and this opportunity culminated in writing a book. While doing research for a project on a European city, her attention was "accidentally" captured by intriguing information about a woman who was considered a sexual deviant for her time. Immediately, the historian sensed that this material could be "a very different project than anything else I had ever done." She attributes this opportunity to a combination of the data presenting itself to her with her own instinct that it would be a fruitful study. As she explained, "[O]ne friend said the archives smiled upon me. Then again, if I hadn't thought it was interesting and worth writing about, the book wouldn't have been written."

Although minimized in her recounting of the story, two components created the possibility for her research. Her prior feminist orientation implicitly valued women as historical agents, which meant that she was open for her interest to be piqued. There was also space within the discipline for such a question to be granted scholarly merit. In fact, women's history was becoming a "hot topic."

Even though this economic historian regards her entry into women's history as serendipitous ("It began by accident!"), it became more than a brief divergence from her mainstream scholarly path. When asked how this work in women's history differed from her other knowledge work, she pointed to both form and content: "It's a different kind of writing. Women's history is a more narrative approach. . . . It involved me reading up on questions of patriarchy and the like. I realized how much I hadn't read that had to do with women's issues."

Her brief foray into women's liberation literature and emerging feminist theory provided her with a language to articulate a feminist scholarly perspective. She found a way to uncover the subjective experiences of oppression, while simultaneously being rewarded for expanding the boundaries of historical inquiry in an intellectually exciting way.

Viewing this research project in women's history as a dramatic departure in her own scholarly career, this historian was initially concerned about the reception from her history colleagues at a high-prestige university. She worried about her colleagues whom she knew pursued more mainstream disciplinary topics. For a moment, she considered keeping it a secret: "I toyed briefly with not telling anyone here that I was working on it because I was afraid of how it might be perceived, especially as I was coming up for tenure. But I decided not to. One reason was a practical reason that people would wonder what I was working on. Then it also just didn't seem right."

In spite of the risk, she presented some of the research to her colleagues in the department. She was relieved when she realized that they were intellectually engaged in her topic: "It went very well. I was amazed. Some of the issues that I deal with are at the intersection of sex and power. They are interested in sexuality. And power they understand very well. They were very supportive and made good suggestions, and I was much relieved." Her work was warmly received not only as respectable scholarship but actually as a "hot topic" given that issues about sexuality and power were being discussed in cross-disciplinary study groups.

In retrospect, the entire experience had profoundly altered the course of her scholarship. What began as an "interruption," she realized, "turned out to be not an interruption at all but . . . [a] fundamental [shift] in my outlook as a historian. My whole view of people is much deeper. . . . And all of my writing has just changed forever. There is no going back to the way I did it before. Even in writing a mainstream project . . . I'm more aware of the complexity of human motivation, of the uses and misuses of power, of how individuals and institutions affect each other."

Underlying this profound shift in her work as an historian was a new understanding that scholarship could be both an intellectual and emotional endeavor. In her words,

I had realized on an intellectual level that I was uncovering some of the past. . . . But it's one thing to realize it on an intellectual level and another to . . . realize how far back and how rich and how complicated and how painful some of those times are. It's like seeing a patient in a hospital beginning to recover memory. [T]hat's something that is emotionally very charged. . . . And that for me has been a very moving experience. There were times when I was close to tears. . . . For me it is a revelation at the emotional level—to think through fully what repression of history does to people and has done to women. And in that sense it is an issue I felt most keenly with the [sexuality] issue . . . , but extending it from there you can see what has been done to women's history and the history of the poor and the history of all the oppressed. I was aware of the expression that history was written by the victors. And again, I could understand that on an intellectual level, but to experience emotionally what that means for me—I'm just beginning to understand what that means. It is a very enriching experience.

Women's history led her to create knowledge in a way that entailed deeper intellectual and emotional involvement. She realized, in contrast, "how utterly superficial" her research would have been if she had not had "this interruption, so to speak." The data that she "stumbled upon accidentally" was a catalyst for a new scholarly trajectory into women's history as well as for a fresh approach to her more mainstream scholarship. And her feminist commitments were further enriched by the rewards she accrued for producing creative historical research.

As all of these illustrations from the discipline of history suggest, Pathfinders found natural openings to raise previously unasked questions. For the most part these new questions were linked to uncovering new historical material. By demonstrating the ways in which women have been hidden from history, Pathfinders have contributed important scholarship to the canon and established women's history as a legitimate subfield and specialization. Yet, like their feminist colleagues in literature, this kind of innovation is rather conventional in the sense that it does not force a major reexamination of the nature of historical study. In fact, some feminist historians noted the absence of critique about the premises and standards of the discipline (Scott, 1986). By posing gender as a category of analysis for the entire discipline, rather than for only a subfield, the ambition is to rethink fundamental conceptual frameworks, and basic assumptions about periodization and chronology. In addition, feminist contributions to the discipline are not as visible in the area of theory.

By adding women to the canon, women scholars enlarged the domain of history and redefined what counted as historically significant. Of the Pathfinders in the three disciplines, historians had to move away from their discipline the least in order to develop and nurture feminist scholarly agendas. That Pathfinders were able to do both mainstream history and/or women's history by the 1980s is evident in the ability of feminist historians to publish their work in a range of journals, from the *Journal of American History*, a special issue of *American Historical Review*, to the *Journal of Social History*. At the same time, however, early work by feminist historians was also published in *Feminist Studies*, noted one observer. Other articles have appeared in *Signs* and *Women and History*, an occasional journal by the Institute for Historical Research in New York for scholars in women's history, especially those without an institutional base. One Pathfinder in history began her career with successful publications in both a mainstream history journal and a feminist journal.

Clearly within history it was possible to focus scholarship centrally on women and to remain in the discipline. Another Pathfinder explained that her approach was to formulate research simultaneously in two distinct ways for two different audiences. She described the realization that this was a possibility: "It became quite clear . . . that it wasn't going to work just to do [this major project] and simply include gender and women. In fact, [they are] a separate set of problems that have to be approached as central rather than just a part of the other problem. . . . It seemed to be clear to me that there was going to have to be two books here and then it worked out very nicely." This historian found a creative way to make gender central while still addressing what she saw as the "broader concerns" of the discipline. She crafted her research to culminate in two separate books, each with a different emphasis and story line. While she acknowledged the tension between feminist and scholarly interests, she explained that "it didn't paralyze me. It was in the back of my mind, but I was able to do what I wanted to do."

Being "committed to both" has meant that her primary identity "shifts a lot." There are times when "a focus on women is what I want to deal with. . . . It's very gripping for me and I want to do that." In fact, she suggested that sustaining her feminist motivation "to pursue what is practically and intellectually relevant" kept her from feeling bored with standard history: "History looked duller after shifting my focus centrally to women." Not only has women's history allowed her to create knowledge that she considered both feminist and scholarly, but it also provided her with an intellectual stimulation that otherwise would not be present in her regular disciplinary work.

Within history, the search for a convergence between feminist and scholarly agendas has been the least problematic of the three disciplines. Not only have feminist historians been the most successful in reconciling that tension in their academic lives, but they have received the most disciplinary rewards for identifying a new subject matter that is seen as intellectually exciting. Their feminism provided them with a new angle of vision to ask previously unexplored questions. Like feminist historians, Pathfinders in sociology reported a struggle to reconcile the same tension. But they had more difficulty in establishing a kind of scholarship and disciplinary location in which they could be both feminists and sociologists.

SOCIOLOGY

In contrast to history, Pathfinders in sociology found fewer intellectual resources for combining their feminist and sociological interests. In searching out research topics that would both sustain a feminist agenda and count as sociology, Pathfinders were likely to focus on women as subject matter and then attempt to make theoretical innovations. Sociology, at least nominally, has long acknowledged male-female differences as worthy topics of sociological study. Theory, on the other hand, was a most fruitful location for contributions that would be considered as major analytical departures.

Guided by their feminist perspective, Pathfinders in sociology were drawn to adopt a critical stance toward male-centered theoretical accounts in the discipline. In theoretical reconceptualizations, these women paid attention to sources and mechanisms of male-female inequality and difference and worked to create new theory that would take their insights into account.

While not offering the Pathfinders as wide an opening as social history, sociology in the late 1960s did provide feminist thinkers with a critical vantage point from which to reflect critically upon prevailing sociological theory. Radicals from the New Left constructed an ideological critique of sociology, especially the dominant paradigm of functionalism, for its conservative bias. The critical perspective from the Left was an important precursor to feminist thinking. Bernard (1973) observed:

As the Sociology Liberation Movement had accused sociologists of cultivating a power-oriented sociology, creating not a science of society but a science of just one segment of society, honed to help it exploit the other segments, so, in a similar vein, these women charged that sociology was not a science of society but a science of male society and that it did not necessarily have great relevance for women. Just as the Sociology Liberation Movement charged that sociological research was on the side of the power structure, these women charged that it had been on the side of men. (p. 77)

The leftist critique assisted feminist Pathfinders in two ways: it set a precedent that allowed for critique, and its language was useful in opposing and subsequently deconstructing traditional sociology for the ways in which it functioned as an instrument of patriarchy.

Although Pathfinders were directly exposed to this radical trend in sociology to differing degrees, it provided substantial impetus for oppositional thinking and served as important intellectual antecedents to feminist theory. As one interviewee explained, those who were in graduate school at Brandeis, for example, found "a little oasis" from the rest of sociology because of the German Jews who had migrated there. The faculty were oriented to classical European sociology and critical theory, instead of to the functionalism of Merton and Parsons, which dominated American sociology. These graduate students learned quickly that "functionalism was a bad word there." But even sociologists in more mainstream departments around the country became aware of the growing momentum of radical critiques of sociology's dominant paradigm.

Feminism in its own right came to provide a valuable angle of critique for Pathfinders in sociology. Two feminist sociologists in my study were particularly successful, not only in finding a way to integrate their feminist and sociological interests but also in making significant theoretical contributions to the discipline. One is credited with creating a new subfield, the sociology of emotions. The other contributed highly respected theoretical insights into women's experience of abortion.

The Pathfinder who invented the subfield of emotions illustrates how a feminist perspective could identify new terrain as sociologically significant. She attributed her motivation to develop a previously unexplored line of inquiry to the dramatic revelation that something was missing from sociological theory: "The legitimacy of developing empathy for the subject [of a study] . . . was missing from the canon itself. It seemed unimportant, not an important piece of knowledge to be had; whereas to me it looked like this huge boulder in the field. . . . And to ignore feelings was to ignore the biggest clue we have about how people work, what motivates them, . . . and the way they socially located themselves." Out of this recognition she elevated emotions and feelings to a new level, by suggesting that they constituted valuable sociological data and therefore warranted theoretical attention.

In demarcating this unexplored area, she explained she was not at the time self-conscious of the fact that she was legitimating a "women's realm." Rather, she saw it as a profound line of critique of the discipline: "Although it isn't anything that comes to me by temperament in particular . . . , I became critical of the field for not making room for this. I feel like I went into a "no man's land" and sort of made something up. Basically I theorized a portion of experience that people recognize and know is true. If we really want to understand women's experience, and indeed anybody's experience, we have to understand feelings." While she was not motivated by an explicit feminist agenda, she suggested that a feminist perspective was implicitly a springboard for her scholarly inquiry. Her scholarship, as she characterized it, has had "as its basic premise honoring the experience of women . . . and feelings."

In contrast to those Pathfinders who more directly sought to translate feminist commitments into a scholarly agenda, she regards her approach as deriving from a mix of personal experience and disciplinary ideas: "I don't think it was something someone else was saying in a different way that I then was legitimating in the academy. It works for a lot of others that way. But it didn't feel like that to me. It felt much harder to do in a way. . . . [While] I drew some encouragement from the women's movement, the intellectual content I think came from my experience of [growing up] watching skeptically the acting that went on, my interest in emotions and feelings and my reading of Goffman."

Her experience of making the initial connections was a definite feeling of moving herself out of mainstream sociology: "I felt out there in left field. [This kind of] sociology felt bizarre." Nevertheless, she pioneered a new subfield that was in the Weberian tradition of *verstehen* sociology, an approach which had been introduced to her in graduate school as having little legitimacy.

To reconcile her feminist perspective with her academic work, this sociologist created a new agenda for sociological theory. Characterizing her scholarly contributions rather modestly, she sums up the innovation in this way: "It just felt like something I wanted to do. Given the climate of the times, I was permitted to do it."

Another Pathfinder made a substantial contribution to sociological theory in her study of abortion. In contrast to the implicit feminist agenda of her colleague who studied emotions, this Pathfinder was motivated by an explicit feminist agenda that she was trying to reconcile within the parameters of conventional sociology. She began her important scholarly contributions on abortion with her dissertation. Her choice of topic was not only guided by intellectual interest but also infused with political commitment: "I found abortion very interesting. And I had found a question which was, how come there was so much abortion when there was so much contraception available in this society? I remember when I did the review of the literature . . . I had a fine feminist outrage at the existing explanations of the 'authorities' about why women didn't use contraception. So it may have been that I actually did reading . . . that sort of galvanized me."

She recalled that the experience of writing the literature review felt like "I was very clearly dialoguing with these idiots, as I saw them, who'd written these stupid theories about why contraceptive use wasn't more prevalent." She then developed her interest into a dissertation in spite of the absence of faculty support for it. As she described it: "When I wanted to write my dissertation the faculty couldn't understand why anyone would be interested in abortion, or women, or contraception." She found no acknowledgement that this previously unexplored topic was worthy of theoretical attention or had potential sociological import. She decided to pursue it anyway because it captured her interest.

This case is striking in that her research culminated in a book that has since received widespread acclaim. Analyzing abortion from a feminist perspective, she connected it with larger disciplinary concerns about theories of human decision-making. She then did a follow-up study on abortion, in which she contributed important theoretical insights about the politics of abortion controversy by framing it as a debate within wider political movements. Creatively carving out a space for her work in the canon, she combined prevailing language in the discipline and standard sociological methods (e.g., some statistics) with the qualitative methods that would capture the deeply subjective and highly diverse concerns of her women subjects.

Within sociology this Pathfinder made a significant theoretical contribution as a result of trying to reconcile her feminist and scholarly interests. While she attributed sociology's receptivity to chance ("I've been lucky. . . . I was at the right place at the right time"), she actually infused the available disciplinary resources with the commitments she brought from her experiences in the women's liberation movement to theorize about "an unexplored part of social life." Her scholarly work was energized by her feminist agenda.

The feminist theoretical advances made by these two Pathfinders have not overturned the way people do sociology, nor have they challenged long-standing theoretical conceptions such as stratification, organizations, or authority. Yet their contributions are noteworthy because of the processes they went through in creating new knowledge. From feminist points of view, they discovered previously neglected problems for inquiry. Their insights not only challenged some domains within the discipline, but their knowledge work has been invigorated by the fact that they worried about a political and intellectual agenda.

Feminist research has not resulted in a fundamental, definitive rethinking of sociological inquiry. Nor has a major subfield emerged, as it has in history. Nonetheless, some observers do suggest that several subfields within sociology have been influenced by the addition of gender as a variable. Thorne and Stacey (1985), however, assert that simply adding gender to sociological studies is quite superficial and unsatisfactory and should even be considered an unfortunate co-opting by the discipline of feminist prodding.

One direction in feminists' quest for a distinctive feminist sociology has been to search for a "feminist methodology." Feminist sociologists have drawn upon an increasingly visible interpretive tradition within the social sciences as well as the radical branch of sociology that has roots in Marxist and critical theory. Both sets of traditions offered fertile ground for feminist thinking because they tend to be reflexive about the circumstances in which knowledge is developed (Smith, 1979).

Feminist scholars have been attracted to methodological presuppositions that acknowledge the role of social-historical locations in the production of knowledge. Although feminist sociologists have preferred qualitative methods, such approaches certainly existed before feminists attempted to create a mode of inquiry into the particularities of women's experiences and thereby enrich theoretical understandings. While discussions of a feminist methodology have been aimed at sharpening the vision of a sociology of, by, and for women, the notion of feminist methods is not widely understood, and if understood at all, is not taken seriously by mainstream sociology. The methodological efforts by feminist sociologists have not been as noteworthy as their theoretical contributions.

Feminist sociologists have not been able to establish a niche in the discipline like that of women's history, but they have created a vibrant intellectual community, which has made substantive contributions to theory and transcended several sociological specializations. In fact, one illustration of this is the establishment of *Gender and Society*, a journal dedicated to publishing feminist sociology. Yet the fact that feminist scholars wanted to establish this journal also indicates their difficulty in getting their work published in mainstream journals. At that time, such a journal was not created within the field of history, presumably because finding an outlet for work that is both feminist and historical had not been as problematic.

Thus, in contrast to history, sociology has been much less hospitable to women faculty who shifted their scholarly focus to center on women but also sought to stay within the discipline. In fact, five of six Pathfinders in sociology have done research on women and identify themselves politically as feminists. Yet none of the Pathfinders in sociology at the time of my interview identified herself as doing something called feminist sociology.

Pathfinders in sociology expressed more of a disjuncture between being both feminist and sociological. As one scholar explained, she was uncomfortable with considering herself a feminist sociologist, because "I don't want to be thought of as a woman who is interested in women and not sociology." A reluctance to take on the identity of a feminist sociologist is even more clear in the case of a scholar who considers herself a conventional sociologist. Although she has studied gender differences during her career, "I would never call myself a feminist scholar."

Several Pathfinders in sociology told me that they feel "pulled in two different directions" by their interests in feminism and in scholarship. As one of them explained, in spite of her own academic success in creatively negotiating between the two, the tension persists: "It seems to me that being a feminist scholar is a real tension because to the extent that you're a feminist, you're part of a political movement, and to the extent that you're a scholar, you're trying to find out, with all due humility for how difficult it is, something that you think of as the truth, that transcends what you want to hear." She is located in a tenured faculty position within a sociology department at a high prestige research university, and she has the opportunity to be part of a lively community of feminist scholars with similar interests.

Feminist sociologists have been more likely to find a convergence between the two in cross-disciplinary networks. In intellectual communities that go beyond the discipline, they have been able to draw upon concepts and ideas from feminist colleagues in anthropology, political theory, history, and literature, thereby acquiring intellectual resources that would not be available otherwise. In fact, such networks may be more necessary for sociologists than for historians, who have already established a niche for a feminist intellectual community within their discipline. The exposure to ideas outside of sociology is clearly valuable, and it can even be more challenging as an intellectual pursuit. As this feminist sociologist pointed out: "What I'm interested in cross-cuts a lot of different disciplines, and it's both a curse and a blessing because you can sort of go out and read and talk to other people across a wide range of disciplines, but then you're always anxious because you think, 'Oh my God, there's the perfect study out there, or the perfect footnote that I didn't read.' . . . The interdisciplinarity is simultaneously very enriching and somewhat anxiety-provoking."

The interview data in this study suggest that, in an effort to be both feminist and sociological, these Pathfinders have benefited from cross-disciplinary networks for originating and sustaining their feminist critiques much more than their counterparts in history. Although these efforts have been theoretically fruitful, feminist scholars have not achieved a foothold within the discipline to fundamentally challenge the nature of sociological inquiry, although they have made attempts to, theoretically. In contrast, philosophy has been even less hospitable to feminist ideas than sociology. Feminist philosophers have had an even more pressing need for cross-disciplinary support, and sometimes have had to leave the discipline entirely in order to develop their feminist scholarship.

PHILOSOPHY

Of the three disciplines, philosophy has sustained the most extreme tension between feminist and scholarly interests. Philosophy has been unreceptive to feminist ideas in two fundamental ways. First, intellectually, the scholarly presuppositions of philosophy are fundamentally incompatible with feminist concerns. Second, pragmatically, philosophy is dominated by scholars who have a restricted vision, who do not count feminist analyses as real philosophy. Both the intellectual content and practice of philosophy leave feminist philosophers facing formidable challenges and often unable to reconcile their divergent interests.

Of the seven Pathfinders in philosophy, only three identified themselves as doing any feminist philosophy. The other four do conventional philosophy. And only one of those four sees herself as a feminist, which she described as "not relevant" to her scholarship.

In the process of trying to reconcile their feminist and scholarly concerns, the three who consider themselves feminist philosophers have not, for the most part, directed their attention to creating innovations in either subject matter or theory. They have been drawn primarily to rethinking philosophic method. In trying to reconceptualize philosophy, these Pathfinders have tried to integrate their feminist understandings of the world by challenging the nature and methods of philosophical inquiry.

One notable commonality from my interviews with Pathfinders in philosophy was that these women tended to focus more on their perceptions of disciplinary constraints and less on their actual contributions. This may reveal an important paradox for feminists in philosophy: through the process of trying to generate feminist scholarly questions, scholars have come to learn what philosophy cannot do for them. In fact, their preliminary efforts to redefine what counts as philosophical inquiry might indicate that they have to either suppress their feminism and do standard philosophy or suppress their philosophical interests and move out of philosophy.

Pathfinders identified three major ways the discipline constrained their efforts to generate feminist questions: the maleness of philosophy, the absence of texts by women, and the dominance of analytic philosophy. Each warrants some elaboration.

In characterizing philosophy as male, my informants did not simply call attention to the fact that most philosophers are male. Rather, they suggested that the canon is male in the sense that it keeps women invisible and silent (Grimshaw, 1986). Two premises have made philosophical discourse male: universalism and abstract reasoning. Philosophical problems have always been considered, or alleged to be, universal. Since philosophy has always implicitly equated the class of human beings with the class of men, male ways of reasoning and acting have been adopted without question as human. A related assumption is that one ought to focus on the abstract and rational in order to achieve truth and goodness.

By implication, then, the universal and abstract mandate of philosophy negates the philosophical significance of women, if women are seen as more particularistic and relational, which many contemporary feminists have proposed. (See, for example, Gilligan, 1982.) The challenge for feminists was first to make "the woman question" a bona fide philosophical problem (Gould, 1976). Pathfinders suggested that a whole range of human activity that feminists take to be humanly important is completely neglected in philosophy (e.g., caretaking of various sorts, nurturance, and so on). While feminists have struggled to establish that women constitute appropriate subject matter for the discipline, it was an even more radical proposition to assert that women have some unique perspective to share from their experience as women. Only later did feminist scholars working in ethics and moral development argue that women have a distinct moral voice which could alter the maleness of philosophy, and in so doing improve upon philosophical understandings. (See for example Noddings, 1984, and Gilligan, 1982.)

A second obstacle Pathfinders reported was the absence of texts. "Philosophy is based on texts," according to one scholar. "Most subfields have some sort of bible that you can look to for readings and discussion." So there has been little, except for work by men, on which to build feminist arguments and textual criticism. The absence of texts for feminism contrasted markedly with Marxism, where there were volumes of texts. Unlike feminism, a Pathfinder described, Marxist scholarship "has seven million thousand footnotes. . . . It's extremely articulated. It's full of hair-splitting. It's finely argued. It's elaborated. There are tombs and tomes of obscure argumentation that you need to dig through."

In searching for appropriate texts for feminist philosophy, two women philosophers told me that they considered Susan Griffin's work on human nature as an important metaphysical contribution. Yet Griffin's work does not resemble academic philosophy in form: it is often considered nonacademic literature, perhaps only finding its way into philosophy through teaching materials but not through scholarly citations. So, early on, feminist thinkers would be drawn to material outside the academic canon.

A third problem for feminist scholars was that the dominant orientation in Anglo-American philosophy is analytic. Neither the substance nor the form of analytic philosophy offered resources for those who wanted to take a feminist approach. One Pathfinder suggested that the concerns of the analytic tradition ("language, logic, and a lot of technical stuff") were just not interesting to her. She preferred questions about "life, death, and how to live." She elaborated:

[Analytic philosophy] cuts up whole pictures into discreet units that can be manipulated numerically and logically. It gets the messy, soft, gooey, feminine stuff out of them to get it real hard and crisp and clean and make it into a science. . . . Instead of big issues like how people live their lives, or what's it all about Alfie, or what the analytic folks would say were "loosey goosey" things, they tend to focus on issues which have some kind of practical consequences, but which can be treated without personal involvement. . . . [Even the question of] justifications for knowledge [is dealt with] as a very abstract general issue, and you don't have to talk about what people with that knowledge might do with their lives or what people should do with that knowledge . . . or what kind of system do we have here in which knowledge is generated or whatever.

In other words, neither the substantive orientation nor the method of analytic philosophy nurtured feminist concerns.

An underlying premise of analytic philosophy is that of detached inquiry, which is in direct contrast to the interested character of feminist scholarship. This theme is elaborated upon by feminists who seek to directly challenge the core of philosophy. According to one observer, "[P]hilosophy, above all, thinks of itself as the activity of disinterested reason. And so to have any sort of agenda is a kind of debasement of philosophy."

Of course, one approach that feminist scholars used was to challenge the idea that philosophy is the activity of pure reason and to argue that all intellectual activity is "interested" in some way. Drawing upon the rhetoric of critical theory and the Left, subsequent feminist tracts have developed this argument, which is aimed at reorienting the discipline's fundamental imperative.

The cumulative message from Pathfinders was that philosophy provided no help in generating questions for inquiry that interested them. As one scholar lamented, "It was very hard for me to begin work because the work wasn't done yet. And until it's started it's hard to know what to do. [And] you are always challenged from people who have a defined or articulated methodology going back a couple thousand years." In the absence of natural intellectual openings for feminist ideas, philosophy has been "a hard nut to crack," a metaphor suggested by several women I interviewed.

While this portrait of philosophy suggested no intellectual avenues for feminist thinking, in reality, potential openings for feminist thinking could be found in very small cracks within philosophy's subfields. One Pathfinder suggested that such openings often go unnoticed by her colleagues who, "unfortunately, are more comfortable with a victim stance." She condemned her feminist colleagues for characterizing philosophy as "an absolutely oppressive, nonreformable patriarchal canon." If it were, she suggests, "no feminist scholarship could ever have begun, nor feminists hired."

On closer inspection, the edges of the discipline had some opportunities, in addition to those subfields that were more sensitive to contemporary societal issues. As Sherman (1980) suggests, moral and political philosophy were possible locations for raising concerns about social justice. Applied ethics was also open to concerns about abortion, rape, marriage, and preferential hiring, as evidenced by some of the more topic-oriented work by feminist philosophers in the early 1970s.

As in the early stages of women's history, the early input of academic women in philosophy was additive. For example, one philosopher formulated a dissertation topic that focused on a woman philosopher. A professor of contemporary continental philosophy actually made the suggestion, after she applied for a Fulbright to study in Europe:

Imagine: there I was the only woman in this mass of male students. . . . This professor . . . suggested I study Simone de Beauvoir. My immediate feeling was, is she a philosopher? Could I do a dissertation on her? He didn't know shit about her, but he knew about me and he knew that she was a philosopher. . . . I had never heard of doing a dissertation on a woman. . . . I had never read anything [in philosophy] on a feminist. . . . I had nothing to go on except this man's confidence in me. And my own interest. It was very frightening.

Supported by an advisor, she set out to do a new kind of dissertation in philosophy, a topic that appealed to her because it fit with her feminist commitments. It was almost a surprise that she could, in effect, do some scholarly research that would incorporate any of those interests.

However, the early career experience of this Pathfinder was atypical. No other feminist philosophers that I interviewed had experienced this kind of encouragement to consider feminist ideas as significantly philosophical. The more common experience was to have a vague sense of feminist intention but a lack of particular vision for its potential. In reflecting on trying to generate feminist philosophical questions in the mid-1970s, another Pathfinder recalls being "puzzled about what we could do":

We saw some standard ethical problems to tackle as our issues. And we thought it was important to develop philosophical arguments in support of feminist positions on those questions. But beyond that I think most of us were really at a loss to see what the relation was between our work as philosophers and our political commitments as feminists. . . . I'm not sure how interested I myself was in feminist scholarship at the time or what I perceived were the possibilities for it in my field. I didn't see how interesting it would turn out to be. I had no idea of my future direction.

So, early on, she had no sense of the possibilities, nor of the resources, but only a vague notion that she might find a way to integrate her feminism with her scholarship by addressing some ethical questions.

So, feminist scholars in philosophy were compelled to innovate without having a preconceived notion of what they would create. As one Pathfinder remembered, she knew feminist ideas might result in "changes that would disrupt standard philosophical methods, but . . . I couldn't identify what they would be." She thought that two traditional philosophical problems seemed to offer "tremendous potential: the mind/body problem and the existence of the external world." But she didn't "know what it might look like" to reconsider those problems.

Even more common was the experience of another Pathfinder who entered graduate school and more or less systematically moved from one subfield to another, searching for a hospitable location within the canon. It is interesting that, in the late 1960s, she began graduate school still believing that women should be subordinate. She reported that, by excluding herself from the general category of women, she became intellectually male-identified:

I thought I was a strong-headed exception, and I did accept the thought of women being subordinate. Even when I read Aristotle and he said, "Come brothers, let us reason together," I just included myself with the honorary men. When he made his offensive remarks about women being cows and incapable of friendship, I didn't identify with women at the time and was . . . pretty male-identified. I only had male teachers and male texts to study. To be a philosopher meant to be male-identified.

A few years later, having developed a feminist perspective, she realized the misogynist views of Aristotle and others were "major flaws lacking in wisdom, political responsibility, and ethical respectability." It became increasingly clear to her that the canon reflected "an inadequate comprehension of half the population."

Since she was concerned with "how to live well as an individual in a social community," ethics and political philosophy became attractive subfields for her. Yet even within ethics, the emphasis was on metaethics, which she found unsatisfactory: "There were burning social issues—civil rights for Blacks, the sexual revolution, the Vietnam War, freedom of speech—just really urgent personal and social issues. And our ethics classes had nothing to do with them. Nothing to do with the community and social well-being. I felt out of balance in that regard because I wanted to be engaged in the historical changes that were going on and wanted to do something." Nonetheless, guided by her idealism, she stuck with philosophy because it seemed to fit with her agenda for social change: "The slogan was around that knowledge was power and knowledge enables us to understand . . . life and to make good choices."

Deeply concerned about these issues, she became attracted to texts in existentialism: "Some of the philosophy, about the meaning of life, was very exciting and some of it was overly abstract and a bit tedious." She felt comfortable with the general orientation of existentialism, which she interpreted "as a philosophy of rebellion." From existentialism, she studied Marxism and then, in an informal way, feminism. She combined those three analytic perspectives for her dissertation, in a study on the dialectics of violence and love in the leftist movement. Yet, in spite of her progress in identifying hospitable schools of thought in philosophy, she was uncomfortable with philosophic method throughout graduate school. She found the method to "have an overemphasis on analysis. The work had to be hard and cutting, insightful and challenging. It was a very aggressive kind of training—to be challenging and critical and antagonistic and to break down others' positions. . . . Though I succeeded very well in learning [it], I felt it was a masculinization of me to succeed in that fashion, in a way that is actually a setback for my spirit and personality." As a woman, she felt that she was trained with "a different set of values" that did not exclusively value reason. "I think for a lot of women our primary training . . . is to be loving. . . . The conflict for me was that the [philosophical] training I was getting had nothing to do with being loving in the world. I've always found that disparity a hard one to adjust to."

In addition to its overemphasis on analysis, she was uncomfortable with the philosophic method because of its atheism: "Having spiritual values was looked down on as mushy-headed and sentimental and soft-minded." Philosophy's intolerance for spiritual values and nonaggressive analysis became two significant influences on the development of her scholarly interests in feminist theory.

So, for this Pathfinder, trying to reconcile her feminist and philosophical interests meant challenging philosophic method. Her preliminary efforts entailed envisioning a holistic philosophy that would resolve the mind/body split, which she had found problematic both in theory and practice:

The mind-body split was not just a theory we studied, but a practice that we were disciplined in, so that the intellectuality didn't have anything to do with the emotions. The emotions arise out of the body and physical responses to the experience we have. Either pleasure or pain or fear or anger or what have you. These are embodied experiences in ... interactions with our environment and other people. ... As long as philosophy disregards the emotional life, it is disregarding that part of our physical experience which is crucial to making good decisions.

Through her scholarship she attempted to "bring the heart and mind back together again." She attributed the source of her ambitions to feminism: "a new view of history that feminists have formed." She drew on resources from the women's movement, the peace movement, and radical feminists working against violence: "all of them have been continuing sources of support," providing validation for her perspective and a language with which to formulate her ideas. Her scholarship quite literally developed out of the interplay between philosophy and these nonacademic sources.

Guided by her feminist commitments to create a new kind of philosophy that addressed the need to unite mind and body, this philosopher left her faculty position in the philosophy department and moved into women's studies. She preferred women's studies as a location because it was a stimulating "political and intellectual and emotional climate which has been enormously valuable" to her scholarship: "I felt it was important to have some separate space and autonomy, to develop on our own terms, not always tied to a male audience or male criteria. ... I feel that in my development as a thinker, as a woman thinker, a feminist, and a philosopher, it's been invaluable to be able to develop my thinking freely within the context of an autonomous women's studies program."

This decision to move emerged out of the realization that "I felt that it was too difficult to push my ideas into philosophy [because] of its narrow constraints." In order to develop her ideas, she had to physically and intellectually separate herself from the discipline. Ten years later, having "developed a well-formed holistic perspective," she then felt ready to move back into philosophy.

Her attempts to reengage in a dialogue with philosophy colleagues were encouraging. Initially, she was apprehensive: "I had qualms or anxieties about presenting something as unorthodox, philosophically speaking, as a talk on fertility, sexuality, and rebirth, but actually my colleagues were passively receptive and supportive. ... [They] feel that I'm reworking the material in a new way and have been appreciative."

Somewhat surprised, she considered this receptivity to be significant progress, given what it had been like for women in philosophy 15 years earlier. As she recalled the earlier era, "It was a major production to even hire a woman in philosophy. ... In my first job I was told by the chair that he didn't think women could do philosophy."

Even though she was encouraged by her current colleagues' responses, she felt that her work was still "beyond the domain of philosophy, and therefore not genuine philosophy." She would not consider giving a paper to the APA because it would be considered "too bizarre or simply just not rational discourse." The interdisciplinary nature of her scholarly work has been a drawback, as she described: "Although it [may be] part of philosophy of religion and [or] part of the history of philosophy, it's really about the meaning of life. But real philosophy is the pursuit of wisdom. I reach for that. But it's a more multidisciplinary approach than a strict philosophical approach. It combines philosophy, esthetics, history of art, anthropology, some sociology."

As a Pathfinder doing feminist philosophy, she has found the most support for feminist ideas outside the boundaries of the discipline. Although her scholarship has been perceived as highly innovative feminist philosophy within feminist circles, it remains unclear whether she can succeed in persuading her disciplinary colleagues that it indeed counts as philosophy.

This Pathfinder's efforts to reconcile her feminist and philosophical interests dramatically illustrate how feminist philosophers may feel the need to choose between these two as alternatives. One path would be to suppress their feminist interests and work on standard philosophical problems in conventional ways. The other path would be to forsake the disciplinary interests, at least temporarily, as this Pathfinder did. This would mean pursuing new questions and orienting them primarily toward a nonphilosophical audience. Indeed, as she attested, the drive to be feminist may be so powerful that one would seek colleagues elsewhere.

Two other Pathfinders made preliminary attempts to redefine in more feminist terms what counts as philosophical inquiry, although at the time of the interviews they had thus far not felt the need to literally leave the discipline in order to be feminist philosophers. They did, however, frequently address a cross-disciplinary audience, and they did identify some primary colleagues as being located outside the discipline.

In grappling with these same issues, one philosopher of science has challenged the adversarial nature of philosophic method. Her feminist agenda had led her to approach philosophy in a constructive rather than destructive mode, which radically challenged the conventional method of argumentation and conduct of discourse in the discipline.

With support from others who self-identified as feminist philosophers, this philosopher of science came to question the value of philosophy's adversarial orientation. According to Moulton (1983), the adversarial method hinders understanding because "conditions of hostility are not likely to elicit the best reason." Moreover, the prescription for debate between adversaries with opposing views is not "merely one among many procedures for philosophers to employ," but it is *the* way of doing philosophy. This method also restricts "the kinds of questions asked and the answers that are thought acceptable" (p. 157).

In this spirit, this Pathfinder tried to invent a constructive mode, rather than the destructive adversarial method. A constructive approach is more difficult to establish than is critique, she thought, since that is what they were trained to do in graduate school. She explained that her agenda is to "construct another way of thinking about women, gender, justice, etc." She contrasted the two modes: "The adversarial method is very destructive. You set up a position and try to show what's wrong with it. Whereas in feminist philosophy, you find instead an attempt to argue toward a position, rather than to show what's wrong with some other position. Even so, that's still argument. But it's a lot harder to develop a constructive argument than a destructive one." So this philosopher of science has actually stayed within her subfield, but tried to develop an innovative approach within it.

Trying to reconcile her interests in feminist theory with the ideals of scientific objectivity, she has explored whether or not it is possible to have a value-free science. In the process of developing her work, she has tried to imagine and construct different alternatives. Throughout this process, her interests have expanded into new areas of natural science. As she explained:

I notice in my own work I have been conscious of trying to say something constructive rather than destructive. And for every destructive thing I say I try to do more than suggest an alternative. I try to flesh out what an alternative might be. For example in a recent paper I decided I was much more interested in thinking about the alternative. I spent a lot of time reading literature in [a natural science discipline] to really understand the alternative. It turns out to be interesting, full of possibilities, something I really want to pursue after I finish my current project.

So in trying to do philosophy differently, she has reached beyond the discipline to find resources that enhance and refine her ideas.

In addition to the philosopher of science, another feminist philosopher has sought to reconcile her feminist and philosophical interests by directly challenging philosophy's intolerance for emotionality. She learned the discipline's imperative early in graduate school: "It is wrong. It is inappropriate. It is out of place." Adapting to this mandate has been a struggle, which she attributed, in part, to coming from a working-class background: "I'm also extremely emotional. It's a working-class thing I'm running into, a working-class kind of style. I swear a lot. I'm very expressive. I grew up with Italians. It does not go over well in philosophy. I've lost my audience."

She also attributed her motivation for bringing emotions into philosophy to her feminist commitments. She feels that philosophy, rather than focusing on abstract hypotheticals, needs to deal with experiences of women. She applauds the efforts of feminist philosophers thus far to bring "greater depth to philosophy. Instead of 'If p therefore q and not r over s,' . . . it has emotion now, it has all kinds of new things. It talks about social dynamics. It talks about pain and alienation. It talks about a lot of things that are real to me."

This Pathfinder has incorporated emotionality into both the content and form of her scholarship; for example, writing on racism and sexism in a passionate way. On more than one occasion she cried while giving a paper; whereupon her colleagues accused her of being manipulative. Her challenge has been to do philosophy in a different way, which means that her colleagues have difficulty responding. She explained what happened at an APA meeting:

It's hard for them to know how to respond to my papers because it doesn't feel like I'm giving new arguments. I said, "But I have some suggestions, I'm making claims here. You could talk about how I'm defining sexism in this field. Or you could just talk about your experiences, about experiences with sexism." The first person to respond said to me from the back of the audience, [a well-respected woman philosopher] said, "I have no intention of talking to you about anything that has happened to me."

The feminist philosophy that she aspires to create departs radically from conventional philosophical inquiry.

Of the three feminist philosophers in this study, this one has had the least success in conventional academic terms at finding a convergence between her feminism and her scholarship. Her efforts have resulted in feelings of frustration and marginality. In spite of the fact that she receives no disciplinary rewards for her efforts, she continues to stay in the discipline, focusing mainly on teaching feminist-oriented courses in the philosophy department.

These three Pathfinders have illustrated the ways that feminist philosophers have had difficulty in reconciling their feminism with the demands of the discipline. More so than in history and sociology, feminist philosophers have shifted to orienting their work toward audiences outside their discipline. But their persistence in developing something called a feminist philosophical agenda suggests that the motivation to be feminist is so powerful that women scholars pursue it regardless of an inhospitable disciplinary context.

One Pathfinder in philosophy explained in detail how she formulated her scholarly direction. Having been trained in an analytic subfield, she unexpectedly came to the following resolution. She recalls serendipitously finding a convergence between her feminist concerns and philosophical interests: "The two became connected but it's not as though I worked out those connections and then acted on what I had worked out. Increasingly I began to apply my philosophical [orientation] to issues of feminist theorizing. Who knows what subterranean connections were being made!" Without intending to create new knowledge in any strategic way, this Pathfinder developed a new intellectual direction for her work.

Her lack of foresight is illustrated by her description of a specific turning point when her feminism and philosophy converged. In the mid-1970s, as a newly established faculty member, she did a paper on pornography which she refers to now as a "shift" and "major break" in her thinking. Motivated by her anger about sexual abuse, she decided to approach it in a scholarly way: "[The paper] was pretty philosophical, using the standard disciplinary tools, but it was also deeply permeated by a commitment to a feminist perspective. . . . I didn't see it as a new direction in my [scholarship]. I understood myself to be doing something different, which was much more linked to my political commitments and personal inclinations. And when that paper was done, I'd go back to focusing on more standard topics."

But she did not go back to standard philosophy. This paper marked a turning point that suggested a new direction for her scholarship. Not only did her intended audience shift, but the fusion of intellect with emotion was new: "And in that paper I saw myself acting as a philosopher in the feminist community, as a feminist contributing to the feminist discourse rather than something I was doing for the philosophical community. . . . It was an extraordinary experience for me—the combination of intellectual and emotional power that I had never had for a philosophical audience. The integration of the two was a real turning point for me."

Not only did she begin to write for an academic audience that extended beyond the philosophical community, but in this instance the intended audience did not even include philosophers. As she explained: "If [my audience] is academic, it tends to be interdisciplinary, and sometimes [it's] not entirely academic." She prefers this outside work to what she considers to be "narrow disciplinary boundaries":

The picture I have is that there are questions and issues that engage a feminist and these can be approached in lots of different ways by the academic disciplines. So I think of myself as a philosopher equipped to do some things and not others, for example, to explore the structure of reasoning. I see myself as having to bring the philosophical work that I can to bear on the larger feminist questions. It's not that I have to drop my philosophical standards when I speak to a feminist audience. It's that I have to make my work relevant in ways that I don't have to when I'm speaking to a philosophical audience that really wouldn't care about how a particular distinction is going to get applied in the world.

So, addressing a feminist audience as a feminist philosopher required translating and reshaping the work to fit a different set of considerations. The "level of detail and distinctions" that are customary in philosophy must "get excised in order to keep the question alive."

Over time, her scholarly agenda developed to reflect both feminist and philosophical values. When asked where her research ideas come from, she responded:

I take the current agenda of feminist thinkers and ask myself, is there something useful philosophy can do here? . . . So I connect up with the questions that are either being addressed in that interdisciplinary community or that ought to be. I look at the presuppositions, assumptions, and discourse and try to work those things out philosophically. After the initial encounter between the philosophical work and the broader concerns, the work develops its own momentum and generates its own sorts of questions. So that it no longer seems appropriate for me to talk about my work as something bridging some gap between analytic philosophy and broader interdisciplinary concerns.

While she was motivated initially by feminist concerns, she has come to respond to the interests of her philosophy colleagues as well: "Walking that boundary between having something to say that will interest members of my discipline as well as people outside it is always a trick. " Earlier in her career, she had not thought it possible to find a convergence between both sets of concerns: "For a long time my professional ties [in philosophy] and my intellectual ties [in feminism] didn't have very much to do with each other. Then as I started to publish and give talks around, they did come together . . . to develop networks across the country."

While working at the intersection of these two sets of colleagues and audiences, she has successfully produced some highly innovative scholarship.

The evolution of this Pathfinder's interests illustrates a pattern of attempting to resolve the tension between feminism and philosophy by satisfying both. In contrast, some of her colleagues have abandoned the standard interests of the discipline entirely. Their view, according to one observer, is that feminists "should not worry about what mainstream philosophy thinks of them. If you think that your job is to make those men change, it's a lost cause. You've given them all the power to determine what philosophy is." In contrast, feminist scholars who became committed to asserting the standpoint of women set out on another path, to develop their feminist scholarship on its own terms far from a disciplinary base.

Feminist philosophers who were proponents of a new kind of philosophical inquiry drew on different resources and encountered different obstacles. Commonly referred to as feminist epistemology, their line of feminist inquiry directly opposes philosophy's posture as a neutral disinterested observer by proposing that knowledge is materially situated (Hartsock, 1983). As Jaggar (1983) explains,

The concept of women's standpoint presupposes that all knowledge reflects the interests and values of specific social groups. Since this is so, objectivity cannot be interpreted to mean destitute of values, and impartiality cannot be interpreted to mean neutrality between conflicting interests. . . . If claims to knowledge are to be objective and impartial, whose interests should they reflect? [One] answer is the interests of women. Given their subordinate status, women have no interest in mystifying reality, so they are likely to develop a clear and more trustworthy understanding of the world. (p. 384)

In privileging women's position as knowers, feminist scholars (many of whom have worked in the philosophy of science) have proposed that the standpoint of women (i.e., the subjugated) is preferable.

Such tenets of this feminist theory are a radical challenge to philosophy, essentially negating the discipline's core premise of objectivity but continuing to speak to the discipline. According to proponents of feminist epistemology, human beings are located in an inescapable "gendered social space"; one can only be located "somewhere in particular." In the words of Haraway (1987), "cut off from passion and position, objectivity becomes a bizarre god-trick—the art of being nowhere comprehensively." By way of contrast, a feminist epistemology aims at enriching philosophical understanding with a more accurate epistemology, replacing the "god-trick" with "views from somewhere."

Two interrelated problems have prevented feminist epistemology from capitalizing its initial contribution. The first is that, as a standpoint, epistemology is widely considered to imply relativism, although Harding (1986) refutes this point. The second is that the line between the concrete and the theoretical becomes blurred. In this sense, traditional philosophy would consider feminist epistemological propositions to be a debasement of philosophy. And even feminist scholars have internalized these criticisms to some extent. As one Pathfinder observed, the feminist philosophy done by women of color often gets set aside as "pretheoretical."

The tensions between feminist perspectives and epistemological features of philosophy have prompted further debates within feminist theory. While a theoretical agenda for feminist philosophy has yet to cohere, these scholars have turned their attention to finding a niche. According to one Pathfinder, this process necessitates first carving out a space by rejecting earlier arguments:

When I think of the canon historically, what is in the canon are attempts to construct ideas, some of which involve a lot of adversarial argumentation in order to carve out a space. So what gets into the canon is work that has something to say in the space that's carved out. Think about Descartes, Hume, and Kant, for instance. All of them argue against predecessors and against some canon they imagine themselves in opposition to and employ destructive arguments. Descartes, for example, employs this method of doubt that conveniently takes care of everything. And then in the space that they've cleared—or imagine themselves to have cleared—they construct something new. So if you think of the canon in that way, I don't know that I'm doing anything different.

In attempting to clear an epistemological space for themselves, feminist philosophers have challenged fundamental conceptions of philosophical significance. The establishment of *Hypatia*, a journal for feminist philosophy, reflects their attempt to create a forum within the discipline for their developing ideas.

Although there have been a few small openings within some subfields and at the edges of the discipline, feminist scholarship has not achieved a stable foundation within the discipline. The lack of receptivity has been compounded by the fact that "it's mostly women engaged in this funny kind of work which just really confirms people's initial prejudice that women can't do real philosophy," one Pathfinder explained. This keeps the status of feminist philosophy "fairly fragile." She continued: "There isn't a location for feminist work in philosophy except to some extent [now] there's some recognition that a lot of women and some men are doing philosophical work that they consider to be inspired by, motivated by, driven by feminist concerns. Some people acknowledge this. Lots don't."

One sign of progress, according to an observer, is that in the mid-1970s a philosopher "might have sneered at it, whereas [increasingly] that same person certainly will be careful about the company in which he or she sneers at it."

Establishing legitimacy for feminist ideas in philosophy, as in sociology and history, has required progress on the idea level as well as the organizational level. Philosophers had more difficulty than those Pathfinders in the other two disciplines. In philosophy, feminists were comparably fewer in number. Several women in this academic generation described being the only person doing feminist work in a philosophy department, and often the only woman. Feeling "embattled" and "cut off or deprived" of collegial relationships within their departments, these scholars were inclined to develop close relationships with feminists in women's studies or in other departments.

The need to find and sustain an intellectual community for feminist scholarly interests was echoed by most, but not all, women of this generation in philosophy. A few of them maintained a "wait and see" attitude about whether or not feminism can be linked to philosophy in a fruitful way. One scholar asserted that a feminist perspective does not constitute a philosophical perspective because, as she understands it, feminists basically put forth one proposition: that women and men should be equal. Unlike the feminist Pathfinders, she heard the term *feminist* and either narrowly construed a feminist agenda or thought it inappropriate to the discipline. This kind of skepticism also appeared as a dominant perception among nonfeminist women scholars in generations that either predated or preceded the Pathfinders.

Unlike in history and in sociology, Pathfinders in philosophy were only in the initial stage of making crude formulations of what an agenda might be. And unlike their colleagues in history and sociology, feminist philosophers tended to deviate more from the disciplinary and departmental base to find resources and audiences for their scholarly ideas. There were simply not enough of them to form an audience that would constitute a viable scholarly community.

The extreme case of philosophy illustrates the inability to successfully resolve the tension between political and scholarly interests. The Pathfinders in this study have not succeeded in challenging what counts as philosophical inquiry in a sustained or systematic way. Yet, more than the Pathfinders in history or sociology, the accounts of women in philosophy dramatically reflect how compelling a feminist agenda may be, since they persisted in their attempts to develop intellectual projects even though those projects were not seen as innovative and even though it meant losing—or never establishing—disciplinary legitimacy.

DISCIPLINARY DIFFERENCES

The contrast in Pathfinders' experiences across the disciplines suggests that attempts to reconcile the tension between feminist commitments and scholarly commitments were ongoing even when disciplines were not receptive to their contributions. This dynamic echoes the reform efforts of those who continued to articulate feminist challenges within inhospitable organizational contexts. Yet within the disciplines, the subject matter itself becomes center stage. In history, Pathfinders expanded the content to place women at the center of historical inquiry. In sociology, their feminist perspective enabled Pathfinders to theorize about previously unexplored categories and dimensions of social experience, even though they experienced some ongoing tensions. And, although less successful in overturning the prevailing mode of disciplinary inquiry, Pathfinders in philosophy sought to challenge the very method of the discipline in order to include insights from women's experience.

Working to be both feminist and scholarly, the women of this academic generation have proposed dramatic intellectual departures from standard ways of thinking in their disciplines. In some cases their intellectual creativity was readily accepted and rewarded as an innovative contribution, as in the subfield of women's history. In fact, finding a convergence between the feminist and historical agenda may be said to have enhanced the likelihood for a successful career for some academic women. In sociology, women did not have the same relative ease and continued to search for research problems that would allow them to be feminists and sociologists at the same time.

Finally, in philosophy, we see the other extreme from history and the unlikely prospect of generating a convergence between feminism and scholarship in the discipline. There were neither natural intellectual openings nor rewards for challenging the dominant adversarial method. Trying to be feminist and scholarly resulted in feelings of frustration and marginality, which left feminist women in philosophy to choose between two alternatives: to work on standard philosophy problems and forsake feminist commitments as not relevant, or to pursue feminist ideas and angles of critique and therefore not be credited with doing real philosophy. Those who chose this latter alternative developed strong extradisciplinary commitments in their intellectual pursuits. In fact, that these commitments may have originated in nonscholarly starting points testifies to the force of their conviction.

In examining the intellectual choices of academic women of this historical era, it becomes clear that Pathfinders searched to define intellectual problems that would sustain both their feminist and scholarly interests and in so doing created new knowledge. Significantly, it also led them to create alternative networks which were both resources and audiences for their knowledge work. Moreover, the accomplishments of this academic generation to establish a feminist scholarly discourse both within and across the disciplines yielded an entirely new set of scholarly possibilities for the generations of academic women who directly preceded and succeeded them, as the next chapter depicts.

6

Alternative Academic Pursuits: The Pathtakers and Forerunners

After the Pathfinders' initial breakthrough, feminist scholarship entered a second stage. By the mid-1970s, the fusion between feminist and scholarly commitments resulted in an increasingly well-articulated body of knowledge and a clear scholarly agenda. The emergence of feminist scholarship created wider and deeper intellectual openings for academic women of other generations, opportunities that had not been available for the Pathfinders.

In this second stage, feminist scholarship intersected with the scholarly careers of academic women of other academic generations. The women who directly followed the Pathfinders entered graduate school at a time when feminist scholarly ideas offered an exciting range of scholarly avenues to explore within their disciplines. These women became Pathtakers in the sense that they could choose between two distinct alternatives. They could embrace feminist ideas as a viable scholarly direction in a disciplinary context. Or, alternatively, since women had achieved an established presence in the academy, they could ignore feminist scholarship and instead choose to pursue a more conventional disciplinary agenda.

The Pathfinders' legacy not only affected those who entered the academy after them. The generation of women who had preceded the Pathfinders also found new intellectual possibilities in the emerging feminist scholarship. These women had built their academic careers on prefeminist scholarly interests. All of the Forerunners in this study were tenured professors at teaching-oriented institutions and worked within expectations for extensive teaching responsibilities. To varying degrees, these women felt stuck—either in their teaching load or in old research agendas. Pursuing feminist ideas became an attractive way to revitalize their academic work. While it was too late for them to take advantage of feminist scholarship as a foundation for building a career, these Forerunners were nonetheless at a potentially fruitful juncture for them to learn about and perhaps embrace the new feminist intellectual paradigm in their teaching, reading, or less active scholarly pursuits.

Each generation's knowledge work cross-pollinated with feminist scholarship in a particular way. Since the Pathtakers were just beginning their careers, they purposefully chose to ignore or build their academic careers through elaborating a feminist scholarly agenda. The Forerunners were already established, but they could choose to transition into new scholarly materials as well. Whether these academic women chose to engage in feminist scholarship or not, the new intellectual possibilities in some way touched the lives of both generations of academic women.

Of course, this sketch of these differences simplifies the rich interview data on the concerns and commitments of each generation of academic women. My purpose is not to offer a full account of their academic paths, but rather to provide the key dimensions of contrast that distinguish them from the generation of Pathfinders who created the initial fusions for feminist scholarship. A description of the different paths of the Pathtakers and the Forerunners portrays some dynamics of knowledge creation after the initial contributions emerged. Specifically, in the perceptions of these two generations, we learn more about the underlying dimensions of the struggles for academic legitimacy that would continue for the new feminist work and for its creators.

THE PATHTAKERS

In important ways, the Pathtakers seemed ideally situated to take advantage of the emerging feminist scholarly agenda. Caught up in the momentum of interest carried by their feminist peers just a few years earlier, the majority of Pathtakers encountered feminist ideas in their coursework as undergraduates or early on in graduate school. There was a sense of intellectual excitement and possibility for feminist ideas to varying degrees in their disciplines, even though pursuing feminist ideas as a foundation for an academic career was still seen as risky. Unlike the Pathfinders, who raised these questions for the first time, the Pathtakers could select intellectual interests that would refine and further elaborate feminist ideas in the academy. Or they could choose not to.

Like the Pathfinders, women in the generation of Pathtakers tended to go to graduate school right after college. Yet Pathtakers did not report the same ambivalence about pursuing graduate work that the Pathfinders expressed. The majority of the Pathtakers said they knew early on that they would pursue a Ph.D. and an academic career. For example, a philosopher "just assumed that's what I would do because I liked philosophy." And a sociologist said, "I always knew I wanted to go to graduate school. It was just a matter of where and what I would study." Another sociologist explained that "my idea of fun was to sit and work out research designs." Unlike the Pathfinders, these women generally embraced the intrinsic worth of academic endeavors.

For in marked contrast to the generation preceding them, these women entered graduate school in a less politicized era. This is not meant to suggest that they were apolitical; in fact, roughly half of them reported having had some feminist political convictions. But even those with feminist politics had a different approach. For example, a sociologist described her outlook: "I believe charity begins at home and conduct my own life to do what I can to support women in my family and in my social groups. . . . I'm concerned about the lives and opportunities of women. . . . But [I don't] dedicate my intellectual academic work to those issues." The difference lies in the fact that this generation of academic women was not primarily motivated by a need to enact a political agenda in their scholarship. And even those women who did want to link a feminist perspective to their academic work did not attest to political motives as a sole or primary factor in their intellectual choices.

Since radical politics and ambivalence about academia were distinctively absent from the Pathtakers' perspectives, the intellectual engagement of graduate training seemed to capture most of their attention and energy. So when they encountered feminist ideas within graduate school, these women were able to capitalize on the accomplishments of their feminist predecessors. Conceptually, they saw a feminist discourse emerging to varying degrees within their disciplines, and they saw how these contributions were regarded within their disciplines. In addition, organizationally, they saw how feminist ideas were being nurtured in growing channels of informal networks that the Pathfinders had already established within departments and across campuses around women's studies programs. These venues made it viable to remain in a discipline and pursue alternative disciplinary interests, including those that were feminist.

The intellectual choices of an economic historian serve to illustrate the viability of a feminist scholarly path in the second stage. She came to build her academic career on feminist scholarship. She began graduate school at a high-prestige university in 1973, immediately after finishing her B.A. in history from that same institution. Going to graduate school was "a natural thing to do" because she saw herself as a professor. Having majored in history in college, she wanted ultimately in some way to have an impact on what was taught in American high school history classes. She recalled her thoughts at the time:

"I remember thinking that I wanted to go back and teach them the right thing. The policies of this country, I thought, were fundamentally predicated on ignorance. I thought, if more people knew the truth, they wouldn't do these wrongs. . . . So I went and immediately applied to graduate school. I decided I didn't want to take any time off. When I got there, I was just enthusiastic about becoming a professor."

Her years in graduate school saw her through two major intellectual shifts, one of which was connecting feminist politics to her historical interests. She described these simply: "First of all I got more interested in social and political history. Secondly, I started to apply my feminist ideas to my scholarship. That's the other very large thing that occurred for me in graduate school."

Although she spoke of this intellectual change in a matter-of-fact tone, embracing a feminist scholarly agenda only came after she recognized that there was a place for a feminist perspective in the academy. It is interesting that she began college being "bothered" by the term *feminist* and not really understanding its meaning. When she entered college, she recalls the president having hailed her incoming class as "the next great feminist generation." Her response to that was decidedly negative: "I had no idea what feminist meant and all I could think of were those ugly blue stockings. I wanted to be active and attractive, to be smart and do everything. And I didn't want to be some dowdy, blue-stockinged woman. This image was in my mind. Within a few weeks, I realized what she was talking about. She was talking about women who were feminists . . . who challenged the academy in a way, by advocating affirmative action and so on."

Gradually it made sense to her, and she applied her new-found "feminist ideology to political action" on campus. She also came to see the value of developing a feminist perspective in her historical research. Her intention to do so was clear and immediate, for such an intellectual "revolution" was already under way in her discipline: "[Historians] didn't include women and left a lot of questions unanswered that can be easily answered when you include women. There was a gradual revolution. It comes out of politics. . . . I knew I would [join it]. Immediately when I realized this possibility of doing feminist scholarship, I decided that if I did economic history, I would apply my economic history to women."

During graduate school she did begin to do research on women in industry, but she chose to leave women out of her dissertation research. She had surmised that her advisor was not someone that she could talk to about her research interests in women. When asked if he had been supportive of that as a scholarly direction, she declared, "No! I shouldn't laugh, but no. He made such crass comments about women and scholarship on women. He . . . advised a friend of mine to do research on women for therapeutic reasons." The fact that he encouraged her friend to pursue research on women made a big impression on her: "I remember my advisor saying, 'That's very good for Cynthia because she doesn't have a great deal of self-confidence and working on women helps her to build up her self-confidence, and it boosts her ego a little bit.' Clearly he had no sympathy for feminist work or feminist approaches on their own. He thought it was fine if she would look into a topic area with women because it was therapeutic for her. But it wouldn't lead anywhere, since it's not really a field, and it's not real history."

So, even though her advisor saw research on women as being "peripheral" and "unimportant," she decided "not to fight with him on it." Instead of doing a dissertation on women, she chose a more conventional topic in economic history, developing her ideas about women on the side. Many of the sources she read had to do with women, but she saved them for the book that she subsequently developed out of her dissertation research: "I thought, I've got to get my dissertation done. I turned my interest to that. But I kept doing stuff with feminist scholarship and then as soon as my dissertation was done, I went into doing much more work on . . . women."

Pursing research on women after the dissertation was a common intellectual pattern among her women peers who were not able to find dissertation advisors who believed that women's history was legitimate scholarship. Following the dissertation, she explained, "I did take a different direction. I've known a lot of people who've done that—all women, who have done their dissertation on a topic that was encouraged in graduate school. As soon as they finished that, they went off and switched their fields and started to consider women rather than just men in their work."

She characterized her subsequent research as "really social history. It's the only place where you can easily get feminism to apply." She focused on "forgotten women," which she felt was "long overdue" scholarship. When asked to identify the sources for her choice of intellectual problems to work on, she said that at first they came from "my own head," but always with a conviction of "wanting to change the research in the discipline." In the mid-1970s, when she first became interested in research on women, she found little in the discipline to draw upon. But increasingly she found more women identifying interesting intellectual projects in history. The development of her research interests since is clearly entangled with her effort to reconcile a feminist scholarly agenda and a conventional disciplinary agenda.

The discipline, she perceived, has given her mixed messages. Reflecting on doing feminist scholarship since graduate school, she said that "including women is not that threatening. Most people have at least come to accept the idea that women are people." But a part of her research does make her disciplinary colleagues "uncomfortable." She characterized it as "the multidisciplinary or antidisciplinary aspect of a feminist approach." Her research reflects these features in several ways: "I find myself borrowing a lot from other people. Concepts can be borrowed. I see myself as a social scientist because, like other social scientists, I like to look at the complexities of a situation. Change over time isn't the only interesting thing to look at. . . . But I am a historian."

Looking back over her career, she observed that her interest has always sought to expand disciplinary boundaries. She saw this orientation as implicit in feminist scholarship: "The beauty of feminist scholarship is that you open up your mind and get rid of limits, you get rid of disciplinary boundaries. You're supposed to get rid of that and start anew. If you have limits, no matter what the limits are, whether it's the boundaries of the discipline or certain subjects that can't be talked about in the institution, it's very contradictory to the fundamental goals of feminist scholarship." In fact, she said that she "always used work from other disciplines. Most of the books I cite are not history books."

Having maintained a scholarly trajectory of feminist research since graduate school, she not only has drawn her interests from a variety of sources, but has also found her primary scholarly identity in a network of women academics. Since graduate school, she has established a network of scholars who do work on women: "I have a whole new group of people that I deal with for feminist scholarship. With very few exceptions, the new network is all made up of women. Almost all these women took a path similar to mine. They also did work on more mainstream issues—i.e., male issues—for their dissertations and the first book. Almost without exception they are now spending most of their time working on women." She indicated that the scholars in this network are located in different disciplines, although some are also in history, and many are social scientists.

She viewed her network of feminist scholars as a primary intellectual community, valuable precisely because of its integrative approach:

I've found [with] those of us who do feminist scholarship . . . how even if we're working on different topics, how well our work integrates, how hard we try to blend our work, how hard we try to find common threads. . . . I don't want to give you the impression that we're all weak and wimpy and don't want to step on other people's toes and unwilling to criticize just because it's a woman who is presenting something that has to do with women. One does criticize when it needs to be. We're smarter [because] we're attempting to construct a whole as opposed to the individualistic aspects of this stuff.

Implicit in this process of creating feminist scholarship, she suggested, is "a political perspective." The task is political because the scholars want to create new categories of analysis. She acknowledged that the new categories are "political, but so are the old categories. The old categories were derived because people held certain values that they thought were neutral but they're not. The old values were masculine. . . . There are people who denigrate [feminist scholarship] and say that [we] are being so political and that [we] should be value-free." She supposed that if they referred to their research as gender research, it might be seen as "more neutral." Unlike feminism, she suggested, "gender is scientific, it's clean, it doesn't involve emotions or anything like that."

In spite of her explicitly feminist intention to transgress boundaries and indulge her interest in what she sees as her "multidisciplinarity," she felt that her discipline has been receptive to her foray into feminist scholarship. Yet at the same time, she is conscious of having had her vision restricted by her earlier disciplinary training:

I think within the discipline, I think a lot of people are willing to start to listen because they think it might be something new and creative and everybody is interested in that. . . . In terms of success in just writing a paper, interesting work, I think it's much more imaginative and creative not to be bound by discipline. I'm so trained as a historian that it's very hard not to be a historian. But I'm so thrilled when I read things that aren't history and I learn so much from sociologists and anthropologists.

One way that feminist scholarship has been problematic for its practitioners is in their uncertainty and at times insecurity about finding an audience: "My gut feeling is that multidisciplinary approaches scare people a great deal more because it upsets their world. That's just in terms of success in getting an audience." This historian wants her scholarship to be considered by "multiple audiences," including conventional historians, feminist scholars in history, and feminist scholars outside of history. The result, however, is that "I fall between the cracks."

On the local level, this historian has felt that her feminist scholarship makes her "a little bit out of step" with her colleagues. Within her department, the presence of an older tenured woman—a Forerunner—has "made my experience in this place far better." In her position, as a self-identified feminist scholar, she has come to rely on this woman's "powerful influence" in the department and "constant source of support." But she has found her primary intellectual community among feminist scholars in other departments. She finds the women's studies faculty to be "academically the most stimulating group on campus: "The only time I have a really good intellectual discussion here is [with that] group."

In retrospect, she thought that both her colleagues in her department and the members of the feminist scholarly community have influenced the direction of her scholarship thus far. As she herself suggested, they "affect the kinds of things you choose to write about because you want to get some support. Not only monetary support to go to conferences and such but you also want to be able to talk to your colleagues about what you're doing."

In reflecting on the contexts in which she works, she feels tremendously excited about pursuing a career as a feminist scholar in history. Yet communicating with historians who do not share a feminist perspective is a constant pressure and source of anxiety: "I would very much like it if I didn't have to explain things so much. I would very much like it if I didn't have to curb some of my ideas for fear people are going to say 'there she goes again.'" In spite of the fact that she has thus far developed a successful career based on research on women, and that she has a feminist intellectual community that includes but goes beyond her disciplinary framework, she has still yearned for an academic setting where feminist interests could be expressed fully and taken seriously. In her words, "I would love to be able to share these ideas with the anger and passion. . . ."

In contrast to this historian doing feminist scholarship, a woman in philosophy pursued a more conventional scholarly path. She ended up specializing in history of philosophy, teaching at a high-prestige university. Her intellectual biography reflects no inclination to engage feminist scholarly ideas.

Like the historian, this philosopher entered a well-respected graduate program in 1973. In retrospect, she characterized herself as being naive: "I didn't really know what was out there." As an undergraduate she had studied some history of philosophy, which "did turn out to be what I wanted to go on in." Unlike the historian, though, the philosopher reported that she did not engage in feminist activities while in graduate school. Her awareness and participation was limited to associating with the women's caucus in her department: "Some of the women who were in the classes ahead of us organized a group for all the women. It was very helpful." She appreciated its value as a support group, basically helping them cope with their academic environment but not actively seeking to change it: "A lot of them were talking about our relations to faculty members and a little bit to other graduate students though that was difficult. A lot of it was telling each other that we weren't crazy. That other people were. I don't know how to describe that. It was not [about] . . . changing anything except maybe ourselves. So it was kind of a support group."

On further questioning, she recalled that the women's caucus also obviated a sense of self-doubt that they had each privately held: "That's one of the things we started to talk about a lot, I'd forgotten. . . . We all were convinced that we had been admitted to the graduate program by mistake. And if only they'd known, they just would never have done it. Which is a nice piece of judgment on them. They're so stupid they can't read our work and can't figure out if we're for them or not."

Throughout graduate school she went through a process of clarifying her own talents. She reported that she did extremely well in the required logic courses, but when she got to more advanced stages, she "hit a wall": "I had always thought of myself as someone who had some talent in roughly mathematical areas which in the field of philosophy would come out mostly in logic. But I just hit a wall and realized that what I was really good at was learning ... and working problems but I'm not good at constructing ... mathematical objects and so forth. So it's a difference between being good at reading a short story and writing one."

When I asked her if other women were working in logic, she indicated that, "on the whole, I think, it is men who work in logic." In spite of the fact she was an exception in the specialization by virtue of her gender, gender did not appear to be relevant to her experience of turning away from logic to pursue another specialization.

After a few years in the graduate program, she had been on the verge of dropping out, when an academic advisor told her "it would be silly to quit now." Her ambivalence about the program was rooted in a sense of questioning her own scholarly capabilities. "I just felt that what I did wasn't any good. I didn't know why I was bothering, it was all so painful. I hated ... putting pencil to the paper. I still do but at that time. ... For a while, I found it very hard to read philosophy. I just couldn't concentrate." The advisor's encouragement got her through the qualifying exams.

After that point, much to her surprise, she found it "relatively easy" to come up with a dissertation topic. She went back to the first seminar she had taken, in which she had written a paper about epistemology: "I thought, why not just do that since this is turning out to be on my mind? I can remember being sort of surprised. Oh, I can write a thesis on that, too. So that seemed to be a nice idea." Having identified a viable topic, she then managed to finish graduate school in a total of four years (which is shorter than the national average) and secured an attractive postdoctoral appointment (which is a rarity in her discipline).

For the most part, this philosopher spent much of her time in graduate school, as well as for a few years thereafter, contemplating whether or not history of philosophy should be her specialization. In fact, she was surprised to learn other philosophers considered her specialization in this subfield to be an important philosophical question in itself: "The question why work in history of philosophy was thought to be itself an extremely important and philosophical question, which was news to me. I tried thinking about that a little bit on my own [in graduate school], but I didn't know how to go about it." She soon found a niche within the discipline with colleagues who were interested in these same concerns.

The development of her research agenda reflected how she has pursued "whatever it is that's on my mind." At the same time, she has found her philosophy colleagues to be "extremely stimulating." Working within the history of philosophy has felt intrinsically worthwhile to her. She maintained that having a historical perspective on what counts as philosophy is crucial, because without being historically sensitive, one cannot properly approach any philosophical work: "It's as if you tried to categorize all the noises in the world into music and nonmusic without understanding or knowing anything about what has been music to date in different cultures. Or every patch of ink on a surface classified as pictorial or nonpictorial without knowing anything of its history or context that makes a patch of ink a work of art."

In the course of gaining confidence in her academic career and chosen scholarly specialization, she had never considered working from a feminist perspective. Although she considers herself a feminist, she said that feminist scholarly questions "never really seemed that interesting. . . . It didn't feel that interesting." As a result, she was not aware of what feminist philosophy entails: "I don't know the literature and I don't know people who are working in it. I'm really out of it." Moreover, she was uncertain whether or not feminist questions belong in philosophy. She has had a sense that "there certainly is some problem of legitimacy. . . . But this is all third-hand because I don't know that much about all this."

Her criterion for whether feminist questions are worth pursuing was an internalized notion about what is significant within philosophy:

My own sense is that what makes something distinctively philosophical is the feeling that the very idea of something is either paradoxical or somehow necessarily unsatisfying. This is somehow incomplete and we haven't really gotten to the ground of it. Something's wrong somewhere. It's the job of the philosopher to try to think about how the reality of one side's wrong and the other side's right. So that would be one kind of example. The other is just, say if you're giving reasons for why you believe something.

Given what she believed to be reasonable starting points for philosophy, she doubted that it would be fruitful to attempt to develop a feminist philosophical agenda:

I think a lot of people share my sense that there are a number of extremely important political and psychological questions that need to be addressed from a feminist perspective. . . . I think there are a tremendous number of pressing questions . . . that need to be talked about. Whether philosophers are going to be any better at talking about them is another question. And whether they're distinctively philosophical again is something I doubt. Certainly there's been a lot of press about pornography for example.

To think this through further, she indicated during the interview, she "would have to read more stuff than I've read." She then invited me to talk with "a study group of graduate students [in the department] who read some feminist . . . literature. They know more about it than me." She summed up her own orientation to feminist ideas: "It is not interesting enough for me to waste my time on it."

As the interview came to a close, I raised the questions of whether or not there is a feminist way of knowing and whether women know differently than men. She responded with a philosophical analysis of this question and suggested that "if there was something in these questions that was going to be philosophically provoking," it would be of value to explore a range of outlooks, not only a feminist one: "If I were to try to get a handle on this I think I would [ask] is there a Christian way of living or outlook? Are the rich really different from the poor? . . . Certainly being a woman or being a feminist or being man or being a bigot or any of these things . . . sound like the sources that qualify."

I also asked about some other topics that have been identified by feminist philosophers, which she located in the subfield of applied ethics. "My own feeling is that the examples are ones that aren't in a sense really philosophical. They are . . . interesting and important" but not philosophically.

Regarding whether or not feminist input would be useful in the discipline in any sense, she did indicate a feeling that feminists in the discipline could transform "the practice and conduct of the profession." This would mean "encouragement of women who are interested in philosophy at every stage of the way." So, her sense of feminist questions is that they are not fundamentally valuable for philosophical pursuits. But she did express some interest in engaging with feminist ideas as a nonacademic endeavor: "I don't read as much as I would like to of feminist literature, but I hit the big ones as they come out." As for scholarship, however, she chooses to remain indifferent to feminist ideas in her field.

In summary, the women in the generation of Pathtakers, who began their careers once feminist scholarship was already established as an option, expressed orientations that diverged considerably from the academic women a few years before them. Either they followed a scholarly path that promised rewards and success in their discipline, or they proceeded along the feminist path initially charted by the Pathfinders who kept their disciplinary commitments in the foreground. Neither path seemed to entail the kind of feminist engagement in scholarship that the Pathfinders expressed. As one Pathtaker suggested about her feminist predecessors, "their scholarship was what they are living, which for me isn't always the case. It's only one part of my life."

THE FORERUNNERS

The women of the generation of Forerunners were already in tenured positions when feminist scholarly ideas intersected with their academic careers. Many of them reported having felt stuck, so that their introduction to feminist scholarship enlivened their intellectual lives. Although all of the Forerunners in this study were faculty at lower-prestige institutions, where heavy teaching responsibilities tend to thwart the active pursuit of research agendas, many Forerunners reported a newly acquired excitement about incorporating feminist scholarly ideas into their teaching and, where possible, into their reading and upcoming research.

Like the Pathtakers, the women of this older generation could choose either to embrace or to ignore feminist ideas. Of the five Forerunners I interviewed, the three who became interested in feminist scholarship were historians; the two who were not interested were located in sociology and philosophy, respectively. A brief description of one woman from each orientation points to some of the dynamics in considering whether to pursue new intellectual interests and sheds further light on the struggle for legitimacy experienced by feminist scholarship.

A woman of this generation who came to specialize in European history reported that she built her career on the conventional disciplinary agenda and much later developed her interests in women's history. This intellectual shift occurred 20 years after she had entered graduate school in 1956.

Like most academic women of her generation, this historian began graduate school purely out of a love of learning and the scholarly life. She was genuinely engaged with her discipline, and less concerned with launching a successful career: she said she had not preconceived "a formal plan": "It was just so clear that I would do it. I don't think I ever formally decided to do it. It was something that grew out of my interests, out of my extreme interest in learning. . . . When I was an undergraduate, I had no idea of where I'd end up, whether it would be languages, literature; for a while I seriously thought of chemistry, . . . law, [and] history of science."

She became attracted to history because "from my reading I realized that history includes almost everything I am interested in." Once she was in graduate school, she "gave very little thought to my later career." As she explains, "it was really done more out of a love of learning. I went ahead because I so enjoyed it." Finances were not a worry since she was married and she received grants.

At the high-prestige university she attended, she studied European history, focusing exclusively on the period before 1800. Having grown up in Europe, she was drawn to the historical material which felt "close to me" and "meaningful." As she described, "I absorbed this interest from my teachers [when I was growing up]. And I continued to work on it out of familiarity." She then came to specialize in the Renaissance and Reformation periods because of "a quite outstanding professor" she had encountered in graduate school. She described receiving consistent mentoring from two faculty, both men, who were "unbelievably helpful. The two men under whom I worked not only were supportive but became my very close friends and remained so. And I think the world of both of them. It was one of those things where the personality and the subject meshed. . . . They are people for whom I have a great deal of respect and affection. It was just like that in graduate school. From the first moment I got along very well with them."

She selected a dissertation topic on the early modern period with these two men as "my first and second reader." While working on her dissertation, she was asked to teach full-time because one of these professors went on leave. As she explained, "They simply handed me his courses. . . . I was very frightened. Yet I did it. . . . As often in life, things just worked out."

The years in graduate school she described as exciting and happy. She developed a network of peers that remained in touch during the subsequent decades. All of her colleagues were men and all were in history: "Some of the people, all are men—at that time there were no other women in my field—in history, and many of them are people I see regularly or, in some cases, with whom I correspond. It's still very much of a network. In graduate school we'd study together, especially in preparation for exams. Some became personal friends. So it is both a kind of personal and intellectual support network." Outside her specialization, she connected with two women in American history. She referred to them as still "like sisters to me."

Having completed graduate school in the early 1960s, this historian was teaching full-time before the Pathfinders even entered graduate school. She reported having had some political awareness of civil rights issues a few years before that. She wanted to do an independent reading course because "I didn't know a thing about it. . . . I had not seen a Black person until I was 16." A political science professor was willing to work with her on this topic, even though he thought "it was a strange subject for me to be interested in." Although the civil rights movement did not influence her scholarly interests, she indicated that it dramatically affected her subsequent teaching. Students who were "real diamonds in the rough," she explained, she "would've written off" previously because she had been more interested in teaching the elite.

When the women's movement got under way in the late 1960s, she explained, she had been "put off quite a bit originally." She was most uncomfortable with the type of person—"the protagonists"—whom "I found to be extraordinarily unpalatable people." Some of these women became her colleagues, and she was uncomfortable with them: "At the time when I first met these strident, mannish females, it was almost a kind of revulsion I felt toward many of them." Over time, however, she made a dramatic shift, which occurred as feminist scholarship was becoming more visible and gaining momentum. In retrospect, she reasoned, the shift "came not because of the people. It came because of the subject."

Her gradual growing interest in feminist scholarship she attributed to two changes: she became open to social history and she saw the scholarship in women's history improve. Both of these discoveries occurred through her reading, were confirmed by participating in a professional conference, and were clarified in the process of teaching.

Since she started out as "a mainstream historian concerned with intellectual and religious history in the early modern period," she initially had very little interest in social history. "Simply out of curiosity," she began to read beyond the initial feminist publications, which she had considered was "half-baked stuff." She recalled being profoundly influenced by studies on women and families that appeared in the *Journal of Interdisciplinary History*. "I remember very definitely. It included that type of very good work that has nothing to do with pushing a cause beyond the point to which it can be pushed, but which is serious, good social history." By the time articles get to that level, she suggested, they have gone through a process of being judged and weeded out: "What gets published . . . at the very least is thought-provoking and at the best is a new and different perspective."

At the same time, she recalled reading *Signs*, which she cautioned "includes the wheat *and* the chaff." She read the journal regularly because it is "very useful as far as showing what kind of scholarship can be done and what exists." Yet she also noted that "one has to be a bit more judicious when reading *Signs*. Sometimes it can be very abrasive." For instance, she objected to "this continual stridency by writers who deal with the so-called third world." She worried that it is "intellectually not very honest to not admit certain profound social differences" between the Western world and the non-Western world. The journal "bends over backwards" to include this kind of material, which she finds "somewhat repetitive."

In reading feminist scholarship in these journals, she indicated that she was motivated by "an immense amount of curiosity." Since she has never had a faculty appointment at a research university, she felt "extraordinarily fortunate" that she has not been pressured to "publish or perish, [or] to conform precisely to a mold, [where] I couldn't look to the right or to the left." She felt that she has increasingly engaged with feminist scholarly ideas out of "sheer curiosity, but not at all a programmatic approach either pro or con."

In addition to reading, her intellectual curiosity inspired her to attend a meeting of the West Coast Association of Women's Historians. When it began meeting 20 years before the interview, she had found the program uninteresting. Yet, in retrospect, she felt that she "formed a quick and I think inadequate judgment." Several years after its beginnings, when she agreed to go as a favor to a friend, it made her reconsider the substance of the sessions: "It made me re-think a lot of things because I met some very serious, interesting, and dedicated women who were certainly acceptable. And that meeting made me realize for the first time that my judgments were inadequate."

Since then, she has "sort of kept an eye on what they are doing." Even though she is still not interested in a lot of the topics, she realized that she "might go anyway—just for the fellowship. But I don't have that need because I have enough of a network of scholars here." Since her interest in women's history is peripheral to her main academic work, she does not feel a pressing need to go for either the ideas or collegiality.

In addition to attending an occasional conference, she has pursued her feminist intellectual interests by teaching a course on changing family structures with a colleague from psychology. She was fascinated by how they would read the same materials and yet approach them so differently: "I'm more interested in questions of legal structures and she is more interested in the implications for human relations." Since their "personalities meshed nicely," she enjoyed the ongoing cross-disciplinary dialogue, which she would not have had without their feminist intellectual connection.

One dramatic revelation that came out of her experience teaching this course was that chronology is not necessarily the way to approach how family structures change. Since she was a historian, it was a major shift to see that "a chronological frame" may not be the best way to understand family structure, "which is evolving so rapidly." Rather than feeling "constrained" to use the customary "step-by-step, orderly approach" of chronology, she agreed to organize the course around some "some central questions and some peripheral questions." This decision and the course materials were informed by her knowledge of feminist scholarship, which she considers important to her intellectual vitality. "This is why I find women's history interesting, because it isn't a straight jacket. Obviously, it can be, but it doesn't have to be."

From her engagement in feminist scholarship through teaching, reading, and occasional attendance at conferences, this historian came to regard the bulk of women's history as respectable and exciting. "If you judge women historians by their best example, they are really an impressive lot. At their best I find them to be remarkably versatile. . . . If you descend to the mediocre, then you have the same old problem—at its worst it's polemical." She distinguished between a useful analytical approach and one that is destructive. Regarding the latter, she described what makes her uncomfortable:

What bothers me [most] is hate. There is a lot of hate and resentment, . . . a chip on the shoulder attitude in things that have been written. Here again one's personality plays a large role. I do not have much patience with whiners, among my students, my colleagues, etc. I am much more of a doer. And this carries over in my attitude toward feminist scholarship. . . . You can deal with injustice and cruelty . . . but it's how you deal with it. This kind of look at us, poor us, we've been victimized, oh we are always the victims, men have done all these things to us, no, uh-ah—this is bad on the personal level, on the scholarly level. It's not something which gets you anywhere. Even if it's true, that's not the issue here at all, but it's how one deals with it on a scholarly level. . . . I find that the best women's historians, the ones I really admire, can say, for example, here's a situation of subordination, what does it tell us about the mentality of the time, about the social structures, etc.

The best scholarship, she believes, is that "which combines feeling and sensitivity with objectivity."

She has been attracted to women's history because it is a completely new way of looking at women and women's experience. Her interest in women's history "is now very real." It came about because of a change "not only in tone but in seriousness." She sees women's history as very respectable now, and now very much in the mainstream of historical scholarship:

"In women's history we have seen an unbelievable revolution in about a generation. From something which was on the fringes, which was put down often by the men, which was not treated seriously, to something which has made a tremendous impact. . . . But I have to say that the unacademic and the fluffy types intellectually have fallen by the wayside, and what has remained is now remarkable scholarship. . . . In fact, I would go so far as to say that some truly first-rate scholars are now working in history on women's studies, on women's history. And the men, there is no way a serious historian can put this down anymore and be patronizing about it.

In reflecting upon the tremendous intellectual fulfillment she has experienced in the course of her scholarly career, this historian explained the unique position of her academic generation: her "generation was probably the first one that was trained in a traditional mode, but then at a very crucial time was confronted with a very different scholarship." She described that they read a lot of the "great classics" and only later in their careers were "confronted with different ways of looking at things." Social history, she said, "was literally new. It had that kind of freshness to it." In contrast, she characterized that graduate students since then begin by learning about all of this at the outset, and she wondered what would keep them vital in the coming decades.

Coming to read and teach women's history has revitalized her own scholarly agenda: "It adds a tremendously important and satisfying dimension to the kind of history that I studied." She suspects that, "as I perceive it, there is really not a major difference between women's history and simply human history." When her current writing project is completed, she has some ideas that would "definitely move me more in the direction of social history. And I would like to tackle it just for fun, even if they are not too successful." Her work at the time of the interview had absolutely nothing to do with women, she confessed: "I can't even drag women in by the hairs on their head." Even though her primary interest and "closest associations" have been with colleagues who study the Reformation period, she continued to read widely and discuss feminist scholarly interests.

This historian illustrates the change in direction that occurred for some Forerunners, after building their scholarly careers at a time when one's woman-ness was not relevant to one's scholarship. In this case, as in others, turning to feminist scholarship late in her career would not jeopardize her academic reputation. Although she was tremendously impressed with the exciting new questions posed by feminist scholars in her discipline, she herself has not done research that contributes to the growing body of feminist scholarship. She has been actively engaged but, unlike the Pathtakers who embraced feminist ideas, this historian is more a consumer and disseminator—rather than a producer—of feminist ideas.

In contrast to this historian, a sociologist of this generation never became engaged with feminist scholarship and remained uncertain of the potential scholarly value of feminist ideas. Having gotten her M.A. in 1962, she entered a Ph.D. program with full support from a three-year National Institute of Mental Health fellowship; funding was tied to an ongoing program to study the family. In retrospect, she reflects on how she ended up pursuing this academic career path:

"As I sit here now I wonder how I got here. I guess one thing just led to another. Opportunities seemed to come my way, and it seemed a shame not to take advantage of them. It never occurred to me to pursue the Ph.D. if they hadn't offered me that very healthy fellowship. That was a free ticket all the way through graduate school. That'd be hard to pass up."

Once in the doctoral program, she did research in the sociology of the family, even though that was not her primary area of interest. She was more interested in deviance and social psychology. But she connected with a network of peers in working on the family project. In fact, these people—all men—became her colleagues and have remained an ongoing network throughout her career, similar to the Forerunner in history.

When the time came to choose a dissertation topic, this closely knit group ended up choosing related topics. In some sense, they felt obligated to do so because of the NIMH project. But there was no formal contract to that effect. After their dissertations were completed, they published a book together on their research.

Since career opportunities were abundant at that time, this sociologist was not worried about the link between her areas of expertise and the job market. In fact, when she negotiated for her first academic appointment, the institution offered to lighten the teaching load as an incentive to persuade her. It was 1968, and they were beginning to recruit women faculty. She ended up in a position which was primarily teaching. Her subsequent teaching areas reflect an eclecticism consisting of her original interests in deviance and social psychology, symbolic interactionism, which she "liked the most," and research methods. For the first 10 years of her career, she taught in all these areas, priding herself for being versatile and adaptable to departmental needs. When she got tired of "filling in the gaps," she began to do work in the sociology of aging.

The growth of her interest in the sociology of aging indicates that she was interested in taking a new intellectual direction. At first she had been reluctant because "it was a new field for me." She also found that much of the literature "comes from gerontology, and it is so poorly done, so biased and so simple-minded." But she saw that this material could be formulated into a good course, if it were taught from a sociological perspective rather than from a focus on the problems of old people. Her engagement with this material resulted in a long-term project on socialization throughout the life cycle.

This sociologist assessed that her selection of intellectual interests has not been affected by the emergence of feminist scholarship. She has little time or inclination for research, so her teaching interests would be the most likely to reflect any feminist ideas. When asked about the possibility of teaching in the highly visible and popular women's studies program on her campus, she indicated that there has been "nothing compelling for me to put such a course together." And she added, "I don't know what my reaction would be if I were asked to give a course."

While she generally supports the existence of the women's studies program, something about feminist scholarship makes her uncomfortable. About women's studies, she said, "I think it's fine. I'm all for it. I appreciate what they are doing." But she has been decidedly reluctant to connect with the ideas and the people, which she attributes to "my cohort, my age, or the time I got into sociology." And she reminded me that nearly all of her professional colleagues are men.

Separate from her scholarly interests, she did read some of the popular feminist literature when it came out in the late 1960s. "I got all excited about that. They opened my eyes to a new way of looking at male/female relationships and that women weren't taking advantage of available opportunities because they were not knowledgeable about them." But these revelations were not something she considered relevant to her own academic work. "It's fine to see women as victims but that should be separate from an academic milieu."

Over time, she has come to regard material on women or gender as "an area of interest" within sociology, but "not something that has to stand alone." She has considered the politicized and nonacademic quality of some feminist work to be inappropriate: "It could get into trouble if it deals too much with feminist issues as opposed to women's issues." She said that she is not interested in it when it tends to be "a matter of debate and taking sides rather than material that can be analyzed and looked at critically." Her choice has thus been to act as a bystander, neither actively consuming nor contributing to feminist scholarship. She characterized her own stance as "aloof," an effective way of "distancing myself" in order to "weather the changing times" quite well.

During the interview, she communicated to me that she was very satisfied with her career, although she wished she had established some intellectual and social networks locally. "I feel sorry about that. I often wish that were there." One opportunity that had occurred to her was the local Sociologists for Women in Society meetings. "I'm aware of them, but I've never been able to make the meetings." She believed those meetings to fulfill an important function, "for women to get together and talk about their professional goals and what they want out of sociology." She especially liked the idea that men were permitted to attend.

At the end of the interview, she summarized her attitude during the previous 20 years of her career: "You do what you can with what you have." She felt fortunate to have benefited from the opportunities that have come her way. But she had not come to regard feminist scholarly ideas as important new intellectual opportunities.

In summary, the Forerunners usually encountered feminist ideas while teaching, through informal networks on campus, in their professional associations, or as they became visible in their journals and other professional publications. The Forerunners in my study were located at lower prestige institutions, primarily as teachers. Some came to view feminist ideas as intellectual possibilities that could revitalize their own thinking and classroom work. Others felt that since their intellectual commitments were already established, feminist scholarship had little to offer them. In both cases, Forerunners did not themselves opt for making major contributions to the feminist canon. If they chose to pursue any feminist intellectual interest, it tended to be peripheral to their main scholarly identity. If they did contemplate making a shift in their scholarly careers, the possible transition seemed exciting.

Like most of the Pathtakers, the Forerunners have come to feminist ideas intellectually rather than politically. Some even expressed revulsion at the prospect of integrating the political with the scholarly. Since they were not activists like the Pathfinders, the Forerunners tended not to identify with the ideology of the movement, nor to have much political experience. "The idea of organizing tends to be foreign," as one observer suggested. Engaging with feminist scholarly ideas means "you read certain articles or books; it doesn't mean [you have to] organize yourself." This remark was made by a Pathfinder who tried to account for the fact that women of the previous academic generation are not drawn to the intellectual, political, and social networks that the Pathfinders found so essential. Although some Forerunners (mostly in history) have attended an occasional meeting of feminist scholars, these women did not rely on a feminist scholarly network for primary colleagueship. They remained satisfied with the colleagueship in their home departments and disciplines.

SUMMARY

The intellectual choices of the Pathtakers and the Forerunners reflect a number of significant dynamics at work in the second stage of feminist scholarship. The two academic generations on either side of the Pathfinders found different scholarly opportunities for contributing to a feminist scholarly agenda and they had different choices to make.

For the generation of Pathtakers, beginning a career within a feminist paradigm meant that they could develop and refine the feminist discourse initially established by Pathfinders within their disciplines. Through this engagement, this group could simultaneously benefit their careers and work toward furthering the legitimacy of feminist ideas in the academy. The Pathtakers also had a second option—to regard feminist ideas with indifference and simply assume their right to central places in the scholarly life of their disciplines. It is perhaps ironic that the feminist developments they could choose to overlook had contributed mightily to the possibilities for these women to assume mainstream academic roles. The possibility for this alternative—for academic women to participate fully as professionals—marked a new era for women in higher education.

The Forerunners intersected with feminist scholarship at a later career stage. Some of these women pursued feminist intellectual possibilities and in so doing shifted their research and teaching interests. Although not in the scholarly spotlight for their knowledge creation, their academic lives were revitalized if they chose to develop in this new intellectual direction.

Academic women in the generations of Pathtakers and Forerunners thus could and might choose to pursue feminist scholarship if it seemed genuinely interesting to them. This poses a stark contrast to the Pathfinders, who did not perceive themselves as having a choice or making a choice, but rather felt compelled to proceed along uncharted terrain seeking to reconcile the tension between their political commitments and the expectations of conventional scholarship.

When compared to the Pathtakers and Forerunners, the Pathfinders seem to have had both a more difficult and an easier task than the women of these other generations. The difficulty, according to one Forerunner historian, is that the Pathfinders had to be strident, which she thought was an unattractive but necessary stance for the first generation of a movement: "They not only were strident but they really had to be. As pioneers of a movement, these academic women . . . were carriers of the cause. . . . Obviously [they] didn't have the luxury that the next generation had, . . . the luxury of a perspective, of speaking with a soft voice."

In other words, to make it possible for future academic generations of women to speak with a soft voice, the Pathfinders demanded inclusion and had to shout to have their voices heard. Those who came to feminist scholarship after the Pathfinders "didn't have to be on the defensive all the time," according to another historian.

Although the Pathfinders struggled with the challenges of creating new knowledge, it appears that their scholarly contributions and organizational accomplishments were to some extent enhanced by the rebellious climate of that particular historical era. While acknowledging the difficulties of her generation, one Pathfinder in sociology actually suggested that in some ways it may have been easier for the Pathfinders than for feminist scholars of the second stage. She recalled:

In some perverse sort of way it was almost easier for my generation, because . . . it was both the best of times and the worst of times. The problems were very real and very flamboyant and very egregious. But there was also an incredibly rich and exciting and supportive women's movement that let you make sense out of it all in a way which, while painful, wasn't personally crazy-making. You may have felt oppressed, but you didn't feel crazy. . . . On the surface it seems easier because it seems so much more egalitarian. But in a perverse sort of way, that makes it more difficult. . . . They don't have the same sense of the world, the same ideology, or the same movement to support them through it that I did.

Thus, in this second stage, the development of feminist scholarship reflects the possibility for developing contributions to feminist scholarship that are less overtly personal and political. The ways in which the generations of Pathtakers and Forerunners potentially engaged with the Pathfinders' initial fusions of feminism and scholarship reflects the possibility for a clear detachment from the political roots that the Pathfinders nurtured. While the Pathfinders were more compelled to create a feminist scholarly discourse almost over and against their particular social-historical locations, the other two generations had a range of academic options. Essentially, women of this later historical era could be academic women without being feminists. They could also be women scholars working in their disciplines without being feminist scholars.

In contrast to the Pathfinders, these other two academic generations had different stakes and different perceptions of the opportunities for engagement with feminist scholarship. To shape their sense of what was intellectually interesting, a wide range of resources were available, including feminist ideas that were becoming increasingly visible in their disciplinary journals and professional conferences, as well as academic colleagues who to varying degrees identified as feminist or as having feminist scholarly interests. Such different conditions meant that they could engage with feminist scholarship, either centrally or peripherally, without detaching from either their disciplinary scholarship or their academic career trajectories.

7

Changing Conditions for Knowledge Creation

In this study I have explored how women of different academic generations have taken diverse paths in their intellectual and career histories. My analysis of the Pathfinders' retrospective accounts illuminates some of the conditions that created the possibility for them to shape their ideas into feminist scholarship as an academic specialty within and beyond their disciplines. For purposes of contrast, I also portrayed the conditions in which other academic generations of women chose whether or not to make gender central to their academic pursuits.

I have suggested that a dynamic mix of intellectual, political, and organizational conditions shape different possibilities for knowledge work across academic generations. Although their years in graduate school were far from ideal, the Pathfinders did find conditions that fostered their fusions between feminist politics and academic interests: a critical mass of women scholars, epistemological openings in selected disciplines, an abundance of financial aid for doctoral candidates, and a supportive national political movement. At the same time, several factors in their campus settings supported women's studies as areas for interdisciplinary teaching: an organizational climate that espoused academic pluralism, some financial resources to respond to women's requests symbolically if not substantively, and a tolerance if not willingness by campus leaders to establish experimental programs, teaching positions, and courses that were cross-listed by departments.

The translation of women's liberation as a political movement into a visible academic movement is impressive: in 1969 there were 17 women's studies courses, and by 1980 there were over 30,000 women's studies courses, 500 degree programs, and 50 research centers (Howe and Lauter, 1980). The intellectual advancements are noteworthy as well, as DuBois et al. (1985, p. 157) has observed: "the persistence, strength and steady growth of this new scholarship has established the study of women as a focus for academic inquiry, and the critiques of disciplinary bias have rendered problematic much of what was previously assumed to be true in academic fields, the ways that research had long been interpreted, and the assumptions and methodologies guiding its content." While some observers have suggested that academic feminism lost its scholarly momentum within and beyond the disciplines after 1980, Boxer (1998) provided evidence to the contrary: from 1980 to 1995 the total number of dissertations and theses in women's studies increased from 126 to 2,478, with dramatic expansion also in the disciplines studied, with the largest in history and literature, and somewhat less in economics and philosophy but expansion there nonetheless.

With the benefit of hindsight, the emergence of feminist scholarship is quite remarkable. In the 1960s, no one at the time anticipated the difference women would make and the intellectual momentum that would be established by making gender visible within and across the disciplines. Although Black studies had paved the wave for a women's studies agenda, the establishment of feminist scholarship as an academic specialty has generated a degree of intellectual disruption, interpersonal conflict, and curricular transformation that race and class have not yet achieved, although work on race has gained visibility and momentum in the 1990s. To understand the prospects for deeper scholarly revisions around questions of race and class, further analysis of the conditions of graduate education and socialization across the disciplines is needed, which could be gained through intellectual biographies and career histories of scholars who have made race and/or class central to their knowledge work.

The emergence of feminist scholarship captured in this book focuses on the experiences and initial academic contributions of the Pathfinders, women who began graduate school in the mid-1960s. As we have seen, most of them were white middle-class women influenced by a political agenda from the Left, antiwar sensibilities, and ideas from the emerging women's liberation movement. Their accounts tell us that feminist scholarship was created in academic settings that became populated by women students who reflected critically on their life experiences and became receptive in varying degrees to a discourse of women's rights, including the right to be free of discrimination, to be included, to be heard, and to choose. This women's rights movement intersected with disciplinary openings that were forged by these women, establishing women as subjects of study and furthering methodologies with particularistic aims. At the same time, as women students and faculty sought to establish a visible organizational presence, universities typically responded with additive solutions: new courses and later programs, new positions albeit often not tenure track, and new organizational forms (such as women's centers and associations) that stabilized an expanding network.

In spite of such facilitating conditions, the indictment of academic patriarchy and the advocacy agenda that accompanied some of the emerging feminist scholarship directly criticized and challenged many premises and practices of their academic settings. Because of this, the scholarly nature of the field and the academic suitability of its subject matter has continued to be scrutinized by its critics. Indeed, in the course of my research and writing, some of these critics have suggested that feminist scholarship is not a case of new knowledge, knowledge creation, or knowledge advancement. Rather they see it as a symptom of self-interested, value-laden, politically correct, or subversive faculty who have managed to generate "followings" of students and a self-affirming political network. At some campuses these sentiments are expressed with such vehemence and in such a critical mass that they constitute a countermovement to feminist scholarship and other academic specialties such as African-American studies, Native American studies, Latino/Chicano studies, and gay and lesbian studies. In the 1990s deliberations about the merits of research or teaching in any of these areas suggested that their political foundations remain of central concern.

Throughout this book, I have foregrounded the settings where the core sample of academic women worked, most prominently the disciplines in which these scholars developed as graduate students and then as faculty but also to show some variation in the institutional expectations for them to devote their time to teaching or research. In the remainder of this concluding chapter, I think it is essential to examine changes in those conditions and what they portend for the future, in terms of feminist scholarship in particular and knowledge creation more generally. I focus first on the political and then on the organizational.

THE CHANGING POLITICAL CONDITIONS

For the Pathfinders, their sisterhood was powerful. They worked from their life experience, they demonstrated how intentional communities can be formed and sustained, and they illuminated what knowledge work can be like when it is fueled by a hunger to work out deeply felt tensions and beliefs in settings where they experienced some turmoil. Over three decades have passed since the Pathfinders' academic generation entered graduate school. Yet the processes and products of this generation of academic women have continued to be the subject of divergent assessments, from praise to ongoing scrutiny to outright criticism. By the early 1980s, research and teaching for or about academic women had achieved impressive visibility nationally due to the contributions of this generation of second-wave feminist scholars. To their surprise, they simultaneously received blame from several sources, including from successive generations of academic women, and even from some who self-identified as feminist scholars.

The critiques followed several themes. Some sought to minimize the contributions of this generation, claiming that their experience was not genuinely one of oppression since most of them were from white middle-class backgrounds and they were fully supported in graduate school by generous fellowships. Their contributions were also critiqued for being insensitive to, or omitting entirely, differences in sexuality, race, and class. Basically, the critics asserted that these white women who sought to establish gender as a category of analysis did not speak for all women. Furthermore, they asserted that their scholarly contributions were just that, and thus a betrayal to the real activist roots that they claimed to further. As evidence in support of this claim, critics have pointed to the absence of any related academic protests or demonstrations sufficiently oppositional to have campus leaders call out the national guard with riot gear. Moreover, rather than genuinely pursuing altruistic aims of social change, critics characterized the work of these women as self-interested in that they ended up becoming members of a professional class. Some critics have even charged that Pathfinders went into the institution to change it but it changed them, a critique of cooptation that would no doubt dishearten the Pathfinders. Into the 1980s and 1990s, the increased anger and infighting among feminists became so widespread on campuses that many academic women became familiar with "trashing" (Freeman, 1998), a term initially denoting personal attacks within the political movement and an increasingly prevalent practice even among so-called academic sisters.

I can understand that some people today consider the Pathfinders' contributions as graduate students and young faculty to be quite small. Yet I think those critics have lost sight of dramatic insights the Pathfinders offered in this study: how difficult it was for them on a day-to-day basis, how inhospitable were the academic settings at that time for women who wanted to be taken seriously, and how their very inclusion as women who began to speak with women's voices and from women's experiences was highly disruptive and unsettling to the established people and practices in their universities. I think that the Pathfinders' breakthroughs need to be seen as substantial, as they quite literally pushed through foundations and walls of prevailing assumptions in order to make gender visible and to establish women as authoritative participants, whether in classrooms, at disciplinary conferences, or on promotion and tenure committees. Without their contributions, academic women of subsequent decades could not have been able to engage in a more refined discourse about their interests, either with respect to their gender or regardless of it.

THE CHANGING CONDITIONS IN UNIVERSITIES

Just as the intellectual biographies and career histories of the academic women in this study shed light on how broader political conditions influenced universities, they also provide an understanding of the range of organizational possibilities within universities over the past three decades. The Pathfinders identified many additive responses from campus leaders. As enrollments expanded and the proportion of women students increased, the universities established new courses, new academic programs, new teaching positions, new positions to staff a women's studies program or a women's center, and even space for such activities. In some instances these results came from great pressure; in others less pressure was necessary to prompt a change. At times supportive senior male faculty played a role in bringing about these results.

Such expansion was effective at appeasing the demands of women and mediating gender-based conflict in many campus settings. In essence, it was not a zero-sum game; and relative to other academic investments, the expenditures for these items were not great. Of course, as feminist scholars and women's studies faculty sought tenure-line faculty positions and expanded academic programs, cost considerations became more of a factor.

By the mid-1980s, with some variation across campuses nationally, universities became increasingly aware that ongoing additive solutions across the board would not be economically or politically viable as a long-term academic management strategy. Indeed, many campuses were faced with budget cuts and successive demands for retrenchment of academic programs. At the same time, wider public scrutiny of higher education increased, with vociferous criticism and scrutiny of escalating costs and curricular reforms that replaced classical works with politically correct subject matter. Through the 1990s, as public universities were repeatedly criticized for inefficiencies, state revenues fluctuated. Private universities were also at the effect of scrutiny of their tuition and wider economic cycles. Along with cost-cutting strategies and cost-effectiveness rationales, the new academic mandate across many campuses became "change by substitution," where the addition of something new meant that something else had to be eliminated. The organizational climate had shifted to support the restructuring of academic programs in the hope of demonstrating the effort—if not the reality—of achieving cost savings and leaner structures. (For further elaboration, see Gumport, 1993 and 2000a.)

Academic investment came to favor those fields that were revenue-generating and/or most likely to yield knowledge for industrial applications and garner the support of corporate capital (Slaughter, 1997). More humanistic fields, especially those inclined toward particularistic knowledges, identity politics, and advocacy agendas, have been scaled back. One option that has been considered on some campuses was to consolidate such programs into a generic organizational home and degree program, such as cultural studies, a structural move based on the rationale of a potential common ground for agendas in multiculturalism and identity politics. Ironically of course, the emerging divisions among and within different academic feminisms, as well as within a proliferation of postmodern perspectives, suggest that such academic units would achieve little to no intellectual coherence or shared sense of purpose, either in faculty teaching or research activities.

At the close of the 20th century, an unprecedented blending of fiscal and academic interests has reshaped the academic landscape of universities and changed the conditions in which faculty and graduate students engage in knowledge work (Gumport, 1990, 1997, 2000b). Among the many changes, academic units unabashedly compete with each other for resources, such as money, faculty lines, students, and space; graduate students are unionizing in record numbers, and economic costs and benefits are on par with—if not ahead of—prestige considerations in the academic deliberations of university leaders.

Such circumstances raise a significant question of how new areas of knowledge can gain enough resources for institutionalization. Must they meet the imperatives of the marketplace or have an explicit tie to an affluent external sponsor? Without such legitimacy, is it essential for faculty with compatible interests to form a coalition in order to achieve a critical mass? If so, how large is enough? Alternatively, in times of resource scarcity, perhaps a small group of faculty working in an area that has yet to be established would be perceived as less threatening and less expensive. Clearly, the path to establishing legitimacy for new knowledge requires further organizational considerations beyond the initial idea work.

For example, seeking tenure-track faculty lines and promotion reviews are two types of organizational undertakings that invoke the merits and liabilities of the field itself as much as the specifics of the case at hand. What is cutting edge? What is over the edge? What warrants continued investment or new investment by the university? Who decides? These are complex questions that have no standard answers and defy generalizations across university campuses.

Nonetheless, some features of the contemporary context should be noted. In the past two decades, since the academic "star system" of faculty recruitment has been in use among prestige-seeking universities, many faculty appointments have been made in fields that may seem surprising. Faculty stars—both male and female—have been hired (some at six-figure salaries) with specializations in feminist theory, critical theory, critical race theory, and queer theory. The characterizations of each area as academic "expertise" and as "theory" here are important signifiers, in contrast to the earlier more common designation of "studies" in those areas. At the other end of the continuum, over the past two decades, receiving little or no media attention, universities undertake regular reviews of faculty for promotion, and there are plenty of negative tenure reviews of women assistant professors whose records have been deemed insufficient for tenure. A number of these reviews have been reversed at upper levels of the university administration or changed as a result of formal grievances and law suits. Some of the reasons cited in the negative reviews are familiar criticisms levied against the interviewees—especially the Pathfinders—in my study: the publications read more like journalism than scholarship; the candidate was too politically motivated or politically committed; and the favorable "outside" letters in external peer review were made on the basis of membership in a club rather than on the merits of the scholarship. These reasons have surfaced even in disciplines that have been more receptive to feminist scholarship, such as history.

While such a range of judgments may well correspond in part to variations in scholarly achievement and academic records, a determining factor often overlooked is the way that local organizational dynamics put a spin on specific cases. Basically, such academic judgments are about legitimacy. As Spender (1981a, p. 1) explained, there are selection processes at work and they involve power, including "a self-perpetuating power dimension, for those who have power to validate their own models of the world can validate their own power in the process." This means that the organizational resources that are allocated to and within specific academic areas are ever in flux, with some set of knowledge areas likely to be privileged over others, depending upon the prevailing perceptions of quality, need, funding, and institutional legacies. In this sense, both the initial establishment of new academic ideas, and the subsequent process of elaborating them, entail struggles for legitimacy. Their path to legitimacy and possible institutionalization is an uncertain one that must be seen in a relative and contingent light, rather than as absolute or static. This is not to say, for example, that mapping DNA was not a clear scientific advancement. It is only to suggest that the designation of which academic specialties and specialists are most accepted, valued, or deemed innovative is a fluid one. It is always subject to interpretation, one that may be swiftly reversed depending on who judges and under what circumstances.

THE ORGANIZATION OF ACADEMIC KNOWLEDGE

An ongoing challenge for universities and faculty alike is to determine the conditions that foster knowledge creation. For several decades, some members of the academy have expressed the concern that the departmental structure stifles knowledge creation beyond existing departmental parameters. In the 1990s, the academic generation of vocal postmodernists have argued this point, as they have conceptually worked to dismantle established academic categories and distinctions. The general argument is that neither interdisciplinary nor multidisciplinary knowledge work is nurtured in a context where knowledge work is bounded within organizational units that exist primarily for administrative and programmatic convenience.

So in the current university context, scholars who purposefully pursue extradepartmental directions face many unknowns, including uncertain future rewards and evaluation as well as an uncertain basis for collegiality and community. Such uncertainties are particularly daunting for tenure-track assistant professors, whose days and years are marked by the loud ticking of the tenure clock. Universities also face substantial unknowns, as they must determine what resources to allocate to new intellectual terrain. Among their considerations are these: pressure from governing boards, state legislatures, and the wider public to demonstrate productivity in a climate of increased accountability demands; the uncertain feasibility and validity of external peer review; whether the endeavor is an academic specialty suitable for degree-granting status; and if so, whether students will come.

My analysis of the Pathfinders' accounts in this study may shed some light on the ways in which these questions have been answered over the past few decades. As the Pathfinders explained the point of view they held as graduate students and young faculty, they engaged in risky intellectual ventures because they were fueled by a deeply felt passion for the questions they raised. At the same time, they claimed detachment from conventional academic aspirations, which was fortunate since conventional wisdom predicts trouble when one questions highly cherished and previously unchallenged academic assumptions. But in this case, given the wider societal context that legitimated women as participants and questioners, and the precedents for self-proclaimed paradigm-shifting behavior, it worked. Ultimately, it did prove to be knowledge work that had a radical edge, that at its core sought to reshape the boundaries of disciplines and redefine what counts as scholarship. The Pathfinders' accomplishments suggest that the informal organizational structures they created were highly effective supports. Granted, they had the time and the financial fellowships that enabled them to create these structures. Once they became faculty, the constraints changed; yet they were galvanized by collegial support from peers nationally with shared interests beyond their disciplines as well as by interest from the students on their campuses.

Feminist scholars are not the first nor the only academics to suggest that pressure to work within departmental boundaries constrains interdisciplinary or multidisciplinary knowledge work, including work that purposefully erodes boundary distinctions between disciplinary terrains and/or between academic specializations. Since such knowledge work positions itself as subversive in challenging the status quo, scholars who hope to remain in universities must consider whether it will amount to a viable career path. By definition this entails finding a way to frame and articulate one's areas of interest so that they seem cutting edge, yet not over the edge, from the perspective of their departmental and disciplinary audiences. To succeed in the university without doing this is highly improbable, for most tenured university appointments are still made in conjunction with degree-granting programs. There are no simple solutions to the dual challenge of fostering knowledge creation while simultaneously supporting existing knowledge. In most universities the departmental organization of knowledge has historically dominated more as a result of its administrative and programmatic functions than for its intellectual ones. This would suggest that universities can and should set aside resources to support emerging opportunities and facilitate dialogue across academic units. Humanities centers and centers for research on women are good examples of sites on campus that have fostered such innovative exchange.

Beyond that, universities must contend with larger questions, especially in a climate of heightened fiscal awareness where missteps are likely to be widely publicized rather than swept under the rug. These questions include the following: What are the meaningful categories for emerging intellectual interests and expertise? What are the appropriate organizational resources for such areas? What does one do when the disjuncture between organizational structure and intellectual content widens? While such challenges are often cast as academic management problems, I think it is preferable to consider them as symptoms of intellectual vitality and dynamics of knowledge change rather than academic pathologies. It is well-known that much fertile intellectual ground has always been at the boundaries that demarcate academic areas. It is thoroughly conceivable that there are several vital currents of thought within any given university that could be greater than the sum of their parts if they had an infusion of resources or a visible organizational location for dialogue. In this sense, one must not underestimate the significance of organizational structures and resources in supporting and refining nascent ideas.

As universities face a changing mix of political and economic pressures, along with changing social and cultural conditions, their ability to sustain as well as to revise their organization of knowledge is of critical concern. With fewer discretionary resources available today than were available to the Pathfinders in this study, campuses are less likely to smoothly handle impending conflicts over what knowledge to include or exclude in programmatic offerings, over what criteria are appropriate for evaluating specific scholarly contributions, and for determining which organizational form is suitable. The contest over resources continues alongside the evolution of knowledge, and the two have been inextricably linked in deliberations over which expertise is most suitable for degree programs, departments, and faculty billets as well as over which ideas are worthy of dissertations, tenure, and promotion. As universities continue to puzzle over the most appropriate organizational arrangements for existing and emerging fields, decisions will necessarily be incremental and local. Such decisions must involve the most forward-looking individuals on campus, as much is at stake in universities' decision-making. They have cumulative and collective consequences for what counts as knowledge in society, what categories of expertise are valued for academic degrees and future academic positions, how those categories are organized, and how upcoming generations of faculty are socialized. It is still the case that yesterday's knowledge work at the margins may become tomorrow's core concern.

At the same time as illuminating these contemporary knowledge management challenges for universities, my analysis of academic women's career histories and intellectual biographies speaks directly to many of the considerations that remain inherent in pursuing an academic career. My analysis of these pivotal generations foreshadowed a number of dynamics that are still very much at work today: how the attainment of legitimacy is as much an organizational and political achievement as an intellectual one; how the criteria for evaluating a person's academic record remain ambiguous and are themselves contested; how new ideas struggle to compete with and sometimes directly threaten established ones; and how transcending existing boundaries can produce intellectual originality but entail professional risk.

The different experiences of academic women in this study suggest that faculty of every academic generation bring to their work different preconceptions about the parameters of their disciplines, the appropriate foundations for their own scholarship, and their possible futures. In the process of making their own incremental decisions—selecting a graduate school, courses and advisers, paper topics and dissertations, research projects and teaching assignments—these women sought to reconcile tensions within themselves, with others, and within their academic settings. In a fundamental sense, the lesson is that faculty who aspire to create knowledge must each in her or his own way become a pathfinder, engaged in an ongoing process of discovering a way into and through unexplored regions. If faculty are expected to seek and to risk, then universities must explicitly support their endeavors. Further, nurturing a broad range of intellectual pursuits within the academy depends upon support from the wider society to preserve the expectation that such intellectual exploration is essential to the public interest.

Appendix: Notes on the Research Design and Methods

A total of 75 interviews were conducted in the course of this study. In addition to the core interviews with 35 women faculty, I interviewed 20 male faculty who answered questions either as disciplinary observers (five for each of the three disciplines) or as observers of women's studies (five as well). I also conducted interviews with a handful of cognizant deans and department chairs at each level of institutional prestige (high, medium, low) in order to learn about their impressions of the emergence of women's studies and feminist scholarship on their campuses. The purpose of this mixed informant design was to triangulate the data sources and provide me with a richer sense of context to interpret the interviews with my core sample.

As a supplement to the interviews, documents and observational data were gathered from other sources. Where possible, faculty and administrators provided scholarly publications they had written that were relevant to my questions, as well as documents from their files, including internal reports and correspondence that potentially explained some influences on, and justifications for, their work vis-à-vis both disciplinary and university concerns. I also observed a wide range of formal and informal social interchanges among these actors in several kinds of forums over a three-year period. These forums included local and national conferences, local lectures and discussions at one high-prestige research university, and regular meetings of a faculty seminar that was established by feminist scholars for the express purpose of outreach to faculty in traditional disciplines. Extending the research in this way provided me with a broader basis for interpreting the interview data.

INTERVIEWS WITH THE CORE SAMPLE

Making contact to request an interview is a significant part of the data collection process; it marks the beginning of the relationship and affects the actual interview process (Seidman, 1985). For initial contact I used a flexible approach, usually beginning with telephone calls. Some calls were preceded by a letter in which I introduced myself and the study; for others the letter came after my phone call. I was careful to explain the general purpose of my research, what the interview would entail in terms of a time commitment, the nature of the questions, and the assurance of anonymity and confidentiality. If they agreed, I requested that they send a copy of their curriculum vitae, which I used to prepare for the interview. In several cases, I read some of their publications before the interview.

The interviews with these primary informants were semistructured. The general concern was to understand how intellectual interests and career choices were influenced by opportunities and constraints in the primary academic contexts. Since my objectives were to understand their autobiographical experiences and perceptions, I saw my task as twofold: to listen actively and to frame the interview. To accomplish the first, I used a tape recorder and took notes. In order to provide a consistent frame across the interviews, I used an interview guide that outlined topics conducive to eliciting a career narrative. Scholars were asked to describe how they were influenced by their contexts and how they responded to them. The questions covered each stage of their choices, including their perceptions of constraints on and opportunities for career or disciplinary advancement, and their characterizations of their own scholarly contributions, whether primarily disciplinary or groundbreaking in the new field of women's studies.

The actual questions were formulated to probe at a level deeper than the surface autobiographical details that faculty are accustomed to presenting. The lists below are items that I covered to elicit descriptions of their perceptions and experiences in a range of disciplinary and institutional contexts. For example, I asked: "What supports did you receive while you were in graduate school?"; rather than: "Did your dissertation advisor help you obtain your first job?"

Interview Guide for Primary Informants

Section 1: Career History

All of these items were covered in the course of the interview, but not necessarily in this order.

1. Educational Background
   a. degrees received, what year, what institution
   b. dissertation—what topic, design, methodology
   c. dissertation—what assistance (including intellectual, financial, emotional resources)
   d. publications—early experience, who were relevant actors and what influence
   e. first job—how did you get it, who helped you, what job

2. Employment Setting
   a. current—where, how long there, where before
   b. if in academia, what position and percentage of time
   c. if in academia, what tenure track and status
   d. if outside of academia, where

3. Professional Activity
   a. association memberships, caucus or advisory group memberships, what change over time
   b. what functions held in them
   c. publication activities, any editorial board participation
   d. attendance at conferences and meetings—which and frequency
   e. lectures given to professional meetings
   f. papers informally exchanged—with whom, when, what change over time
   g. work with Ph.D./M.A. students on dissertations or theses

Section 2: Intellectual Biography

The focus was to elicit an autobiographical account of each woman's career choices and intellectual interests. I sought a narrative of this evolution through a series of open-ended interrelated questions about opportunities, resources, and constraints available to scholars.

For example:

- How did you end up in graduate school?
- Starting with graduate school, what did the field look like to you? Were you thinking of a particular job?
- Were there any models (people, books, e.g.) in your field available to you? What were sources of intellectual support? How did you choose your advisor? Was there a sense of career opportunities?

- In selecting a dissertation topic, where did your interest originate and how did it evolve? What was your sense of the field? Was this related to a perception of future job opportunities?

- Describe your research interests as they dominated each subsequent stage of your professional career. What scholars (or others) were influential in your thinking and aspirations? What were your thoughts when you got your first academic position? And so on.

The autobiographical data also covered the following topics, which have more of a cross-sectional focus:

1. Research Interests
   a. What do you consider your primary field of study? Secondary? Change over time?
   b. Are these the fields to which your work contributes?
   c. How/where do your work/research interests fit with the rest of the discipline(s)?
   d. Whom do you write for? Whom do you talk with? About what? Has this changed over time?
   e. To what extent do you collaborate? How many projects do you work on? With whom?

2. General Perceptions of Discipline(s)
   a. Describe major shifts in your field in the last 15 years. Any major junctures?
   b. What are the major substantive controversies in your field today?
   c. What is your experience of those controversies? Change over time?

3. Impressions about Scholarship by Women in Your Field(s)
   a. How is scholarship by women received? About women?
   b. Where does it fit in with the rest of the discipline?
   c. What structural features of the discipline do or do not enhance it?
   d. Any thoughts about its future in your field?

Section 3: Reflections on Feminist Perspectives in Academia

My interest here was to present myself as nonjudgmental and without any deeply held convictions toward feminist scholarship. Depending on the comfort level of each interviewee, these topics were discussed easily or with some discomfort. In the event of the latter, I persevered as much as seemed appropriate.

1. Experience of Feminist Scholarship

a. To what extent does it have relevance for you in your professional life? Scholarship? Personal life? Political background?

b. What did you read that marked your initial awareness of feminism? Of feminist scholarship? Were these authors in academic or nonacademic networks? How did the early feminist works influence your readings of scholarly works from your discipline? What changes over time?

c. Did you experience any tension between scholarship and political orientations? If so, how handled?

d. What is your impression of feminist scholarship in your discipline? On the idea level? In reality? Potential/impact/functions/change over time in the academy at large? At your current institution?

e. Do you use feminist theory in your own work? How? What are the benefits? Costs? Thoughts on interdisciplinarity?

f. How do you see the relationship between feminist scholarship/theory and practice/activism? Change over time?

2. Intellectual Community

a. How would you describe your network of professional ties? Multiple networks? What is the basis for association? What common interests? To what degree is it formalized or less visible and informal? Change over time?

b. How would you describe your bonds of intellectual community, and to what extent do they stimulate, motivate, support your work? Change over time?

c. What assumptions guide your work as a scholar? Do you pursue what interests you or what the discipline or the department considers legitimate? What is on the wider political agenda of feminists outside the academy? Any or all of the above? And are you explicit about this in your work? Change over time in last 15 years?

d. How would you describe your involvement in any institutional battles to establish feminist scholarship on campus (either at current institution or elsewhere)? Or in disciplinary battles? If not involved, what are your impressions? What change over time?

The comprehensive interview guide permitted an in-depth exploration of what guided women's intellectual choices and what perceptions they held of organizational and intellectual constraints or potential rewards. The year-by-year approach enabled the scholar to revisit how change unfolded. At each point in their autobiographical recounting, I interjected probes to learn more about specific aspects of their background (i.e., undergraduate, graduate school topics of study, mentors, peers, first academic appointment, etc.) or probes to clarify terms they used that were vague or ambiguous in order to be sure I understood their meaning.

These interviews ranged in length from 45 minutes to 3 1/2 hours, the average length being 1 1/2 hours. The locations varied from interviewees' homes (which was my stated preference in the hope of fewer interruptions), to offices, and, in one instance, a coffee shop. Informants signed a consent form, which explained the nature of the study and described how I intended to disguise their identity in subsequent publication. All interviews with primary informants were taped, except two. In both cases the interviewee said she would feel more comfortable without a tape recorder. In three instances, the interviewee requested to see the transcribed material before I used it in publication. In all cases, they made minor editorial suggestions, and in one case we agreed to remove a passage that she thought might reflect poorly on her colleagues if someone were to determine her identity.

DATA ANALYSIS PROCEDURES

These data collection activities produced several types of data, including the following:

Interview tapes and transcriptions from women faculty in history, sociology, and philosophy, women's studies faculty, disciplinary observers and women's studies observers, women's studies program directors, and cognizant administrators; tapes of public lectures and women's studies programs' histories; field notes and dictation from site visits and conferences; documents from site visits, including women's studies program materials (e.g., proposal to establish itself, annual reports, program history, course syllabi, course enrollment data, fliers, minutes of meetings, confidential memos); faculty curriculum vitae; statistical data on faculty by institution; and campus archival data on women's studies.

Miles and Huberman (1983) advise taking precautions against data overload, that is, collecting too large a volume of data. To prevent this, I reviewed and interpreted data gathered to date on a regular basis, writing notes to myself based on observations, hunches, and methodological reminders. The triangulation of data sources and methods in this exploratory study was an attempt to address the standard social science research concern about validity. Preliminary data analysis and data collection are done together in an interactive way (Glaser & Strauss, 1967; Miles & Huberman, 1983). Preliminary analysis, or data reduction, was based on categories derived from the conceptual framework.

The interview transcripts of the core sample were analyzed according to three basic dimensions:

1. political orientations and their change over time
2. experiences of organizational supports or struggles
3. sense of the discipline and their relationship to its intellectual agendas, and, where relevant, any attempts to establish issues related to women or feminist perspectives in their field.

Analysis of interview data included paying attention to the actual content of disciplinary and institutional paradigms and how these shape the opportunities and constraints which defined the possibilities for feminist scholars.

To organize the data, I also divided each set of elements into "Pre-Ph.D." and "Post-Ph.D." because influences after obtaining the degree tend to be different than those before (Ladd & Lipset, 1972). I proceeded with this analysis by discipline. It is common for categories of analysis to shift in order to achieve greater perceptual and conceptual specificity during the successive stages of a research project (Schatzman & Strauss, 1973). Some categories were previously selected because they were inherent to the conceptualization of the study, such as paradigm, feminist awakening, and political involvement. Other categories along more thematic lines emerged in the course of the analysis, such as experience of isolation or invisibility, "backing into" academia as a career, and the significance of informal networks.

The most dramatic shift in the data analysis was both substantive and procedural. This was the recognition that the data could be organized by viewing the primary informants as generations of academic women. Each generation of academic women received their graduate school training corresponding to a different stage in the wider social conditions and the historical unfolding of academic feminism: the Pathfinders made initial fusions for feminist scholarship, while the Pathtakers had the option of pursuing an already established yet growing feminist scholarly agenda, and a third group—the Forerunners—had established their careers before one ever had a sense that being a woman was relevant to the substance of one's scholarly interests.

METHODOLOGICAL CONSIDERATIONS AND LIMITATIONS

Since my inquiry aimed at advancing our understanding of knowledge creation in academic settings, the design had to be exploratory. The translation of this aim into a research design for understanding the emergence of new knowledge (feminist scholarship) was an ambitious task, which first required making some initial general observations about feminist scholars at work. Feminist scholars have pursued new questions, topics, and methods, even though these were often not at the time considered legitimate scholarly interests. Feminist scholars participate in several networks beyond those that we would normally think would affect their academic work, including social and intellectual networks beyond home disciplines and local campuses, and some entirely outside the academic community. Feminist scholars use different strategies for finding and functioning in their various scholarly/intellectual communities, including skillfully shifting among a wide variety of audiences and scholarly allegiances. Finally, feminist scholars integrate explicit political motivations with intellectual work, advocating transformative aims for higher education through their scholarship.

These initial observations were intriguing in the light of strong university and disciplinary norms that constrain such behaviors. In fact, the emergence and persistence of feminist scholars and their scholarship is a remarkable achievement, given the prevailing professional socialization, organizational culture, and disciplinary mechanisms that are apt to reproduce the status quo. Seen in a different light, however, the critiques offered by early academic feminists may also be viewed as intellectually innovative, seeds of a new paradigm. While their critique extended from disciplinary canons on epistemological levels to postsecondary institutions on organizational levels, the early feminist scholarship was created with few intellectual and organizational resources.

What is most interesting about this phenomenon was most problematic to study. For example, how to define and locate an invisible college of feminist scholars, given that it was a relatively new area of scholarship and that there is enormous variation in what counts as feminist scholarship and who counts as a feminist scholar? How to trace the processes through which disciplines and postsecondary institutions foster or constrain the production of new knowledge? How accurately to render the interdependence among individuals, ideas, and their social settings? After careful consideration of the compromises that would be made, I constructed a research design that placed scholars at the center, mediating intellectual, organizational and political forces within a particular sociohistorical context. Primarily through their autobiographical recounting of experiences and perceptions, I could identify some of the dynamics involved in creating new knowledge and establishing its legitimacy at several levels simultaneously.

Two major sets of methodological issues remain problematic in such an investigation. One concerns the challenges of linking the conceptual framework with appropriate data. The other concerns the distinctive utility of a qualitative and interpretive orientation. The remainder of this chapter describes the considerations that I took into account to address each set of concerns.

Linking the Framework with Data

The investigation of interdependencies among disciplinary, institutional, and political contexts still has several trouble spots that remain problematic. There are three major weaknesses in using sociology of science as a framework: the simplification of interdependencies, the difficulty of discovering emerging paradigms, and the ambiguity of identifying group membership. Empirical studies in the sociology of science tend to simplify reality by restricting the focus of inquiry in order to isolate variables and relationships. Since that was not my aim, I instead sought to investigate the interdependencies involved in knowledge development by foregrounding certain spheres or arenas for analysis. I have done this by choosing the intellectual, organizational, and political. Other aspects of knowledge development are omitted or underplayed. These include the wider intellectual climate, the ideological and socioeconomic functions of higher education, and the role of the consumers (i.e., the student clientele) in defining a scholarly field. In addition, some simplification of the interdependency among the three selected arenas was also required. Mutual influences and outcomes occur simultaneously, or at least not linearly, in interdependent relationships. In this way, the focus for this study was the contexts in which knowledge developed. A wide range of studies that address the question of the impact of feminist scholarship or its specific intellectual, organizational, and political outcomes has already been completed. Howe and Lauter (1980), for example, review the studies on the extent to which feminist scholarship has had impact on the campus and the disciplines. In my investigation, such outcomes are explored only insofar as they suggest how the variations in developments of feminist scholarship (intellectually, organizationally, and politically) point to different generative conditions in either the disciplines or the university settings.

In addition to this kind of simplification, a difficulty with this kind of inquiry is characterizing the nature and function of paradigms. Locating how a paradigm functions in any setting is an ambitious task. It necessitates obtaining information from a variety of informants to search for agreement: a sense of shared problems for scholarly inquiry in a discipline; and an underlying set of shared commitments in an organization. Disciplinary participants then become primarily informants while they are simultaneously subjects. Working with data from them is a necessarily inductive process (Benson, 1983).

This study characterizes the paradigms within which feminist scholars have worked by seeing it through their eyes, in the experiences and perceptions they have had as organizational participants in their disciplines and academic organizations. This approach captures the way in which paradigms are socially constructed and subjectively experienced. At the same time, however, informants vary in terms of the extent of their consciousness or articulateness about disciplinary paradigms. Where I have interpreted the members' accounts, I am interjecting my own understanding into their narrative.

In addition to these two possible limitations, the sociology of science framework includes a third: the challenge of identifying scholars in an emerging field. Obtaining an accurate sense of participants in a field is a critical component to describing and explaining patterns of interaction among the ideas and individuals. It is especially difficult to do if the field is new. Several studies have acknowledged that identification of membership in a field is a formidable challenge.

While March (1965) in his study of the emergence of the field of organizational theory and theorists relied on self-reported disciplinary affiliation of scholars, Crane (1972, 1980) sought to define membership of "research areas," a more precise measure of sharing a specific research agenda. Crane explains that no research area is isolated from others: "social and ideational links hold the various segments of knowledge together and permit the diffusion of ideas from one area to another, but in ways so complex that it is difficult to identify unequivocally a particular research area. Even the labels that scientists use to describe their research problems are constantly changing" (Crane, 1972). (One example is the subfields of physics and their shifting boundaries.) Furthermore, as research areas develop, their size and importance to members are likely to change over time (Crane, 1969).

With this in mind, Kadushin's (1966, 1968) notion of social circle is a good heuristic. Members come together because of shared interests. Being in a social circle is similar to sharing membership in a subculture or social class; "the exact boundaries . . . are difficult to locate" (p. 695). Empirical study of a social circle can attempt to describe the internal orientation of the individual as well as locate individuals in their social relations: In studies "an attempt is made not only to show common values and origins but also participation in common organizations, or, even better, common activities or instances of having been in the same place at the same time" (Kadushin, 1968, p. 695).

There are, of course, shortcomings to using this conceptualization in an inquiry into the emergence and institutionalization of feminist scholarship. Most of the studies that trace the development of a field are quantitative and based on crude measures of productivity and reputation (e.g., citations). In a recent review of the literature, Shenav (1984) concludes that citation measures, in general, tend to be highly skewed, the majority of citations accruing toward just a few scientists while the bulk of scientists have "invisible productivity." Instead of reflecting either ability or merit, Shenav suggests, citation patterns reflect "a distribution of power (in a zero-sum game) among invisible colleges." Yet empirical measures of this sort are further weakened when gender is examined. Not only have women academics on average published less than their male counterparts (Graham, 1972), but it is also likely that frequency and patterns of citation as empirical measures reflect neither the capability nor the work done by feminist scholars within the traditional disciplines. Ferber (1986) confirms this hypothesis for the field of economics and offers one possible explanation: "Most researchers belong to networks within which papers are exchanged so that they will be particularly familiar with the work of other members of the same circle. It is very likely that some degree of sex segregation exists among such networks. . . . Women's organizations within professional [associations] are both a symptom of and a reinforcement for this phenomenon. Ideological affinity is also likely to play a part."

Consequently, the design and methodology for this study have been constructed to explore knowledge creation as process rather than product. In contrast to mainstream sociology of science, this undertaking is an exploratory inquiry into not only the social conditions but also the patterns of association and influence suggested by retrospective intellectual histories of the scholars themselves. Linking graduate education experiences and subsequent occupational choices as a focus of the analysis is also supported by professional socialization literature. (See, for example, Rosen and Bates, 1976.)

In seeking to describe the process of feminist scholarship emerging, the identification of group membership is still problematic in the uncertainty over who is engaging in feminist inquiry. Simply stated, the question is how to determine what scholarly interests "count" as feminist scholarship. At the outset of the study, I was reluctant to impose a narrow definition on the data. I found that what counts as feminist scholarship is highly ambiguous, even among self-identified feminist scholars themselves. The result is that there is little agreement on which scholars and publications constitute the growing scholarly genre. Disputes attempting to sort out membership were evident in informal circles that I observed as well as in publications. (See for example, Stacey, 1983.) Disputes are not uncommon for a new field engaged in establishing a disciplinary ideology (Hagstrom, 1965). As with other new fields, the viability of feminist scholarship may depend on its ability to form some coherence and clarification of the nature of feminist inquiry. At present, there appears to be agreement that feminist scholarship places women at the center of inquiry. But there are still a variety of interpretations of how race and class considerations may be adequately incorporated into a gendered analysis.

Utility of Interpretive Analysis

Although interpretive analyses have become more commonplace in educational research, two issues are often raised about inherent limitations: limited generalizability and interview bias. I shall address each.

In this study I used feminist scholarship as a case study to explore the possible forces at work in the creation of new knowledge. As such, the design was crafted so as to provide a suggestive sense of the elements in the processes for these particular women. At the same time, I sought to understand the wider context in which new genres are created and achieve legitimacy. From this perspective, it is possible that another new academic specialty may have provided greater illumination of these dynamics. Given that this is one case and I have interviewed only a tiny sample of academic women, my aim is to generalize to the plausible concepts in play rather than to offer definitive claims about the field of knowledge or knowledge creation across fields.

Perhaps more significant than the question of generalizability is the issue of interview bias, that is whether the description from my study is an accurate portrayal of the empirical world. My study has several avenues where interview bias may be involved, both in the small sample of academic women and in my interpretation of their accounts. The sample of primary informants is biased toward accounts by people who have done work that has been accommodated by regular departments. The scholarship of more successful disciplinary careers tends to be more cautious than that of faculty in other academic or nonacademic locations. One might maintain that those in extradepartmental locations actually chose to work there anticipating that there would be greater flexibility; or it might be that their scholarly interests actually pushed them out of the more conventional disciplinary/departmental channels. So, the fact that roughly three-fourths of the participants in this study were faculty located in more conventional departments must be taken into account when considering the weight of my findings.

It has been suggested that retrospective accounts of experience are not reliable. Those who make this assertion generally mean one of two things: that the accounts generated in an interview now are likely to deviate from the accuracy of what actually happened a long time ago; or that the account would not be replicated if another interviewer asked the same questions in order to uncover the "same" story. It was obvious that interviewing informants about their experiences and perceptions would likely vary depending upon when the interview was conducted and how I phrased my questions. And it did. My general stance was to present myself and my questions as consistently as possible.

Other kinds of interview bias may be involved, as informants either include or exclude relevant information depending on the rapport established with the interviewer. In some cases, informants may try to fulfill what they perceive to be the interviewer's expectations. In other cases, informants may not trust the interviewer (Angus, 1984). In order to try to minimize this kind of bias, I asked open questions in an informal and nonjudgmental manner, while broadly characterizing my own research interests. Furthermore, concerns about interview bias may be minimized in this study since the emphasis in the findings is on dynamic processes and influences rather than on particular individuals. Of course, one option for presenting the data would be to provide separate portraits of individuals and follow them through the categories of analysis. I decided not to do that for two major reasons. One is that the theoretical focus directs our attention, not to particular individuals, but to the forces at work in the process of developing scholarly interests, a focus best accomplished through conveying patterns punctuated by snapshots from individuals' careers. The second reason not to focus on individuals is to protect their identities. Even having done so, I have in a few instances supplied fictitious information in place of revealing biographical details. While it may still be possible to determine the identity of some women in the study, I attempted to eliminate any commentary from their autobiographical accounts that would put them in a negative light—either personally or professionally. Such adjustments, I believe, are warranted since these women gave generously of their time. I believe these changes have not compromised the integrity of the data analysis and interpretation that I offer throughout the book.

Bibliography

Abramson, Joan. (1975). *The Invisible Woman: Discrimination in the Academic Profession.* San Francisco: Jossey-Bass.

Adkinson, Judith. (1979). "The Structure of Knowledge and Departmental Social Organization." *Higher Education* 8:41–53.

Anderson, Mary, Lisa Fine, Kathleen Geissler, and Joyce R. Ladenson. (Eds.). (1997). *Doing Feminism: Teaching and Research in the Academy.* East Lansing: Women's Studies Program, Michigan State University.

Angus, Max. (1984). *The Mediation and Supplementation of Theoretical Knowledge about Teaching.* Doctoral dissertation, Stanford University.

Apple, Michael. (1982). "Reproduction and Contradiction in Education: An Introduction," in Michael Apple (Ed.), *Cultural and Economic Reproduction in Education.* London: Routledge and Kegan Paul.

Atkinson, Judith. (1984). "What Is Feminist Anthropology?" Public lecture at Stanford University, October 10.

Bannerji, Himani, Linda Carty, Kari Dehli, Susan Heald, and Kate McKenna. (1991). *Unsettling Relations: The University as a Site of Feminist Struggle.* Boston: South End Press.

Barber, Bernard. (1962). *Science and the Social Order.* New York: Collier Books.

Barnes, Barry. (1974). *Scientific Knowledge and Sociological Theory.* London: Routledge Kegan Paul.

Barrett, Michele. (1980). *Women's Oppression Today: Problems in Marxist Feminist Analysis.* London: Villiers.

Beck, Evelyn. (1983). "Self-Disclosure and the Commitment to Social Change." Pp. 285–91 in Charlotte Bunch and Sandra Pollack (Eds.), *Learning Our Way: Essays in Feminist Education.* Trumansburg, NY: Crossing Press.

Bell, Collin, and Howard Newby. (1976). "Introduction: The Rise of Methodological Pluralism," in Collin and Newby (Eds.), *Doing Sociological Research.* New York: Free Press.

Bell, Daniel. (1977). *An Analysis of Undergraduate Curricular Innovation at the University of Houston Central Campus since 1960.* Doctoral dissertation, Stanford University.

Bell, Susan, and Mollie Rosenhan. (1981). "A Problem in Naming: Women Studies–Women's Studies?" *Signs* 6:540–42.

Ben-David, Joseph. (1972). *American Higher Education.* New York: Carnegie Commission on Higher Education.

Ben-David, Joseph, and Randall Collins. (1966). "Social Factors in the Origins of New Science." *American Sociological Review* 3:451–65.

Bennett, William. (1951). *Area Studies in American Universities.* New York: Social Science Research Council.

Benson, J. Kenneth. (1983). "Paradigm and Praxis in Organizational Analysis." *Research in Organizational Behavior* 5:33–56.

Benson, R. (1972). "Women's Studies: Theory and Practice." *AAUP Bulletin* 53 (September) p. 283. Washington, D.C.: American Association of University Professors.

Benston, Margaret. (1982). "Feminism and the Critique of Scientific Method." Pp. 47–66 in Angela R. Miles and Geraldine Finn (Eds.), *Feminism in Canada: From Pressure to Politics.* Montreal: Black Rose Books.

Bernard, Jessie. (1964). *Academic Women.* University Park: Pennsylvania State University Press.

Bernard, Jessie. (1973). "My Four Revolutions: An Autobiographical History of the ASA." *American Journal of Sociology* 4:78.

Bernstein, Basil. (1982). "Codes, Modalities, and the Process of Cultural Reproduction." Pp. 304–55 in Michael Apple (Ed.), *Cultural and Economic Reproduction in Education.* London: Routledge and Kegan Paul.

Blau, Peter Michael. (1973). *The Organization of Academic Work.* New York: John Wiley and Sons.

Blume, Stuart (Ed.). (1977). *Perspectives in the Sociology of Science.* New York: John Wiley and Sons.

Bok, Derek. (1980). "Reflections on Academic Freedom: An Open Letter to the Harvard Community," in *Harvard Gazette* (April 11).

Bowles, Gloria, and Renate D. Klein (Eds.). (1983). *Theories of Women's Studies.* London: Routledge and Kegan Paul.

Bowles, Samuel, and Herbert Gintis. (1976). *Schooling in Capitalist America.* New York: Basic Books.

Boxer, Marilyn. (1982). "For and About Women: The Theory and Practice of Women's Studies in the United States." Pp. 237–72 in Michelle Z.

Rosaldo, Barbara C. Gelpi, and Nannerl O. Keohane (Eds.), *Feminist Theory: A Critique of Ideology*. Chicago: University of Chicago Press.

Boxer, Marilyn. (1998). *When Women Ask the Questions*. Baltimore: Johns Hopkins University Press.

Brown, Richard H. (1978). "Bureaucracy as Praxis: Toward a Political Phenomenology of Formal Organizations." *Administrative Science Quarterly* 23:365–82.

Brubacher, John Seiler, and Willis Rudy. (1976). *Higher Education in Transition: A History of American Colleges and Universities: 1936–76*. New York: Harper and Row.

Bunch, Charlotte. (1979). "Not by Degrees: Feminist Theory and Education," in Charlotte Bunch and Sandra Pollack (Eds.), *Learning Our Way: Essays in Feminist Education*. Trumansburg, NY: Crossing Press.

Carnegie Commission. (1977). *Missions of the College Curriculum*. San Francisco: Jossey-Bass.

Chamberlain, Mariam. (1982). "A Period of Remarkable Growth: Women's Studies Research Centers." *Change* 14 (April): 24–29.

Clark, Burton R. (1983). *The Higher Education System: Academic Organization*. Berkeley: University of California Press.

Clark, Burton R. (1984). "The Organizational Conception." Pp. 106–31 in Burton R. Clark (Ed.), *Perspectives on Higher Education*. Berkeley: University of California Press.

Cole, Stephen, and Jonathan Cole. (1967). "Scientific Output and Recognition: A Study in the Operation of the Reward System in Science." *American Sociological Review* 32:377–90.

Coyner, Sandra. (1983). "Women's Studies as an Academic Discipline: Why and How to Do It?" Pp. 46–71 in Gloria Bowles and Renate Duelli-Klein (Eds.). (1983). *Theories of Women's Studies*. London: Routledge and Kegan Paul.

Coyner, Sandra. (1983). "The Institutions and Ideas of Women's Studies: From Critique to New Construction." *Journal of Educational Thought* 73 (August): 112–33.

Coyner, Sandra. (1993). "Feminist Research Methods." *NWSA Journal* 5 (spring): 111–19.

Crane, Diana. (1969). "Social Structure in a Group of Scientists: A Test of the Invisible College Hypothesis." *American Sociological Review* (June): 335–52.

Crane, Diana. (1972). *Invisible Colleges: Diffusion of Knowledge in Scientific Communities*. Chicago: University of Chicago Press.

Crane, Diana. (1980). "An Exploratory Study of Kuhnian Paradigms in Theoretical High Energy Physics." *Sociological Studies of Science* 10:23–54.

Cruse, Harold. (1969). "The Integrationist Ethic as a Basis for Scholarly Endeavors." Pp. 4–12 in Armstead L. Robinson (Ed.), *Black Studies in the University*. New Haven: Yale University Press.

Culberton, R. (1975). "Criminal Justice Education—For What?" *Michigan Academician* 8:167–78.

Daniels, Arlene K. (1975). "Feminist Perspectives in Sociological Research." Pp. 340–80 in Marcia Millman and Rosabeth M. Kanter (Eds.), *Another Voice: Feminist Perspectives in Social Life and Social Science.* New York: Anchor Books.

de Beauvoir, Simone. (1953). *The Second Sex.* Translated and edited by H.M. Parshley. New York: Knopf.

DiMaggio, Paul J., and Walter W. Powell. (1983). "The Iron Cage Revisited: Institutional Isomorphism and Collective Rationality in Organizational Fields." *American Sociological Review* 48:147–58.

Dinnerstein, Dorothy. (1976). *The Mermaid and the Minotaur.* New York: Harper Collins.

Dressel, Paul L. (1971). *College and University Curriculum.* Berkeley: McCuthchan.

Dressel, Paul L., Craig Johnson, and Philip M. Marcus. (1970). *The Confidence Crisis.* San Francisco: Jossey-Bass.

DuBois, Ellen, Gail Kelly, Elizabeth Kennedy, C. Korsmeyer, and L. Robinson. (1985). *Feminist Scholarship: Kindling in the Groves of Academe.* Urbana: University of Illinois Press.

Duncan, Simon S. (1974). "The Isolation of Scientific Discovery: Indifference and Resistance to a New Idea." *Science Studies* 4:109–34.

Eisentein, Zillah R. (Ed.). (1974). *Capitalist Patriarchy and the Case for Socialist Feminism.* New York: Monthly Review Press.

Elguea, J. (1984). *Sociology of Development and Philosophy of Science: A Case Study in Contemporary Scientific Growth.*" Doctoral dissertation, Stanford University.

Elkana, Yehuda, Joshua Lederberg, Robert Merton, Arnold Thackary, & Harriet Zuckerman (Eds.). (1978). *Toward a Metric of Science: The Advent of Science Indicators.* New York: John Wiley and Sons.

Evans, Mary. (1982). "In Praise of Theory: The Case for Women's Studies." *Feminist Review* 12:61–73.

Faris, Robert E. (1964). "The Discipline of Sociology," in R. Faris (Ed.), *Handbook of Modern Sociology.* Chicago: Rand McNally and Company.

Farkas, Janos. (1974). "The Science of Science as a New Research Field and Its Function in Prediction." Pp. 254–68 in Richard Whitley (Ed.), *Social Processes of Scientific Development.* London: Routledge and Kegan Paul.

Fenton, W. (1947). *Area Studies in American Universities for the Commission on Implications of Armed Services Educational Programs.* Washington, D.C.: American Council on Education.

Ferber, Marianne A. (1986). "Citations: Are They an Objective Measure of Scholarly Merit?" *Signs* 11:381–89.

Fildes, Sarah. (1983). "The Inevitability of Theory." *Feminist Review* 14:62–70.

Finkelstein, Martin. (1984). *The American Academic Profession.* Columbus: Ohio State University Press.

Firestone, Shulamith. (1970). *The Dialectic of Sex.* New York: Morrow.

Foucault, Michel. (1973 reprint). *The Order of Things: An Archaeology of Human Sciences.* New York: Vintage Books.

Fowlkes, Diane L., and Charlotte S. McClure. (1983). *Feminist Visions: Toward a Transformation of the Liberal Arts Curriculum*. Birmingham: University of Alabama Press.

Freeman, Jo. (1973a). "The Origins of the Women's Liberation Movement." *American Journal of Sociology* 78 (January) 4: 792–811.

Freeman, Jo. (1973b). "Women on the Move: The Roots of Revolt," in Alice S. Rossi and Ann Calderwood (Eds.), *Academic Women on the Move*. New York: Russell Sage.

Freeman, Jo. (1998). "The Origins of the Women's Liberation Movement," in Rachel Blau DuPlessis and Ann Snitow (Eds.), *The Feminist Memoir Project*. New York: Three Rivers Press.

Freeman, Jo (Ed.). (1989). *Women: A Feminist Perspective Fourth Edition*. Mountain View, CA: Mayfield Publishing Company.

Friedan, Betty. (1963). *The Feminine Mystique*. New York: Norton.

Fuller, Steve. (1988). *Social Epistemology*. Bloomington: Indiana University Press.

Gardner, Howard. (1985). *The Mind's New Science: A History of the Cognitive Revolution*. New York: Basic Books.

Geertz, Clifford. (1983a). "Blurred Genres: The Refiguration of Social Thought." Pp. 19–35 in Clifford Geertz (Ed.), *Local Knowledge*. New York: Basic Books.

Geertz, Clifford. (1983b). "The Way We Think Now: Toward an Ethnography of Modern Thought." Pp. 147–66 in Clifford Geertz (Ed.), *Local Knowledge*. New York: Basic Books.

Geertz, Clifford. (1988). *Works and Lives: The Anthropologist as Author*. Stanford: Stanford University Press.

Gerson, Kathleen. (1985). *Hard Choices: How Women Decide about Work, Career, and Motherhood*. Berkeley: University of California Press.

Gieryn, Thomas F. (1983). "Boundary-Work and the Demarcation of Science from Non-Science: Strains and Interests in Professional Ideologies of Scientists." *American Sociological Review* 48:781–95.

Gilligan, Carol. (1982). *In a Different Voice: Psychological Theory and Moral Development*. Cambridge: Harvard University Press.

Giroux, Henry, and Peter McLaren. (1994). *Between Borders: Pedagogy and the Politics of Cultural Studies*. London: Routledge.

Glaser, Barney G., and Anselm L. Strauss. (1967). *The Discovery of Grounded Theory: Strategies for Qualitative Research*. Chicago: Aldine.

Goodman, W. (1984). "Women's Studies: The Debate Continues," in *The New York Times Magazine*, April 22.

Gould, Carol. (1976). "The Woman Question," in C. Gould and M. Wartofsky (Eds.), *Woman and Philosophy: Toward a Theory of Liberation*. New York: Capricorn Books, Putnam and Sons.

Gouldner, Alvin W. (1970). *The Coming Crisis of Western Sociology*. New York: Avon Books.

Graham, Patricia A. (1972). "Women in Academe." Pp. 261–76 in Constantina Safilios-Rothschild (Ed.), *Toward a Sociology of Women.* New York: John Wiley and Sons.

Griffith, G., and N. Mullins. (1972). "Coherent Social Groups in Scientific Change: 'Invisible Colleges' May Be Consistent throughout Science." Pp. 959–96 in *Science,* September 15.

Grimshaw, Jean. (1986). *Philosophy and Feminist Thinking.* Minneapolis: University of Minnesota Press.

Gumport, Patricia J. (1988). "Curricula as Signposts of Cultural Change." *The Review of Higher Education* 12 (autumn) 1: 49–62.

Gumport, Patricia J. (1990). "Feminist Scholarship as a Vocation." *Higher Education* 20 (October) 3: 231–43.

Gumport, Patricia J. (1993). "The Contested Terrain of Academic Program Reduction." *Journal of Higher Education* 64 (May/June) 3: 283–11.

Gumport, Patricia J. (1997). "Public Universities as Academic Workplaces." *Daedalus* 126 (fall) 4: 113–36.

Gumport, Patricia J. (2000a). "Academic Restructuring: Organizational Change and Institutional Imperatives." *Higher Education* 39: 67–91.

Gumport, Patricia. (2000b). "Learning Academic Labor." *Comparative Social Research* 19:1–23.

Hagstrom, Warren O. (1965). *The Scientific Community.* New York: Basic Books.

Haraway, Donna. (1987). Presentation at American Philosophical Association Annual Meetings, March 22. San Francisco.

Harding, Sandra. (1986). *The Science Question in Feminism.* Ithaca: Cornell University Press.

Hartsock, Nancy. (1983). "The Feminist Standpoint: Developing the Ground for a Specifically Feminist Historical Materialism." Pp. 283–310 in Sandra Harding and Merrill B. Hintikka (Eds.), *Discovering Reality.* Dordrecht, Holland: D. Reidel.

Hefferlin, J. B. Lon. (1969). *Dynamics of Academic Reform.* San Francisco: Jossey-Bass.

Hill, S. (1974). "Questioning the Influence of a 'Social System of Science': A Study of Australian Scientists." *Science Studies* 4:135–63.

Hochschild, Arlie. (1975). "Inside the Clockwork of Male Careers," in Florence Howe (Ed.), *Women and the Power to Change.* New York: McGraw-Hill.

Hodgkinson, Harold L. (1970). *Institutions in Transition: A Profile of Change in Higher Education.* Berkeley: Carnegie Commission on Higher Education.

Howe, Florence. (1975). *Women and the Power to Change.* New York: McGraw-Hill.

Howe, Florence, and C. Ahlum. (1973). "Women's Studies and Social Change." Pp. 393–423 in Alice S. Rossi and Ann Calderwood (Eds.), *Academic Women on the Move.* New York: Russell Sage.

Howe, Florence, and Paul Lauter. (1980). *The Impact of Women's Studies on the Campus and the Disciplines.* Washington, D.C.: National Institute of Education.

Jacklin, Carol. (1984). "Changes in the Field of Psychology." Public lecture at Stanford University, October 24.

Jaggar, Alison M. (1983). *Feminist Politics and Human Nature.* Totowa, NJ: Rowan and Allanhead Publishers.

Jencks, Chrisopher, and David Reisman. (1977). *The Academic Revolution.* Chicago: University of Chicago Press.

Kadushin, Charles. (1966). "The Friends and Supporters of Psychotherapy: On Social Circles in Urban Life." *American Sociological Review* 31 (October): 786–802.

Kadushin, Charles. (1968). "Power, Influence, and Social Circles: A New Methodology for Studying Opinion Makers." *American Sociological Review* 33 (October): 685–99.

Keller, Evelyn Fox. (1985). *Reflections on Gender and Science.* New Haven: Yale University Press.

Keller, Evelyn Fox et al. (1987). "Competition and Feminism: Conflicts for Academic Women." *Signs* 12 (spring): 493–511.

Kelly, Joan. (1984). *Women, History, and Theory.* Chicago: University of Chicago Press.

Kerr, Clark. (1973). "The Foreword" in Carl Kaysen (Ed.), *Content and Context: Essays on College Education.* New York: McGraw-Hill.

King, M. D. (1980). "Reason, Tradition, and the Progressiveness of Science," in Gary Gutting (Ed.), *Paradigms and Revolutions.* Notre Dame, IN: University of Notre Dame Press.

Klotzburger, K. (1973). "Political Action by Academic Women," in Alice Rossi Ann Calderwood (Eds.), *Academic Women on the Move.* New York: Russell Sage.

Koedt, Anne. (1970). "The Myth of the Vaginal Orgasm." Pp. 198–207 in Ellen Levine, Anita Rapone, and Anne Koedt (Eds.), *Radical Feminism.* New York: New York Times Book Company.

Koedt, Anne, Ellen Levine, and Anita Rapone. (1971). "Editorial from Notes from the Third Year," in Anne Koedt, Ellen Levine, and Anita Rapone (Eds.), *Radical Feminism.* New York: New York Times Book Company.

Kuhn, Thomas S. (1962). *The Structure of Scientific Revolutions.* Chicago: University of Chicago Press.

Ladd, E., and S. Lipset. (1972). "Politics of Academic Natural Scientists and Engineers." *Science* 76:1091–100.

Langland, Elizabeth, and Walter Gove. (1981). *A Feminist Perspective in the Academy: The Difference It Makes.* Chicago: University of Chicago Press.

Lauter, Paul, and Florence Howe. (1978). *The Women's Movement: Impact on the Campus and Curriculum.* Washington, D.C.: National Conference Series.

Law, John. (1973). "The Development of Specialties in Science: The Case of X-Ray Protein Crystallography." Pp. 123–52 in Gerald Lemaine et al. (Eds.), *Perspectives on the Emergence of Scientific Disciplines.* The Hague: Mouton.

Lemaine, Gerard, Roy MacLeod, Michael Mulkay, & Peter Weingart (Eds.). (1976). *Perspectives on the Emergence of Scientific Disciplines.* Chicago: Aldine.

Levine, Arthur. (1978). *Handbook on Undergraduate Curriculum*. San Francisco: Jossey Bass.

Lewis, Gwendolyn L. (1980). "The Relationship of Conceptual Development to Consensus: An Exploratory Analysis of Three Subfields." *Social Studies of Science* 10:285–308.

Light, Donald W., Jr. (1974). "Introduction: The Structure of Academic Professions." *Sociology of Education* 47 (winter): 1–28.

Lindsey, Duncan. (1978). *The Scientific Publication System in Social Science*. San Francisco: Jossey-Bass.

Lipset, Seymour M. (1976). *Rebellion in the University*. Chicago: University of Chicago Press.

Lodahl, Janice, and Gerald Gordon. (1972). "The Structure of Scientific Fields and the Functioning of University Graduate Departments." *American Sociological Review* 37 (February): 57–72.

Looser, Devoney, and E. Ann Kaplan. (1997). *Generations: Academic Feminists in Dialogue*. Minneapolis: University of Minnesota Press.

MacDonald, Madeline. (1980). "Sociocultural Reproduction and Education." Pp. 13–25 in Rosemary Deem (Ed.), *Schooling for Women's Work*. London: Routledge and Kegan Paul.

MacKinnon, Catharine. (1983). "Feminism, Marxism, Method, and the State: Toward Feminist Jurisprudence." *Signs* 8 (summer): 635–58.

MacKinnon, Catharine. (1987). "A Feminist University," in opening remarks for a conference entitled "A Feminist University," public lecture at Stanford University, May 2.

Mandelbaum, Seymour J. (1979). "The Intelligence of Universities." *Journal of Higher Education* 50 (November/December): 697–725.

Mannheim, Karl. (1936). *Ideology and Utopia*. London: Routledge and Kegan Paul.

March, James G. (1965). *Handbook of Organizations*. Chicago: Rand McNally.

Masterman, M. (1970). "The Nature of a Paradigm," in Imre Lakatos and Alan Musgrave (Eds.), *Criticism and the Growth of Knowledge*. Cambridge: Cambridge University Press.

Mayhew, Lewis B., and Pat Ford. (1971). *Changing the Curriculum*. San Francisco: Jossey-Bass.

McIntosh, Peggy, and Elizabeth Minnich. (1984). "Varieties of Women's Studies." *Women's Studies International Forum* 7: 139–48.

McRobbie, Angela. (1982). "The Politics of Feminist Research: Between Talk, Text, and Action." *Feminist Review* 12 (October): 48–59.

Merton, Robert. (1942, reprint 1973). "The Normative Structure of Science." Pp. 267–85 in Norman W. Storer (Ed.). (1973). *The Sociology of Science: Theoretical and Empirical Investigations*. Chicago: University of Chicago Press.

Merton, Robert K. (1945, reprint 1973). "Paradigm for the Sociology of Knowledge." Pp. 7–40 in Norman W. Storer (Ed.), *The Sociology of Science: Theoretical and Empirical Investigations*. Chicago: University of Chicago Press.

Merton, Robert K. (1957, reprint 1973). "Priorities in Scientific Discovery." Pp. 286–324 in Norman W. Storer (Ed.), *The Sociology of Science: Theoretical and Empirical Investigations*. Chicago: University of Chicago Press.

Merton, Robert K. (1969, reprint 1973). "The Perspectives of Insiders and Outsiders." Pp. 99–136 in Norman W. Storer (Ed.), *The Sociology of Science: Theoretical and Empirical Investigations*. Chicago: University of Chicago Press.

Meyer, John W. (1977). "The Effects of Education as an Institution." *American Journal of Sociology* 83: 55–77.

Meyer, John W., and Brian Rowan. (1977). "Institutional Organizations: Formal Structure as Myth and Ceremony." *American Journal of Sociology* 83: 340–63.

Miles, Matthew B., and A. Michael Huberman. (1983). *Analyzing Qualitative Data*. New York: Center for Policy Research.

Miles, Matthew B., and A. Michael Huberman. (1984). *Qualitative Data Analysis*. Beverly Hills, CA: Sage Publications.

Millet, Kate. (1970). *Sexual Politics*. Garden City, NJ: Doubleday.

Mills, C. Wright. (1967). *Sociological Imagination*. New York: Oxford University Press.

Milman, Marcia, and Rosabeth Kanter (Eds.). (1975). *Another Voice: Feminist Perspectives on Social Life and Social Science*. New York: Anchor Books.

Mitchell, Juliet. (1973). *Women's Estate*. New York: Random House.

Mok, Albert and Anne Westerdiep. (1974). "Societal Influences on the Choice of Research Topics of Biologists." Pp. 210–23 in Richard Whitley (Ed.), *Social Processes in Scientific Development*. London: Routledge and Kegan Paul.

Morlock, L. (1973). "Discipline Variation in the Status of Academic Women," in Alice Rossi and Ann Calderwood (Eds.), *Academic Women on the Move*. New York: Russell Sage.

Morrison, J. (1973). *The Rise of the Arts on the American Campus*. Carnegie Commission on Higher Education. New York: McGraw-Hill.

Moulton, J. (1983). "A Paradigm of Philosophy: The Adversary Method." Pp. 149–64 in Sandra Harding and Merrill B. Hintikka (Eds.), *Discovering Reality*. Dordrecht, Holland: D. Reidel.

Mulkay, Michael J., and David O. Edge. (1974). "Cognitive, Technical, and Social Factors in the Growth of Radio Astronomy." *Social Science Information* 12:25–61.

Mullins, Nicholas C. (1973). "The Development of Specialists in Social Science: The Case of Ethnomethodology." *Science Studies* 3:245–73.

Nelson, B. (1974). "On the Shoulders of the Giants of the Comparative Historical Sociology of Science-in Civilizational Perspective." Pp. 13–20 in Richard Whitley (Ed.), *Social Processes in Scientific Development*. London: Routledge and Kegan Paul.

Nelson, G. (1987). "Harvard Approves Women's Studies Honors Concentration." P. 14 in *Second Century Radcliffe News*, April 14.

Neyman, Elzbieta. (1977). "Scientific Career, Scientific Generation, Scientific Labour Market." Pp. 71–94 in Stuart Blume (Ed.), *Perspectives in the Sociology of Science*. New York: John Wiley and Sons.

Noddings, Nel. (1984). *Caring: A Feminine Approach to Ethics and Moral Education*. Berkeley: University of California Press.

Oakley, Ann. (1981). "Interviewing Women: A Contradiction in Terms." Pp. 30–43 in Helen Roberts (Ed.), *Doing Feminist Research*. London: Routledge and Kegan Paul.

Oberschall, Antony. (1972). "The Institutionalization of American Sociology." Pp. 187–251 in Antony Oberschall (Ed.), *The Establishment of Empirical Sociology: Studies in Continuity, Discontinuity, and Institutionalization*. New York: Harper and Row.

Pfeffer, Jeffrey. (1981a). "Management as Symbolic Action: The Creation and Maintenance of Organizational Paradigms." *Research in Organizational Behavior* 3:1–52.

Pfeffer, Jeffrey. (1981b). *Power in Organizations*. Marshfield, MA: Pitman.

Pfeffer, Jeffrey, Gerald R. Salancik, and Huseyin Leblebici. (1976). "The Effect of Uncertainty on the Use of Social Influence in Organizational Decision-Making." *Administrative Science Quarterly* 21: 227–45.

Price, Derek J. de Solla. (1965). "Networks of Scientific Papers." *Science* 49 (July): 510–15.

Pusey, Michael R., and Robert E. Young (Eds.). (1979). *Control and Knowledge: The Mediation of Power in Institutional and Educational Settings*. Canberra: Australian National University.

Rich, Adrienne C. (1979). "Taking Women Students Seriously," in Adrienne C. Rich (Ed.), *On Lies, Secrets, and Silence: Selected Prose, 1966–78*. New York: Norton.

Rosaldo, Michelle Z., and Louise Lamphere (Eds.). (1974). *Women in Culture and Society*. Stanford: Stanford University Press.

Rosen, Bernard C., and Alan P. Bates. (1976). "The Structure of Socialization in Graduate School." Pp. 154–67 in Ronald Pavalko (Ed.), *Sociology of Education*. Itasca, IL: Peacock Publishers.

Rosenberg, Rosalind. (1982). *Beyond Separate Spheres: Intellectual Roots of Modern Feminism*. New Haven, CT: Yale University Press.

Ross, Janice. (1997). *The Feminization of Physical Culture: The Introduction of Dance into the American University Curriculum*. Doctoral dissertation, Stanford University.

Ross, R. Danforth. (1976). "Academic Innovations: Two Models." *Sociology of Education* 49 (April): 146–55.

Rossi, Alice S., and Ann Calderwood (Eds.). (1973). *Academic Women on the Move*. New York: Russell Sage Foundation.

Rowbotham, Sheila. (1973). *Woman's Consciousness, Man's World*. New York: Penguin Books.

Roy, Rustum. (1979). "Interdisciplinary Science on Campus: The Elusive Dream." Pp. 161–96 in Joseph J. Kockelmans (Ed.), *Interdisciplinarity and Higher Education*. University Park: Pennsylvania State University Press.

Ruddick, Sara, and Pamela Daniels (Eds.). (1977). *Working It Out: 23 Women Writers, Artists, Scientists, and Scholars Talk about Their Lives and Work*. New York: Pantheon Books.

Rudolph, Frederick. (1962). *The American College and University: A History*. New York: Vintage Books.

Rudolph, Frederick. (1981). *Curriculum: A History of the American Undergraduate Course of Study since 1936*. San Francisco: Jossey-Bass.

Schatzman, Leonard, and Anselm Strauss. (1973). *Field Research: Strategies for Natural Sociology*. Englewood Cliffs, NJ: Prentice Hall.

Scheffler, Israel. (1965). *Conditions of Knowledge*. Chicago: University of Chicago Press.

Schein, Edgar H. (1985). *Organizational Culture and Leadership*. San Francisco: Jossey-Bass.

Schramm, Sarah S. (1979). *Plow-Women Rather than Reapers: An Intellectual History of Feminism in the United States*. Metuchen, NJ: Scarecrow Press.

Schuster, Marilyn, and Susan VanDyne. (1984). "Placing Women in the Liberal Arts: Stages of Curriculum Transformation." *Harvard Educational Review* 54:413–28.

Scott, Joan. (1986). "Gender: A Useful Category of Analysis." *American Historical Review* 91:1053–75.

Scott, Robert L. (1979). "Personal and Institutional Problems Encountered in Being Interdisciplinary." Pp. 306–27 in Joseph J. Kockelmans (Ed.), *Interdisciplinarity and Higher Education*. University Park: Pennsylvania State University Press.

Scott, W. Richard. (1981). *Organizations: Rational, Natural, and Open Systems*. Englewood Cliffs, NJ: Prentice Hall.

Seidman, Earl. (1985). "Interviewing the Faculty: Discovering What Faculty Really Experience and Do," in Earl Seidman (Ed.), *In the Words of the Faculty*. San Francisco: Jossey-Bass.

Shapiro, J. (1982). "Women's Studies: A Note on the Perils of Markedness." *Signs* 11:717–21.

Sheehy, Gail. (1981). *Pathfinders*. New York: William Morrow and Company.

Shenav, Yehouda. (1984). Unpublished manuscript, Department of Sociology. Stanford University.

Sherman, Nancy. (1980). "Philosophical Issues in Feminism-A Review Essay." *Harvard Educational Review* 50 (February): 86–91.

Showalter, Elaine. (1971). "Introduction: Teaching about Women." Pp. i–xii in Elaine Showalter and Carol Ohmann (Eds.). *Female Studies IV*. Pittsburgh: KNOW.

Simeone, Angela. (1987). *Academic Women: Working towards Equality*. South Hadley, MA: Bergin and Garvey Publishers.

Slaughter, Sheila. (1997). "Class, Race, and Gender and the Construction of Postsecondary Curricula in the United States." *Journal of Curriculum Studies* 29, no. 1: 1–30.

Smith, Dorothy. (1979). "A Sociology for Women." Pp. 135–87 in Julia A. Sherman and Evelyn T. Beck (Eds.). *The Prism of Sex*. Madison: University of Wisconsin Press.

Spender, Dale. (1981a). *Men's Studies Modified: The Impact of Feminism on the Academic Disciplines*. Oxford: Pergamon Press.

Spender, D. (1981b). "The Gatekeepers: A Feminist Critique of Academic Publishing," in Helen Roberts (Ed.), *Doing Feminist Research*. London: Routledge and Kegan Paul.

Spender, Dale. (Ed.). (1980). *Man-Made Language*. London: Routledge and Kegan Paul.

Spiegel-Rosing, Ina, and Derek J. deSolla Price (Eds.). (1977). *Science, Technology, and Society: A Cross-Disciplinary Perspective*. London: Sage Publications.

Stacey, Judith. (1983). "The New Conservative Feminism." *Feminist Studies* 9 (fall): 559–83.

Stacey, Judith, and Barrie Thorne. (1985). "The Missing Feminist Revolution in Sociology." *Social Problems* 32 (April): 301–16.

Stanley, Liz, and Sue Wise. (1983). *Breaking Out: Feminist Consciousness and Feminist Research*. London: Routledge and Kegan Paul.

Sternhell, C. (1984). "The Tenure Battle: The Women Who Won't Disappear." *Ms. Magazine*, October.

Stimpson, Catharine R. (1975). "The New Feminism and Women's Studies." *Change* 5:43–48.

Storer, Norman W. (1966). *The Social System of Science*. New York: Holt, Rinehart and Winston.

Strathern, Marilyn. (1987). "An Awkward Relationship: The Case of Feminism and Anthropology." *Signs* 12:276–92.

Swidler, Ann, and Jorge Arditi. (1994). "The New Sociology of Knowledge." *Annual Review of Sociology* 23:305–29.

Taylor, Charles. (1966). "Marxism and Empiricism," in Bernard Williams and Alan Montefiore (Eds.). *British Analytical Philosophy*. New York: Humanities Press.

Trow, Martin. (1977). "Departments as Contexts for Teaching and Learning," in Dean E. McHenry et al. (Eds.), *Academic Departments*. San Francisco: Jossey-Bass.

Veysey, Laurence. (1973). "Stability and Experiment in the Undergraduate Curriculum." Pp. 1–64 in Carl Kaysen (Ed.). *Content and Context: Essays on College Education*. New York: McGraw-Hill.

Walker, Robert H. (1958). *American Studies in the United States: A Survey of College Programs*. Baton Rouge, Louisiana: Louisiana State University Press.

Watkins, B. (1979). "Feminism: A Last Chance for the Humanities?" Paper presented at the National Women's Studies Association annual meeting, June 1, Laurence, Kansas.

Weber, Max. (1946). "The Social Psychology of World Religions," in *From Max Weber: Essays in Sociology*, H. H. Gerth and C. Wright Mills (Eds.). New York: Galaxy.

Weingart, Peter. (1974). "On a Sociological Theory of Scientific Change." Pp. 45–68 in Richard Whitley (Ed.), *Social Processes of Scientific Development*. London: Routledge and Kegan Paul.

White, Harrison C., and Cynthia A. White. (1965). *Canvases and Careers: Institutional Change in the French Painting World*. New York: John Wiley and Sons.

Whitely, Richard. (1972). "Black Boxism and the Sociology of Science," in Richard Whitley (Ed.), *The Sociology of Science, Sociological Review Monograph No. 18, Keele University*. Pp. 1–10. London: Routledge and Kegan Paul.

Whitley, Richard. (1974). "Cognitive and Social Institutionalization of Scientific Specialties and Research Areas." Pp. 69–95 in Richard Whitley (Ed.), *Social Processes in Scientific Development*. London: Routledge and Kegan Paul.

Wood, Donna. (1979). *Women's Studies Programs in American Colleges and Universities: A Case of Organizational Innovation*. Doctoral dissertation, Vanderbilt University.

Wood, Donna. (1981). "Academic Women's Studies Program." *Journal of Higher Education* 52 (March–April): 155–72.

Worboys, M. (1976). "The Emergence of Tropical Medicine: A Study in the Establishment of a Scientific Specialty," in R. MacLeod, Gerard Lemaine, Michael Mulkay, P. Weingart (Eds.), *Perspectives on the Emergence of Scientific Disciplines*. The Hague: Mouton.

Wynne, B. (1979). "Physics and Psychics: Science, Symbolic Action, and Social Control in Late Victorian England," in Barry Barnes and Steven Shapin (Eds.), *Natural Order: Historical Studies of Scientific Culture*. London: Sage.

Young, Michael F. (Ed.). (1971). *Knowledge and Control: New Directions for the Sociology of Knowledge*. London: MacMillan Press.

Zabel, A. (1947). *A Comparison of the Status of American Literature and English Literature in Representative American Universities and Colleges for the Year 1939–1940: As Evidenced by the Number and Types of Courses Offered and the Professional Status of Teachers*. Doctoral dissertation, Stanford University.

Zelditch, Morris, Jr. (1962). "Some Methodological Problems of Field Studies." *American Journal of Sociology* 67:566–76.

Ziman, John M. (1981). *Puzzles, Problems, and Enigmas*. London: Cambridge University Press.

Zinn, Howard. (1980). *A People's History of the United States*. New York: Harper and Row.

Index

academic generations, core sample and interview data, 54. *See also* Appendix: Notes on the Research Design and Methods

academic knowledge, changing organization of in universities, 157–163

academic patriarchy, xiv, 155

academic pluralism, xiv

affirmative action, as institutional remedy, 59

Afro-American studies, history of, 14

alternative framework, 23; assumptions of, 24; organizational paradigms, 24, 26

American Philosophical Association (APA), 122

American Sociological Association (ASA), discrimination in hiring, 80

American studies, 11; emergence of, 12; interdisciplinarity and struggle for legitimacy of, 13

antiwar, xv; movement, 34; Pathfinder dissertation topic, 87

area studies, emergence of, 12–13

atheism, in traditional philosophical method, 120

Bay Area Women's Research Group, 35

Berkshire Conference on the History of Women, 36

Bernard, Jessie, 33

biochemistry, 1

Black studies, xv; history of, 14

chemistry, 1

Chicano studies, 14

civil rights, 22, 32

Civil Rights Act of 1964, 32

Clark, Burton, 4. *See also* knowledge creation

Commission on the Status of Women, 32

community, scientific, 19. *See also* Kuhn, Thomas S.

computer science, 1

consciousness raising, 27. *See also* knowledge change

consensus, Kuhnian construct, 19

About the Author

PATRICIA J. GUMPORT is Associate Professor of Education, Stanford University.